Pocket

BUSINESS
ITALIAN
DICTIONARY

English-Italian/Italian-English

Inglese-Italiano/Italiano-Inglese

PH Collin

Peter Blanchard
Sylvia Berlincioni

A & C Black

Originally published by Peter Collin Publishing

Third edition published 2003
Second edition published 2002
First published in Great Britain 1995

A&C Black Publishers Ltd
38 Soho Square
London WID 3HB

British Library Cataloguing in Publications Data

A catalogue record for this book is
available from the British Library

ISBN 0 7136 7736 8

Text computer typeset by A&C Black

Preface

This pocket dictionary is designed for any business person, student or traveller who needs to deal with the language of business. It contains over 5,000 essential business terms in Italian and English with clear and accurate translations.

Abbreviations

adj	adjective
adv	adverb
f	feminine
fpl	feminine plural
m	masculine
mf	masculine *or* feminine
mpl	masculine plural
n	noun
v	verb

Prefazione

Questo dizionario si rivolge a studenti e uomini d'affari che utilizzino la lingua inglese in ambito commerciale. Contiene più di 5000 termini indispensabili con traduzioni chiare e accurate.

Abbreviazione

adj	aggettivo
adv	avverbio
f	femminile
fpl	femminile plurale
m	maschile
mf	maschile *o* femminile
mpl	maschile plurale
n	sostantivo
v	verbo

Contents

Indice

Inglese-Italiano
English-Italian

Aa

A1 di prima classe
abandon abban-
donare o lasciare
abandon an action
rinunciare ad
un'azione (f)
abatement
riduzione (f)
abroad all'estero
absence assenza
(f) o mancanza (f)
absent assente
absolute monopoly
monopolio (m)
perfetto
**accelerated depreci-
ation** ammorta-
mento (m)
accelerato
accept (v) *[agree]*
accettare
accept (v) *[take
something]*
accettare
accept a bill
accettare una
cambiale

**accept delivery of a
shipment** prendere
in consegna un
carico di merce
**accept liability for
something**
assumersi la
responsabilità di
qualcosa
acceptable
accettabile o
soddisfacente
acceptance
accettazione (f)
**acceptance of an
offer** accettazione
(f) di un'offerta
**acceptance
sampling** campi-
onatura (f) per
accettazione
**accommodation
address** indirizzo
(m) di comodo
accommodation bill
cambiale (f) di
favore o effetto (m)
di comodo
according to
conformemente a
account conto (m)

account executive
direttore (m)
del servizio market-
ing *o* direttore delle
vendite
account for
rendere conto
account in credit
conto (m) in credito
account on stop
conto (m) bloccato
account: on
account in acconto
accountant
ragioniere (m) *o*
ragioniera (f) *o*
contabile (m)
accounting
contabilità (f)
accounts depart-
ment reparto (m)
contabilità
accounts payable
conti (mpl) passivi
accounts receivable
conti (mpl) attivi
accrual importo
(m) maturato
accrual of interest
maturazione (f)
degli interessi

accrue maturare *o*
accumularsi
accrued interest
interesse (m)
maturato
accumulate
accumulare *o*
accantonare
accurate accurato *o*
preciso
acknowledge
receipt of a letter
accusare ricevuta di
una lettera
acknowledgement
conferma (f)
acquire a company
entrare in possesso
di una società
acquisition
acquisizione (f) *o*
acquisto (m)
across-the-board
uniforme *o*
indiscriminato
act (v) *[do some-*
thing] agire
act (v) *[work]*
funzionare
act of God causa
(f) di forza maggiore

acting facente funzione di o sostituto
acting manager direttore (m) facente funzione
action [lawsuit] azione (f) o causa (f)
action [thing done] azione (f)
action for damages causa (f) per risarcimento
actual effettivo o reale
actuals prezzi effettivi (mpl) di vendita
actuarial tables tavole (fpl) attuariali
actuary attuario (m)
ad valorem ad valorem o in base al valore di
ad valorem tax tassa (f) ad valorem
add aggiungere o sommare
add on 10% for service aggiungere il 10% per il servizio

add up a column of figures sommare una colonna di cifre
addition [calculation] addizione (f) o somma (f)
addition [thing added] aggiunta (f)
additional addizionale o supplementare
additional charges spese (fpl) supplementari
additional premium premio (m) addizionale
address (n) indirizzo (m) o recapito (m)
address (v) indirizzare o rivolgere la parola a qualcuno
address a letter or a parcel indirizzare una lettera o un pacco
address label etichetta (f) indirizzata
address list lista (f) di indirizzi

addressee desti-
natario (m)
adequate adeguato
o sufficiente
adjourn aggiornare
o rimandare
adjourn a meeting
aggiornare una
riunione
adjudicate in a
dispute pronun-
ciarsi in una
vertenza
adjudication
aggiudicazione (f) *o*
giudizio (m)
adjudication tribunal
tribunale (m) di
arbitrato
adjudicator
giudice (m)
adjust adattare *o*
adeguare
adjustment acco-
modamento (m) *o*
accordo (m)
administration
amministrazione (f)
o gestione (f)
administrative
amministrativo

administrative
expenses spese (fpl)
di amministrazione
admission
ammissione (f)
admission charge
spese (fpl)
d'ammissione *o*
spese d'entrata
admit *[confess]*
ammettere
admit *[let in]* far
entrare
advance (adj)
anticipato
advance (n)
[increase]
aum-ento (m)
advance (n) *[loan]*
anticipo (m)
advance (v)
[increase]
aumentare
advance (v) *[lend]*
prestare
advance booking
prenotazione (f)
anticipata
advance on account
anticipazione (f)
su un conto

advance payment
pagamento (m)
anticipato
advertise fare
pubblicità o
reclamizzare
**advertise a new
product** reclamiz-
zare un nuovo
prodotto
advertise a vacancy
pubblicare un'in-
serzione (f) per un
impiego disponibile
advertisement
annuncio (m) pubblic-
itario o pubblicità (f)
advertiser
inserzionista (m) o
chi fa pubblicità
advertising pubblic-
ità (f) o reclame (f)
advertising agency
agenzia (f) di
pubblicità
advertising budget
budget (m)
pubblicitario
**advertising cam-
paign** campagna
(f) pubblicitaria

**advertising man-
ager** direttore (m)
della pubblicità
advertising rates
tariffe (f) delle
inserzioni
pubblicitarie
advertising space
spazio (m)
pubblicitario
advice note bol-
letta (f) d'avviso
advise *[tell what
happened]* infor-
mare o avvisare
advise *[what
should be done]*
consigliare o racco-
mandare
adviser *or* **advisor**
consulente (m)
affidavit attes-
tazione (f) ufficiale
affiliated affiliato
o associato
affirmative
affermativo
afford
permettersi o
avere i mezzi
economici

after-sales service
assistenza (f) post-
vendita alla clientela
after-tax profit
utile (m) al netto
delle imposte
agency agenzia (f)
agenda ordine (m)
del giorno
**agent [representa-
tive]** agente (m) o
rappresentante (m)
**agent [working in an
agency]** agente (m)
**AGM (= annual
general meeting)**
Assemblea (f)
Generale degli
Azionisti
agree [accept]
accettare
agree [approve]
approvare
agree [be same as]
concordare o
corrispondere a
**agree to do some-
thing** acconsentire a
fare qualcosa o
accettare di fare
qualcosa

**agree with [be
same as]**
concordare o cor-
rispondere a
**agree with [of same
opinion]** essere
d'accordo con
agreed convenuto o
concordato
agreed price prezzo
(m) concordato
agreement
accordo (m)
agricultural agri-
colo o agrario
aim (n) scopo (m)
o proposito (m)
**aim (v) avere
lo scopo di**
air aria (f)
air freight
trasporto (m) merci
via aerea
**air freight charges
or rates** spese tras-
porto merci via aerea
air letter lettera
(f) aerea
air terminal
terminal (m) della
compagnia aerea

airfreight (v)
trasportare merci
via aerea
airline linea (f)
aerea o compagnia
(f) aerea
airmail (n) posta
(f) aerea
airmail (v) spedire
per posta aerea
airmail sticker
etichetta (f) di
posta aerea
airport aeroporto (m)
airport bus autobus
(m) dell'aeroporto
airport tax tasse
(fpl) aeroportuali
airport terminal
terminal (m)
airtight packaging
imballaggio (m)
ermetico
all expenses paid
tutte le spese pagate
all-in totale o globale
all-in price prezzo
(m) tutto compreso
all-risks policy
polizza (f) contro
tutti i rischi

allocate stanziare
allow [agree]
accettare o ammettere
allow [give] accor-
dare o cedere
allow [permit] per-
mettere
**allow 10% for
carriage** calcolare
10% per il trasporto
allow for calcolare
o dedurre
**allowance for
depreciation** accan-
tonamento (m) al
fondo di
ammortamento
alphabetical order
ordine (m) alfabetico
alter modificare o
cambiare
alteration modifica
(f) o cambiamento (m)
alternative (adj)
alternativo
alternative (n)
alternativa (f)
amend correggere
amendment emen-
damento (m) o
rettifica (f)

American (adj)
americano
American (n)
Americano, -ana
amortization
ammortamento (m)
amortize
ammortare *o*
ammortizzare
amount [of money]
ammontare (m) *o*
importo (m)
amount owing
importo (m) dovuto
amount paid
importo (m)
pagato
amount to
ammontare a
analyse *or* analyze
analizzare
analyse the market potential analizzare
il potenziale del
mercato
analysis analisi (f)
announce annunciare
announcement
annuncio (m)
annual annuale *o*
annuo

annual accounts
rendiconti (mpl)
annuali
annual general meeting (AGM)
Assemblea (f)
Generale degli
Azionisti
annual report
relazione (f)
annuale al bilancio
annually
annualmente
answer (n)
risposta (f)
answer (v)
rispondere
answer a letter
rispondere a una
lettera
answer the telephone rispondere
al telefono
answering machine
segreteria (f)
telefonica
answering service
servizio (m)
segreteria telefonica
antedate
retrodatare

apologize scusarsi
apology scusa (f)
appeal (n) *[against a decision]* ricorso (m) *o* appello (m)
appeal (n) *[attraction]* richiamo (m)
appeal (v) *[against a decision]* ricorrere in appello *o* appellare
appeal to (v) *[attract]* attirare
appear sembrare
appendix appendice (f)
applicant for a job candidato (m) a un posto di lavoro
application domanda (f) *o* istanza (f)
application for a job domanda (f) d'impiego
application form modulo (m) per domanda di assunzione
apply for *[ask for]* chiedere
apply for a job fare domanda d'impiego

apply in writing fare domanda scritta
apply to *[affect]* riguardare
appoint nominare
appointment *[job]* impiego (m) *o* posto (m)
appointment *[meeting]* appuntamento (m)
appointment *[to a job]* nomina (f)
appointments book agenda (f)
appointments vacant impieghi (mpl) disponibili
appreciate *[how good something is]* apprezzare
appreciate *[increase in value]* aumentare di valore
appreciation *[how good something is]* apprezzamento (m)
appreciation *[in value]* rivalutazione (f)

appropriate (v)
[funds] destinare
approval
benestare (m)
approval: on
approval in prova *o*
in esame
approve the terms
of a contract
approvare i termini
di un contratto
approximate
approssimativo
approximately
approssimativamente
arbitrate in a dis-
pute arbitrare una
vertenza
arbitration arbi-
trato (m)
arbitration board *or*
arbitration tribunal
tribunale (m) arbi-
trale
arbitrator arbitro (m)
area *[of town]* zona
(f) *o* quartiere (m)
area *[region]* area
(f) *o* regione (f)
area *[subject]*
campo (m)

area *[surface]*
superficie (f)
area code codice
(m) di zona
area manager
direttore (m) di
zona
argument discus-
sione (f) *o* disputa (f)
arrange *[meeting]*
stabilire *o*
organizzare
arrange *[set out]*
sistemare *o*
disporre
arrangement *[com-*
promise]* intesa (f)
o accordo (m)
arrangement *[sys-*
tem]* sistemazione
(f) *o* disposizione (m)
arrears arretrati
(mpl)
arrival arrivo (m)
arrivals arrivi (mpl)
arrive arrivare
article *[clause]*
clausola (f)
article *[item]*
articolo (m) *o*
prodotto (m)

articles of associa-
tion atto (m)
costitutivo di soci-
età o statuto (m)
societario
articulated lorry or
articulated
vehicle camion/
autocarro (m)
articolato o veicolo
articolato
as per advice come
consigliato
as per invoice
come da fattura
as per sample
come da campione
asap (= as soon as
possible) al più
presto possibile o nel
più breve termine
ask [someone to do
something] chiedere
(a qualcuno di fare
qualcosa)
ask for [ask a price]
chiedere (un prezzo)
ask for [something]
chiedere o domandare
ask for a refund
chiedere un rimborso

ask for further
details or particu-
lars chiedere ulteri-
ori dettagli o parti-
colari
assembly [meeting]
assemblea (f)
assembly [putting
together] assem-
blaggio (m) o
montaggio (m)
assembly line catena
(f) di montaggio
assess accertare o
stabilire il valore
assess damages
accertare i danni
assessment of
damages accerta-
mento (m) dei danni
asset bene (m) o
cespite (m)
asset value valore
(m) patrimoniale (di
imprese)
assets and liabili-
ties attività (fpl)
e passività (fpl)
assign a right to
someone attribuire
un diritto a qualcuno

assignee asseg-
natario (m)
**assignment [ces-
sion]** cessione (f) o
trasferimento (m)
assignment [work]
incarico (m)
assignor cedente
(m) o parte ven-
ditrice (f)
assist assistere
assistance aiuto
(m) o assistenza (f)
assistant assis-
tente (mf) o collab-
oratore (m)
assistant manager
vice direttore
associate (adj)
associato
associate (n) asso-
ciato (m) o socio (m)
associate company
società (f) collegata
association
associazione (f)
assurance
assicurazione (f)
assurance company
compagnia (f) di
assicurazione

assurance policy
polizza (f) di
assicurazione
**assure someone's
life** assicurare
la vita di qualcuno
attach attaccare o
unire
attack attaccare o
assalire
attend (meeting)
assistere a
attend to
occuparsi di
attention
attenzione (f)
attorney
procuratore (m)
attract attrarre
attractive salary
stipendio (m)
interessante
auction (n) asta (f)
auction (v) vendere
all'asta
auction rooms sala
(f) di vendita
all'asta
audit (n) revisione
(f) contabile
audit (v) verificare

audit the accounts
verificare i conti
auditing revisione
contabile (f) o
certificazione (f)
auditor revisore (m)
ufficiale dei conti
authenticate auten-
ticare o legalizzare
authority autorità (f)
authorization
autorizzazione (f)
authorize *[give per-
mission]* autorizzare
authorize payment
autorizzare un
pagamento
authorized
autorizzato
availability
disponibilità (f)
available disponibile
available capital
capitale (m)
disponibile
average (adj) medio
average (n) media (f)
average (n) *[insur-
ance]* avaria (f)
average (v) calco-
lare una media

average price
prezzo (m) medio
avoid evitare
await instructions
attendere istruzioni
award (n) giudizio
(m) arbitrale
award (v) assegnare
**award a contract to
someone** aggiudi-
care un contratto a
qualcuno

Bb

back (n) dorso (m)
o retro (m)
back orders ordi-
nazioni (fpl) inevase
back payment
pagamento (m) degli
arretrati
back tax
imposta (f)
arretrata
backdate retrodatare

backer sostenitore (m) *o* avallante (m)
backhander bustarella (f)
backing appoggio (m) *o* aiuto (m)
backlog lavoro (m) arretrato
backup (adj) *[computer]* di salvaguardia
backup copy copia (f) di riserva
backwardation deporto (m)
bad buy cattivo acquisto (m)
bad debt credito (m) inesigibile
bag borsa (f)
bail someone out ottenere la liberazione (su cauzione) di qualcuno
balance (n) bilancio (m) *o* bilancia (f)
balance (v) bilanciare
balance (v) *[a budget]* pareggiare un budget
balance brought down *or* **brought forward** saldo (m) da riportare
balance carried down *or* **carried forward** saldo (m) riportato
balance due to us saldo (m) dovuto
balance of payments bilancia (f) dei pagamenti
balance of trade bilancia (f) commerciale
balance sheet bilancio (m) d'esercizio
ban (n) interdizione (f)
ban (v) interdire *o* vietare
bank (n) banca (f)
bank (v) depositare in banca *o* avere un conto in banca
bank account conto (m) bancario
bank balance saldo (m) in banca

bank base rate
tasso (m) ufficiale
di sconto
bank bill [GB]
effetto (m) bancario
bank bill [US] ban-
conota (f)
bank book libretto
(m) di versamento
bank borrowings
prestiti (mpl) bancari
bank charges
spese (fpl) bancarie
bank credit credito
(m) bancario
bank deposits
depositi (mpl) bancari
bank draft assegno
(m) circolare
bank holiday
giorno (m) di
chiusura degli
sportelli bancari o
festa (f) nazionale
bank loan prestito
(m) bancario
bank manager diret-
tore (m) di banca
bank statement
estratto (m) conto
bancario

bank transfer
bonifico (m)
bankable paper
effetti (mpl) banca-
bili o strumenti
(mpl) scontabili
banker banchiere
(m) o funzionario
(m) di banca
banker's draft
assegno (m) circolare
banker's order
ordine (m) bancario
banking attività (f)
bancaria
banking hours
orario (m) di banca
banknote
banconota (f)
bankrupt (adj)
fallito
bankrupt (n)
fallito (m)
bankrupt (v) fare
fallire
bankruptcy
fallimento (m)
bar chart dia-
gramma (m) a barre
bar code codice
(m) a barre

bargain (n)
[cheaper than
usual] affare (m) o
occasione (f)
bargain (n) [deal]
affare (m)
bargain (n) [stock
exchange] vendita
(f) di realizzo
bargain (v)
contrattare o tirare
sul prezzo
bargain offer
offerta (f)
d'occasione
bargain price
prezzo (m)
d'occasione
bargaining contrat-
tazione (f)
bargaining position
situazione (f)
contrattuale
bargaining power
potere (m)
contrattuale
barrier barriera (f)
barter (n) baratto
(m) o scambio (m)
barter (v)
barattare

bartering scambio
(m) di merci e
prodotti
base (n) [initial
position] base (f)
base (n) [place]
base (f)
base (v) [in a
place] essere di
base a o avere la
propria sede in
base (v) [start to cal-
culate from] basarsi
base year anno (m)
di base
basic (adj) [most
important] di base
o fondamentale
basic (adj) [simple]
di base o basilare
basic discount
sconto (m) di base
basic tax tassa (f)
di base
basis base (f) o
fondamento (m)
batch (n) [of
orders] gruppo (m)
batch (n) [of
products] partita
(f) di merci

batch (v) mettere insieme
batch number numero (m) di partita
batch processing elaborazione (f) di massa
bear (n) *[Stock Exchange]* ribassista (m)
bear (v) *[carry]* portare
bear (v) *[interest]* fruttare
bear (v) *[pay for]* sostenere
bear market mercato (m) al ribasso
bearer portatore (m) *o* portatrice (f)
bearer bond obbligazione (f) al portatore
begin cominciare *o* iniziare
beginning inizio (m)
behalf: on behalf of a nome di *o* per conto di
belong to appartenere a

below-the-line expenditure spese (f) straordinarie
benchmark punto (m) di riferimento
beneficiary beneficiario (m)
benefit (n) beneficio (m) *o* utilità (f)
benefit from (v) trarre vantaggio da
berth (n) ormeggio (m)
berth (v) ormeggiare
best (adj) migliore
best (n) il meglio
best-selling car automobile (f) di grande successo
bid (n) *[at an auction]* offerta (f)
bid (n) *[offer to buy]* offerta (f)
bid (n) *[offer to do work]* offerta (f) d'appalto
bidder offerente (m)
bidding offerta (f)
bilateral bilaterale
bill (n) *[US]* banconota (f)

bill (n) *[in a restaurant]* conto (m)
bill (n) *[in Parliament]* progetto (m) di legge
bill (n) *[list of charges]* fattura (f) o bolletta (f)
bill (n) *[written promise to pay]* effetto (m) o cambiale (f)
bill (v) fatturare
bill of exchange cambiale (f)
bill of lading polizza (f) di carico
bill of sale fattura (f) o atto (m) di vendita
billing fatturazione (f)
billion *[UK]* bilione (m)
billion *[US]* miliardo (m)
bills for collection effetti (mpl) all'incasso
bills payable effetti (mpl) passivi o cambiali (fpl) da pagare

bills receivable effetti (mpl) attivi o cambiali (fpl) da incassare
binding vincolante
black economy economia (f) nera
black list (n) lista (f) nera
blacklist (v) inserire in una lista (f) di proscrizione
black market mercato (m) nero
blame (n) biasimo (m) o colpa (f)
blame (v) biasimare
blank (adj) in bianco o vuoto
blank (n) spazio (m) o vuoto (m)
blank cheque assegno (m) in bianco
blister pack pacco (m) con confezione 'blister' (in plastica trasparente con personalizzazione)

block (n) [building]
palazzo (m)
block (n) [of shares]
pacchetto (m)
(azionistico)
block (v) bloccare
block booking noleg-
gio (m) in blocco
blocked currency
valuta (f) bloccata
blue chip titolo (m)
di prim'ordine
blue-chip invest-
ments investimenti
(mpl) in titoli di
prim'ordine
board (n) [group of
people] Consiglio
(m) di
Amministrazione
board (v)
imbarcarsi
board meeting riu-
nione (f) del con-
siglio di amminis-
trazione
board of directors
Consiglio (m) di
Amministrazione
board: on board a
bordo

boarding card or
boarding pass
carta (f) d'imbarco
boardroom sala (f)
riunioni
bona fide in buona
fede
bond [borrowing by
government]
obbligazione (f)
bonded warehouse
magazzino (m)
doganale
bonus gratifica (f)
o premio (m)
bonus issue emis-
sione (f) gratuita di
azioni o aumento (m)
gratuito di capitale
book (n) libro (m)
book (v) prenotare
book sales vendite
(fpl) registrate
book value valore
(m) contabile
booking regis-
trazione (f) o
prenotazione (f)
booking clerk imp-
iegato (m) alla
biglietteria

booking office ufficio (m) prenotazioni
bookkeeper contabile (mf) *o* ragioniere (m)
bookkeeping contabilità (f)
boom (n) sviluppo (m) favorevole dell'economia *o* boom (m)
boom (v) prosperare
boom industry industria (f) che si è sviluppata rapidamente
booming fiorente
boost (n) spinta (f)
boost (v) lanciare
border frontiera (f)
borrow prendere a prestito *o* mutuare
borrower mutuatario (m)
borrowing mutuo (m)
borrowing power potere (m) per ricorrere al prestito
boss (informal) capo (m)

bottleneck strozzatura (f) (nel processo aziendale)
bottom fondo (m)
bottom line nodo (m) della questione
bought ledger mastro (m) dei conti dei creditori
bought ledger clerk responsabile (m) del mastro dei conti dei creditori
bounce *[cheque]* respingere
box number casella (f) postale
boxed set presentazione (f) in cofanetto
boycott (n) boicottaggio (m)
boycott (v) boicottare
bracket (n) *[tax]* fascia (f)
bracket together raggruppare
branch settore (m)
branch manager direttore (m) di filiale

branch office
filiale (f)
brand marchio (m)
o marca (f)
brand image
immagine (f) del
prodotto
brand loyalty
fedeltà (f) alla marca
brand name marca
(f) o nome del
prodotto
brand new nuovo di
zecca
breach of contract
inadempimento (m)
del contratto
breach of warranty
violazione (f) di
garanzia
break (n) pausa (f)
break (v) *[contract]*
rompere
**break an agree-
ment** infrangere un
accordo
break down (v)
[itemize] det-
tagliare
break down (v)
[machine] rompersi

break down (v)
[talks] arenarsi *[di
trattative]*
break even (v)
giungere al punto di
pareggio
**break off negotia-
tions** sospendere
le trattative
break the law vio-
lare la legge
breakages rotture
(fpl) o danni
(mpl)
breakdown (n)
[items] ripartizione (f)
breakdown (n)
[machine] guasto (m)
breakdown (n)
[talks] rottura (f)
breakeven point
punto (m) di pareg-
gio fra costi e ricavi
bribe (n) tangente
(f) o bustarella (f)
bribe (v) corrompere
(con denaro o doni)
brief (v) dare
istruzioni
briefcase borsa (f)
o cartella (f)

bring portare
bring a civil action intentare causa civile
bring in apportare o rendere
bring out lanciare
British britannico *o* inglese
brochure fascicolo (m)
broke (informal) al verde
broker broker (m)
brokerage *or* **broker's commission** commissione (f) di mediazione
brown paper carta (f) da pacco
bubble pack confezione (f) a bolla di plastica trasparente
budget (n) *[government]* bilancio (m) dello Stato
budget (n) *[personal, company]* bilancio (m) preventivo *o* budget (m)
budget (v) budgettare

budget account *[in bank]* contabilità (f) di bilancio
budgetary budgetario *o* relativo al budget
budgetary control controllo (m) budgetario
budgetary policy politica (f) di budget
budgeting preparazione (f) del budget
building society istituto (m) di credito fondiario
built-in incorporato *o* inserito
bulk volume (m) *o* grande quantità (f)
bulk buying acquisto (m) in massa
bulk shipments spedizione (f) in massa
bulky voluminoso
bull *[stock exchange]* speculatore al rialzo
bull market mercato (m) al rialzo

bulletin bollettino (m)
bullion oro (m) in verghe
bureau de change ufficio (m) cambio
bus autobus (m)
business [com-merce] affari (mpl)
business [company] impresa (f)
business [discus-sion] affare (m)
business address indirizzo (m) d'ufficio
business call telefonata (f) d'affari
business card biglietto (m) da visita
business centre centro (m) d'affari
business class classe (f) business
business equip-ment apparec-chiatura (f) d'ufficio
business hours ore (f) d'ufficio
business letter let-tera (f) d'affari

business lunch pranzo (m) d'affari
business premises locali (mpl) d'azienda o locali commerciali
business strategy strategia (f) com-merciale
business transac-tion transazione (f) commerciale
business trip viaggio (m) d'affari
business: on busi-ness per affari
businessman or **businesswoman** uomo (m) d'affari o donna (f) d'affari
busy occupato
buy (v) comperare
buy back riacquistare
buy for cash com-perare in contanti
buy forward com-perare a termine
buyer [for a store] responsabile (m) di un ufficio acquisti

buyer *[person]* compratore (m)
buyer's market mercato (m) al ribasso
buying acquisto (m)
buying department ufficio (m) acquisti
by-product prodotto (m) derivato

Cc

cable address indirizzo (m) cablografico
calculate calcolare
calculation calcolo (m)
calculator calcolatore (m)
calendar month mese (m) solare
calendar year anno (m) solare
call (n) *[for money]* richiesta (f) di pagamento

call (n) *[phone]* chiamata (f)
call (n) *[stock exchange]* opzione (f) d'acquisto
call (n) *[visit]* visita (f)
call (v) *[ask to do something]* invitare
call (v) *[meeting]* convocare
call (v) *[phone]* chiamare
call off a deal disdire un affare
call rate tasso (m) su prestiti a breve
callable bond obbligazione (f) redimibile
campaign campagna (f)
cancel cancellare o annullare
cancel a cheque annullare un assegno
cancel a contract annullare un contratto
cancellation cancellazione (f) o disdetta (f)

cancellation clause
clausola (f) di
rescissione
cancellation of an
appointment revoca
(f) di una nomina
candidate can-
didato (m)
canvass procacciare
canvasser piazz-
ista (m) o propa-
gandista (m)
canvassing propa-
ganda (f)
canvassing tech-
niques tecniche
(f) di propaganda
capable of capace di
capacity *[ability]*
abilità (f) o
capacità (f)
capacity *[produc-*
tion] capacità (f)
produttiva
capacity *[space]*
capacità (f)
capacity utilization
utilizzo (m) della
capacità produttiva
capital capitale (m)
o capitali (mpl)

capital account
conto (m) capitale
capital assets
immobilizzazioni
(fpl)
capital equipment
immobilizzi (mpl)
tecnici
capital expenditure
spese (fpl) conto
capitali
capital gains plus-
valenza (f)
capital gains tax
imposta (f) sulle
plusvalenze
capital goods beni
(mpl) strumentali
capital loss perdita
(f) di capitale
capital-intensive
industry industria
(f) a forte assorbi-
mento di capitali
capitalization capi-
talizzazione (f)
capitalization of
reserves capitaliz-
zazione delle riserve
capitalize capita-
lizzare

capitalize on trarre vantaggio da
captive market mercato (m) controllato da un solo fornitore
capture impadronirsi
carbon copy copia (f) carbone
carbon paper carta (f) carbone
carbonless autocopiante
card [business card] biglietto (m)
card [material] cartoncino (m)
card [membership] tessera (f)
card [postcard] cartolina (f) postale
card index (n) schedario (m)
card phone telefono (m) a schede
card-index (v) schedare
card-index file fascicolo (m) dello schedario

card-indexing schedatura (f)
cardboard cartone (m)
cardboard box scatola (f) di cartone
care of (c/o) presso
cargo carico (m)
cargo ship nave (f) da carico
carnet [document] carnet (m)
carriage trasporto (m)
carriage forward porto (m) assegnato
carriage free franco di porto
carriage paid porto (m) pagato
carrier [company] trasportatore (m) o impresa (f) di trasporti
carrier [vehicle] camion (m)
carry [approve in a vote] far approvare
carry [have in stock] avere
carry [produce] produrre

carry [transport]
portare o
trasportare
carry forward
riportare a nuovo
carry on a business
svolgere esercizio
d'impresa
carry over a bal-
ance riportare un
pareggio
cartel cartello (m)
carton [box] car-
tone (m) o imballo
(m) di cartone
carton [material]
cartone (m)
case (n) [box]
cassa (f)
case (n) [suitcase]
valigia (f)
case (v) [put in
boxes] imballare
cash (adv) in
contanti
cash (n) [money]
denaro (m) contante
cash a cheque
incassare un assegno
cash account conto
(m) di cassa

cash advance anticipo
(m) in contanti
cash and carry
supermercato (m)
all'ingrosso
cash balance saldo
(m) di cassa
cash book libro
(m) cassa
cash card tessera
(f) prelievo contanti
cash deal transazione
(f) sul disponibile
cash deposit depos-
ito (m) in contanti
cash desk sportello
(m) di cassa
cash discount
sconto (m) cassa o
sconto per paga-
mento in contanti
cash dispenser
cassa (f)
automatica prelievi
cash float fondo
(m) di cassa
cash flow flusso
(m) di cassa
cash flow forecast
previsioni (fpl)
del flusso di cassa

cash flow statement rendiconto (m) del flusso di cassa

cash in hand fondo (m) di cassa

cash offer offerta (f) reale o offerta per contanti

cash on delivery (c.o.d.) pagamento (m) alla consegna

cash payment pagamento (m) in contanti

cash price prezzo (m) per contanti o condizioni (fpl) per pagamento in contanti

cash purchase acquisto (m) per contanti

cash register registratore (f) di cassa

cash reserves riserva (f) di cassa

cash sale vendita (f) per contanti

cash terms condizioni (fpl) per pagamento in contanti

cash till contenitore (m) di contanti

cash transaction transazione (f) sul disponibile

cash voucher pezza (f) giustificativa di cassa

cashable incassabile

cashier cassiere (m) o cassiera (f)

cashier's check *[US]* assegno (m) di cassa (spiccato dalla banca su se stessa in favore di terzi)

casting vote voto (m) decisivo

casual work lavoro (m) saltuario

casual worker lavoratore (m) saltuario

catalogue catalogo (m)

catalogue price prezzo (m) di catalogo

category categoria (f)

cater for
provvedere di generi
alimentari
caveat emptor 'l'ac-
quirente presti la
dovuta attenzione'
ceiling limite (m)
massimo
ceiling price prezzo
(m) massimo
cellular phone tele-
fono (m) cellulare
central centrale
central bank banca
(f) centrale
central purchasing
acquisto (m)
centralizzato
centralization
centralizzazione (f)
centralize
centralizzare
centre centro (m)
**CEO (= chief execu-
tive officer)** Direttore
Generale (m)
certificate
certificato (m)
**certificate of
approval** certificato
(m) di accettazione

**certificate of
deposit** certificato
(m) di deposito
**certificate of guar-
antee** certificato
(m) di garanzia
certificate of origin
certificato (m)
d'origine
**certificate of regis-
tration** certificato
(m) d'iscrizione
certificated
certificato
**certificated bank-
rupt** debitore (m)
autorizzato al con-
cordato preventivo
**certified account-
ant** revisore (m)
ufficiale dei conti o
(in US) ragioniere
(m) iscritto all'albo
certified cheque
assegno (m) a
copertura garantita
certified copy
copia (f) autentica
certify certificare o
autenticare
cession cessione (f)

chain *[of stores]*
catena (f)
chain store negozio
(m) che fa parte di
una catena
chairman *[of commit-*
tee] presidente (m)
chairman *[of com-*
pany] presidente (m)
chairman and man-
aging director
presidente e ammini-
stratore delegato
Chamber of
Commerce Camera
(f) di Commercio
change (n) *[cash]*
spiccioli (mpl)
change (n)
[difference]
cambiamento (m)
change (v) *[money]*
cambiare
change hands
essere venduto
change machine
macchina (f)
che cambia denaro in
spiccioli
channel (n)
canale (m)

channel (v)
canalizzare
channels of distri-
bution canali (mpl)
di distribuzione
charge (n) *[in*
court] accusa (f)
charge (n) *[money]*
carico (m)
charge (n) *[on*
account] addebito (m)
charge (v) *[money]*
far pagare
charge a purchase
addebitare un
acquisto
charge account
conto (m) personale
charge card carta
(f) di credito
chargeable
caricabile
charges forward
pagamento (m) a
carico del destinatario
charter (n) noleg-
gio (m)
charter (v) noleggiare
charter an aircraft
noleggiare un
aeroplano

charter flight volo (m) charter

charter plane aeroplano (m) a noleggio

charterer noleggiatore (m) (di navi, aerei)

chartering noleggio (m)

chase *[an order]* dare la caccia a

chase *[follow]* inseguire

cheap economico *o* a basso prezzo

cheap labour manodopera (m) a basso prezzo

cheap money denaro (m) a buon mercato

cheap rate tariffa (f) ridotta

check (n) *[examination]* controllo (m)

check (n) *[stop]* arresto (m)

check (v) *[examine]* esaminare *o* controllare

check (v) *[stop]* arrestare

check in *[at airport]* presentarsi al check in

check in *[at hotel]* firmare il registro

check out *[of hotel]* lasciare libera la camera dell'albergo

check sample campione (m) (statistico) di controllo

check-in *[at airport]* controllo (m) passeggeri

check-in counter check in (m)

check-in time ora (f) di accettazione

checkout *[in supermarket]* cassa (f)

cheque assegno (m)

cheque (guarantee) card carta (f) assegni

cheque account conto (m) assegni

cheque book libretto (m) assegni

cheque number numero (m) dell'assegno

cheque stub
matrice (f)
dell'assegno
cheque to bearer
assegno (m) al
portatore
chief (adj)
principale
chief clerk capo
(m) ufficio
**chief executive
(officer)** direttore
(m) generale
choice (adj) di
prima qualità
**choice (n) [choos-
ing]** scelta (f)
**choice (n) [items
to choose from]**
scelta (f)
**choice (n) [thing
chosen]** scelta (f)
choose scegliere
Christmas bonus
gratifica (f)
natalizia o
tredicesima (f)
chronic cronico
chronological order
ordine (m) crono-
logico

**c.i.f. (= cost, insur-
ance and freight)**
costo (m),
assicurazione (f) e
nolo (m)
circular (n) lettera
(f) circolare
circular letter let-
tera (f) circolare
**circular letter of
credit** lettera (f)
di credito circolare
circulation [money]
circolazione (f)
**circulation [news-
paper]** tiratura (f)
civil law diritto (m)
civile
claim (n) domanda
(f) d'indennizzo
o reclamo (m)
claim (v) [insurance]
rivendicare o pre-
sentare una domanda
d'indennizzo
claim (v) [right]
rivendicare
claim (v) [suggest]
affermare
claimant ricorrente
o chi fa ricorso

**claims depart-
ment** ufficio (m)
indennità
claims manager
responsabile (m)
dei reclami
class classe (f) o
categoria (f)
classification clas-
sificazione (f)
classified ads
annunci (mpl) eco-
nomici (su giornale)
o inserzioni (fpl)
**classified adver-
tisements** annunci
economici
**classified direc-
tory** elenco (m)
classificato
classify classificare
clause clausola (f)
clawback ricuper-
are mediante
tassazione
clear (adj) *[com-
plete]* libero
clear (adj) *[easy to
understand]* chiaro
clear (v) *[stock]*
liquidare

clear a cheque
compensare un
assegno
clear a debt
estinguere un debito
clear profit utile
(m) netto
**clearance certifi-
cate** certificato (m)
di sdoganamento
**clearance of a
cheque** compen-
sazione (f) di un
assegno
clearing *[paying]*
saldo (m) di un debito
clearing bank
banca (f) di
compensazione
clerical impiega-
tizio o d'ufficio
clerical error
errore (m) di
trascrizione
clerical staff personale (m) impiegatizio
clerical work
lavoro (m) d'ufficio
clerk impiegato (m)
client cliente (mf)
clientele clientela (f)

climb salire *o*
ascendere
clinch concludere
definitivamente
clipping service
servizio (m) stralci
giornalistici
close (n) *[end]*
chiusura (f)
close (v) *[after work]*
chiudere *o* finire
close a bank
account chiudere un
conto bancario
close a meeting
togliere la seduta
close an account
chiudere un conto
close down chiud-
ere *o* ospendere
un'attività
close to vicino a
closed chiuso
closed market
mercato (m) chiuso
closing (adj) di
chiusura finale
closing (n)
chiusura (f)
closing balance bilancio (m) di chiusura

closing bid ultima
offerta (f) (di lici-
tazione)
closing date ter-
mine (m) ultimo *o*
data di chiusura
closing price
prezzo (m) di
chiusura
closing stock gia-
cenze (fpl) finali
alla chiusura dell'e-
sercizio
closing time ora (f)
di chiusura
closing-down sale
svendita (f) per
chiusura d'esercizio
closure chiusura (f)
o termine (m)
c/o (= care of) presso
co-creditor credi-
tore (m) in solido
co-director
condirettore (m)
co-insurance
coassicurazione (f)
co-operate cooperare
co-operation coop-
erazione (m) *o*
collaborazione (f)

co-operative (adj)
cooperativo *o*
cooperativa
co-operative (n)
cooperativa (f)
co-opt someone
cooptare qualcuno
co-owner compro-
prietario (m)
co-ownership
comproprietà (f)
COD *or* c.o.d.
(= cash on deli-
very) pagamento
(m) alla consegna
code codice (m)
code of practice
codice (m) di etica
professionale
coding codifica (f)
o codificazione (f)
coin moneta (f)
(metallica)
cold call visita (f)
a freddo
cold start partenza
(f) fredda
cold storage
conservazione (f) in
ambiente
frigorifero

cold store
magazzino (m)
frigorifero
collaboration
collaborazione (f)
collapse (n)
crollo (m)
collapse (v)
crollare *o* cadere
collateral (adj)
collaterale
collateral (n)
garanzia (f)
collaterale
collect (v) *[fetch]*
cogliere *o*
raccogliere
collect (v) *[money]*
recuperare
collect a debt
recuperare un
debito
collect call *[US]*
telefonata (f) a
carico del ricevente
collection *[of*
goods] ritiro (m)
collection *[of money]*
recupero (m)
collection *[postal]*
levata (f)

**collection charges
or collection rates**
spese (fpl)
d'incasso
collective
collettivo
**collective owner-
ship** proprietà (f)
collettiva
**collective wage
agreement**
contratto (m)
salariale collettivo
collector
raccoglitore (m)
commerce
commercio (m)
commercial (adj)
commerciale
commercial (n)
[TV] pubblicità (f)
o spot (m)
commercial attaché
addetto (m)
commerciale
commercial college
scuola (m) superi-
ore di commercio
commercial course
corso (m) a indirizzo
commerciale

**commercial direc-
tory** annuario
(m) commerciale
commercial district
distretto (m)
commerciale
commercial failure
insuccesso (m)
commerciale
commercial law
diritto (m)
commerciale
**commercial trav-
eller** commesso
(m) viaggiatore
**commercial under-
taking** iniziativa
(f) commerciale
commercialization
commercializ-
zazione (f)
commercialize
commercializzare
commission *[com-
mittee]* comitato (m)
commission *[money]*
commissione (f) o
percentuale (f)
commission agent
agente (m)
commissionario

commission rep
rappresentante
(m) commissionario
commit [crime]
commettere
commit funds to a
project affidare
fondi ad un progetto
commitments
impegni (mpl)
commodity merce
(f) o bene (m)
commodity exchange
Borsa (f) Merci
commodity futures
contratti (mpl)
a termine su
materie prime
commodity market
mercato (m)
delle materie prime
common [frequent]
comune o usuale
common [to more
than one] comune
common carrier
vettore (m)
common ownership
proprietà (f) comune
common pricing
prezzi (mpl) correnti

communicate
comunicare
communication
[general]
comunicazione (f)
communication
[message] comuni-
cazione (f)
communications
comunicazioni (fpl)
community
comunità (f)
commute [exchange]
scambiare
commute
[travel] fare il
pendolare
commuter
pendolare (m)
companies' register
Registro (m) delle
SPA
company compag-
nia (f) o società (di
capitali)
company director
amministratore
(m) di società
company law
diritto (m)
societario

company secretary
segretario (m)
del consiglio d'am-
ministrazione
comparability com-
parabilità (f)
comparable parag-
onabile
compare confrontare
o paragonare
compare with
essere paragonabile
comparison con-
fronto (m)
compensate com-
pensare
compensation
compenso (m) o
ricompensa (f)
compensation
 for damage ris-
arcimento (m) di
danni
compete with
someone or **with a**
company
competere con
qualcuno o con
un'azienda
competing (adj) in
concorrenza

competing firms
aziende (f) in con-
correnza
competing products
prodotti (mpl)
che si fanno con-
correnza
competition con-
correnza (f) o com-
petizione (f)
competitive com-
petitivo
competitive price
prezzo (m) allineato
competitive pricing
determinazione (f)
del prezzo di
concorrenza
competitive prod-
ucts prodotti
(mpl) competitivi
competitively
priced con prezzo
competitivo
competitiveness
competitività (f)
competitor concor-
rente (m)
complain (about)
protestare o
reclamare

complaint protesta (f) o reclamo (m)

complaints depart-ment ufficio (m) reclami

complementary complementare

complete (adj) completo

complete (v) finire o portare a termine

completion completamento (m)

completion date data (f) di ulti-mazione

completion of a con-tract adempimento (m) di un contratto

compliance adem-pimento (m)

complimentary in omaggio

complimentary ticket biglietto (m) omaggio

compliments slip cartoncino (m) della società

comply with confor-marsi a o osservare

composition [with creditors] acco-modamento (m)

compound interest interesse (m) composto

comprehensive comprensivo

comprehensive insurance assicu-razione (f) globale

compromise (n) compromesso (m)

compromise (v) venire a un compro-messo

compulsory obbligatorio

compulsory liquidation liquidazione (f) coatta

compulsory pur-chase espropri-azione (f) per pubblica utilità

computer computer (m)

computer bureau ufficio (m) computer

**computer depart-
ment** ufficio (m)
computer
computer error errore
(m) di computer
computer file
archivio (m) (di un
computer)
computer language
linguaggio
(m) di computer
computer listing
registrazione (f)
sul computer
computer printer
stampante (f) lineare
computer printout
tabulato (m)
computer program
programma
(m) di computer
**computer program-
mer** programmatore
(m) di computer
**computer pro-
gramming**
programmazione (f)
di computer
computer services
servizi (mpl) di elab-
orazione elettronica

computer system
sistema (m) elettron-
ico di elaborazione
computer terminal
terminale (m)
di computer
computer time
tempo (m) di
elaborazione
computer-readable
leggibile dal
computer
**computer-readable
codes** codici
(mpl) leggibili dal
computer
computerize
computerizzare
computerized elab-
orato a mezzo
computer
**concealment of
assets** occulta-
mento (m) di beni
concern (n) *[busi-
ness]* azienda (f)
o ditta (f)
concern (n) *[worry]*
preoccupazione (f)
concern (v) *[deal
with]* interessarsi di

concession *[reduction]* agevolazione (f)
concession *[right]* concessione (f)
concessionaire concessionario (m)
conciliation conciliazione (f)
conclude *[agreement]* concludere
condition *[state]* condizione (f)
condition *[terms]* condizione (f)
condition: on condition that a condizione che
conditional soggetto a condizioni
conditions of employment condizioni (fpl) di assunzione
conditions of sale condizioni (fpl) di vendita
conduct negotiations condurre una trattativa
conference *[large]* conferenza (f) o congresso (m)

conference *[small]* riunione (f)
conference phone telefono (m) per conferenze
conference room sala (f) riunioni
confidence fiducia (f)
confidential riservato
confidential report rapporto (m) riservato
confidentiality riservatezza (f)
confirm confermare
confirm a booking confermare una prenotazione
confirm someone in a job confermare l'assunzione di una persona
confirmation conferma (f)
conflict of interest conflitto (m) di interessi
conglomerate conglomerato (m)
connect collegare

connecting flight
volo (m) di
coincidenza
connection
coincidenza (f)
consider considerare
consign consegnare
consignee conseg-
natario (m)
consignment [send-
ing] spedizione (f)
consignment
[things sent,
received] invio (m)
consignment note
lettera (f) di vettura
consignor
mittente (m)
consist of
consistere in
consolidate
consolidare
consolidate [ship-
ments] consolidare
spedizioni
consolidated con-
solidato
consolidated ship-
ment spedizione
(f) consolidata
consolidation
consolidamento (m)

consortium
consorzio (m)
constant costante
consult consultarsi
consultancy
consulenza (f)
consultancy firm
ditta (f) di
consulenza
consultant
consulente (m)
consulting engineer
consulente
(m) tecnico
consumables
generi (mpl) di
consumo
consumer
consumatore (m)
consumer credit
credito (m) al
consumatore
consumer durables
beni (mpl) di
consumo durevoli
consumer goods
beni (mpl)
di consumo
consumer panel
gruppo (m)
selezionato di
consumatori

consumer price index indice (m) dei prezzi al consumo
consumer protection protezione (f) del consumatore
consumer research ricerca (f) di mercato sui bisogni dei consumatori
consumer spending spese (fpl) di consumo
consumption consumo (m)
contact (n) *[general]* contatto (m)
contact (n) *[person]* contatto (m)
contact (v) mettersi in contatto con
contain contenere
container *[box, tin]* contenitore (m)
container *[for shipping]* container (m)
container port scalo (m) per container
container ship nave (f) per trasporto di container
container terminal terminal (m) per container
containerization *[putting into containers]* containerizzazione (f)
containerization *[shipping in containers]* trasporto (m) in container
containerize *[put into containers]* containerizzare
containerize *[ship in containers]* spedire merce in container
contents contenuto (m)
contested takeover acquisizione (f) di controllo contestata
contingency contingenza (f)
contingency fund fondo (m) di previdenza
contingency plan piano (m) di contingenza

continual continuo
continually
continuamente
continuation con-
tinuazione (f)
continue continuare
continuous continuo
continuous feed
alimentazione (f)
continua
**continuous sta-
tionery** moduli (mpl)
a striscia continua
contra account
conto (m) di
contropartita
contra an entry
stornare una
registrazione
contra entry regis-
trazione (f) di storno
contract (n)
contratto (m)
contract (v) contrarre
contract law diritto
(m) contrattuale
contract note fis-
sato (m) bollato
**contract of employ-
ment** contratto
(m) di lavoro

contract work lavoro
(m) a contratto
contracting party
parte (f) contraente
contractor impren-
ditore (m)
contractual
contrattuale
contractual liability
responsabilità
(f) contrattuale
contractually
contrattualmente
contrary contrario
contrast (n)
contrasto (m)
contribute
contribuire
contribution
contributo (m)
**contribution of
capital** apporto (m)
di capitali
contributor
sottoscrittore (m)
control (n) [check]
controllo (m) o
verifica (f)
control (n) [power]
controllo (m) o
potere (m)

control (v) controllare

control a business detenere il controllo azionario

control key tasto (m) di comando

control systems sistema (m) di controllo

controlled economy economia (f) controllata

controller [US] revisore (m) dei conti

controller [who checks] controllore (m)

controlling (adj) controllante

convene convocare

convenient comodo

conversion conversione (f)

conversion of funds conversione (f) di fondi

conversion price or conversion rate tasso (m) di conversione

convert convertire

convertibility convertibilità (f)

convertible currency valuta (f) convertibile

convertible loan stock obbligazioni (fpl) convertibili

conveyance trasmissione (f)

conveyancer notaio (m) o legale (m) che si occupa dei trapassi di proprietà

conveyancing esame (m) dei documenti e stesura degli atti necessari per il trasferimento di proprietà

cooling off period (after purchase) periodo (m) che permette un ripensamento (da parte dell'acquirente)

cooperative society società (f) cooperativa

copartner consocio (m)
copartnership associazione (f) in compartecipazione
cope essere all'altezza
copier copiatrice (f)
copy (n) *[a document]* copia (f)
copy (n) *[book, newspaper]* copia (f) o esemplare (m)
copy (n) *[of document]* copia (f)
copy (v) copiare o riprodurre
copying machine copiatrice (f)
corner (n) *[angle]* angolo (m)
corner (n) *[monopoly]* accaparramento (m) o monopolio (m)
corner shop negozio (m) d'angolo
corner the market accaparrarsi il mercato (m)

corporate image immagine (f) aziendale
corporate name ragione (f) sociale
corporate plan programma (m) aziendale
corporate planning programmazione (f) aziendale
corporate profits utili (mpl) societari
corporation corporazione (f)
corporation tax imposta (f) sulla società
correct (adj) corretto
correct (v) correggere
correction correzione (f)
correspond with someone essere in corrispondenza con qualcuno
correspond with something equivalere a qualcosa
correspondence corrispondenza (f)

correspondent [journalist] inviato (m)
correspondent [who writes letters] corrispondente (mf)
cost (n) costo (m)
cost (v) costare
cost accountant analista (m) dei costi
cost accounting contabilità (f) basata sui conti
cost analysis analisi (f) dei costi
cost centre centro (m) di costi
cost factor fattore (m) costo
cost of living costo (m) della vita o carovita (m)
cost of sales costo (m) delle vendite
cost plus costo (m) più una percentuale
cost price prezzo (m) sotto costo
cost, insurance and freight (c.i.f.) costo (m), assicurazione (f) e nolo (m)

cost-benefit analysis analisi (f) preventiva della convenienza dei costi
cost-cutting riduzione (f) dei costi
cost-effective redditizio
cost-effectiveness redditività (f) dei costi
cost-of-living allowance indennità (f) di contingenza
cost-of-living bonus contingenza (f)
cost-of-living increase aumento (m) del costo della vita
cost-of-living index indice (m) del costo della vita
cost-push inflation inflazione (f) da costi
costing valutazione (f) dei costi
costly costoso
costs spese (fpl)
counsel avvocato (mf)
count (v) [add] contare

count (v) *[include]* includere

counter banco (m)

counter staff personale (m) al banco

counter-claim (n) controrichiesta (f)

counter-claim (v) presentare una controrichiesta

counter-offer controfferta (f)

counterbid controfferta (f)

counterfeit (adj) contraffatto *o* falso

counterfeit (v) contraffare

counterfoil matrice (f)

countermand fermare

countersign contrassegno (m)

country *[not town]* campagna (f)

country *[state]* paese (m) *o* nazione (f)

country of origin paese (m) d'origine

coupon buono (m)

coupon ad materiale pubblicitario con buono

courier *[guide]* guida (f) (turistica)

courier *[messenger]* messaggero (m) *o* corriere (m)

court corte (f) di Giustizia

court case causa (f) legale

covenant (n) convenzione (f)

covenant (v) convenire

cover (n) *[insurance]* copertura (f) assicurativa

cover (n) *[top]* copertura (f)

cover (v) *[expenses]* coprire *o* pagare

cover (v) *[put on top]* coprire

cover a risk assicurarsi contro un rischio

cover charge prezzo (m) del coperto

cover costs
coprire i costi
cover note polizza
(f) provvisoria
covering letter
lettera (f) di
accompagnamento
covering note
polizza (f) provvisoria
crane gru (f)
crash (n) *[accident]*
incidente (m)
crash (n) *[financial]*
crollo (m)
crash (v) *[fail]*
crollare
crash (v) *[hit]*
scontrarsi con
crate (n) cassa (f)
crate (v) imballare
(merce) in casse
credit (n) credito (m)
credit (v) accred-
itare (un conto)
credit account
conto (m) creditori
credit agency agenzia
(f) per reperimento
di referenze
credit balance dif-
ferenza (f) a credito

credit bank istituto
(m) di credito
credit card carta
(f) di credito
credit card sale
vendita (f) con
carta di credito
credit ceiling mas-
simale (m) di credito
o tetto (m) salariale
credit column
colonna (f) dell'avere
credit control con-
trollo (m) del credito
credit entry
registrazione (f)
contabile a credito
credit facilities
agevolazioni (fpl)
creditizie
credit freeze blocco
(m) del credito
credit limit limite
(m) di credito
credit note nota (f)
di accredito
credit policy
politica (f) creditizia
credit rating
grado (m) di solvi-
bilità

credit side avere (m)
o lato (m) dell'attivo
credit-worthy solvibile
credit: on credit a
credito
creditor creditore (m)
cross a cheque
sbarrare un assegno
cross off depennare
cross out cancellare
cross rate cambio
(m) incrociato
crossed cheque
assegno (m) sbarrato
cubic cubico
cubic measure
misure (fpl) cubiche
cum con
cum coupon con
coupon (m)
cum dividend con
dividendo (m)
cumulative
cumulativo
cumulative interest
interesse (m) com-
posto
**cumulative prefer-
ence shares** azioni
(fpl) privilegiate
cumulative

currency moneta
(f) legale
currency conversion
conversione
(f) della valuta
currency note
banconota (f)
currency reserves
riserve (fpl)
valutarie
current corrente
current account
conto (m) corrente
current assets
attività (fpl) liquide
**current cost
accounting**
contabilità (f) a
costi correnti
current liabilities
passività (fpl) correnti
current price
prezzo (m) corrente
**current rate of
exchange** tasso (m)
di cambio corrente
current yield rendi-
mento (m) immediato
**curriculum vitae
(CV)** curriculum
(m) vitae

curve curva (f)
custom clientela (f)
custom-built *or*
custom-made
fatto appositamente
customer
cliente (mf)
customer appeal
richiamo (m) per i
clienti
customer loyalty
fedeltà (f)
dei clienti
**customer satisfac-
tion** soddisfazione
(f) dei clienti
**customer service
department**
ufficio (m) assis-
tenza ai clienti
customs dogana (f)
Customs and Excise
Ufficio Dazio e
Dogana
customs barrier
barriera (f) doganale
customs broker
agente (m) doganale
customs clearance
svincolo (m)
doganale

customs declaration
dichiarazione
(f) doganale
**customs declaration
form** modulo
(m) di dichiarazione
doganale
customs duty dazio
(m) doganale
**customs entry
point** punto (m)
per la dichiarazine
doganale d'entrata
customs examination
controllo (m)
doganale
customs formalities
formalità (fpl)
doganali
customs officer
doganiere (m)
customs official ufficiale (m) di dogana
customs receipt
avviso (m) di
ricevimento
doganale
customs seal
sigillo (m) doganale
customs tariff
tariffa (f) doganale

customs union
unione (f) doganale
cut (n) taglio (m)
cut (v) tagliare
cut down on
expenses ridurre le
spese
cut price (n)
prezzo (m) ridotto
cut-price (adj) a
prezzo ridotto
cut-price goods
merce (f) a prezzo
ridotto
cut-price petrol
benzina (f) a
prezzo ridotto
cut-price store
negozio con merce
a prezzi ridotti
cut-throat competi-
tion concorrenza
(f) spietata
CV (= curriculum
vitae) Curriculum
(m) Vitae
cycle ciclo (m)
cyclical ciclico
cyclical factors
elementi (mpl)
ciclici

Dd

daily quotidiano
daisy-wheel printer
stampante (f) con
testina a margherita
damage (n)
danno (m)
damage (v)
danneggiare
damage survey
perizia (f) d'avaria
damage to property
danno (m) alla
proprietà
damaged
danneggiato
damages
risarcimento (m) dei
danni
data dati (mpl)
data processing
elaborazione (f)
dei dati
data retrieval
ricerca (f) automat-
ica dell'informazione
database base (f)
di dati

date (n) data (f)

date (v) datare

date of receipt data
(f) di ricevimento

date stamp
datario (m)

dated datato

day *[24 hours]*
giorno (m)

day *[working day]*
giorno (m)

day shift turno (m)
di giorno

day-to-day giorno
per giorno

dead (adj) *[person]*
morto

dead account conto
(m) chiuso

dead loss perdita
(f) secca

deadline termine
(m) ultimo

deadlock (n) punto
(m) morto

deadlock (v) essere
a un punto morto

deadweight peso
(m) morto

deadweight cargo
carico (m) lordo

deadweight tonnage
portata (f) lorda

deal (n) operazione
(f) o affare (m)

deal in (v) com-
merciare o negoziare

deal with an order
dare corso ad
un'ordinazione

deal with someone
trattare con qualcuno

dealer
commerciante (m)

dealing *[commerce]*
commercio (m)

dealing *[stock
exchange]*
transazioni (fpl) o
operazioni (fpl)

dear caro

debenture
obbligazione (f) (di
società private)

debenture holder
obbligazionista (m)

debit (n)
adde-bito (m)

debit an account
addebitare un conto

debit balance saldo
(m) debitore

debit column
colonna (f) del dare
debit entry regis-
trazione (f) a debito
debit note nota (f)
di addebito
debits and credits
dare e avere
debt debito (m)
debt collection recu-
pero (m) di crediti
debt collection
agency agenzia (f)
per il recupero dei
crediti
debt collector esat-
tore (m) dei crediti
debtor debitore (m)
debtor side
colonna (f) del dare
debts due credito
(m) esigibile
decentralization
decentramento (m)
decentralize
decentrare
decide decidere
decide on a course
of action decidere
una linea di con-
dotta

deciding decisivo
deciding factor ele-
mento (m) decisivo
decimal (n)
decimale (m)
decimal point
virgola (f) decimale
decision deci-
sione (f)
decision maker
persona (f) che
prende decisioni
decision making
processo (m)
decisionale
decision-making
processes
processo (m) di
decisione
deck piano (m)
deck cargo carico
(m) di coperta
declaration
dichiarazione (f)
declaration of bank-
ruptcy dichiarazione
(f) di fallimento
declaration of
income dichiarazione
(f) dei redditi
declare dichiarare

declare goods to customs dichiarare le merci alla dogana
declare someone bankrupt dichiarare qualcuno fallito
declared dichiarato
declared value valore (m) dichiarato
decline (n) declino (m)
decline (v) *[fall]* rifiutare
decontrol abolire i controlli (mpl)
decrease (n) diminuzione (f)
decrease (v) diminuire
decrease in price diminuzione (f) dei prezzi
decrease in value diminuzione (f) del valore
decreasing (adj) decrescente
deduct dedurre
deductible detraibile
deduction detrazione (f)

deed atto (m)
deed of assignment atto (m) di cessione
deed of covenant atto (m) di donazione
deed of partnership atto (m) costitutivo
deed of transfer atto (m) di trasferimento
default (n) inadempienza (f)
default (v) essere contumace
default on payments inadempienza (f) nel pagamento
defaulter inadempiente (m)
defect difetto (m)
defective *[faulty]* difettoso
defective *[not valid]* privo di validità o viziato
defence *[legal]* difesa (f)
defence *[protection]* difesa (f)
defence counsel avvocato (m) difensore

defend difendere
defend a lawsuit difendere una causa
defendant accusato (m)
defer differire
defer payment differire un pagamento
deferment rinvio (m)
deferment of payment rinvio (m) di pagamento
deferred differito
deferred creditor creditore (m) differito
deferred payment pagamento (m) differito
deficit deficit (m) o disavanzo (m)
deficit financing finanziamento (m) del disavanzo (m)
deflation deflazione (f)
deflationary deflazionistico
defray [costs] pagare
defray someone's expenses sostenere le spese di qualcuno

del credere star del credere
del credere agent agente (m) del credere
delay (n) ritardo (m)
delay (v) ritardare
delegate (n) delegato (m)
delegate (v) delegare
delegation [action] delega (f) o delegazione (f)
delegation [people] delegazione (f)
delete eliminare
deliver consegnare
delivered price prezzo (m) franco
delivery [bill of exchange] cessione (f) di una cambiale
delivery [goods] consegna (f) di merce
delivery date data (f) di consegna
delivery note bolla (f) di spedizione
delivery order ordine (m) di consegna

delivery time data (f) di consegna
delivery van furgone (m) per le consegne
deliveryman uomo (m) delle consegne o fattorino (m)
demand (n) *[for payment]* domanda (f) o richiesta (f)
demand (n) *[need]* domanda (f)
demand (v) domandare
demand deposit deposito (m) a vista
demonstrate dimostrare
demonstration dimostrazione (f)
demonstration model campione (m) per dimostrazione
demonstrator dimostratore (m)
demurrage ritardo (m)
department *[in government]* ministero (m)

department *[in office]* reparto (m) o sezione (f)
department *[in shop]* reparto (m)
department store grande magazzino (m)
departmental dipartimentale
departmental manager capo (m) servizio
departure *[going away]* partenza (f)
departure *[new venture]* nuovo orientamento (m)
departure lounge salone (m) delle partenze
departures partenze (fpl)
depend on contare su
depending on a condizione che
deposit (n) *[in bank]* deposito (m)
deposit (n) *[paid in advance]* acconto (m)

deposit (v) versare denaro

deposit account conto (m) di deposito

deposit slip distinta (f) di versamento

depositor depositante (m)

depository [place] deposito (m)

depot magazzino (m)

depreciate [amortize] ammortizzare

depreciate [lose value] svalutare

depreciation [amortizing] ammortamento (m)

depreciation [loss of value] svalutazione (f)

depreciation rate quota (f) d'ammortamento

depression depressione (f)

deputize for someone rappresentare qualcuno

deputy delegato (m) o sostituto (m)

deputy manager vice direttore (m)

deputy managing director vice amministratore (m) delegato

deregulation deregolamentazione (f) o abolizione (f) della regolamentazione

describe descrivere

description descrizione (f)

design (n) design (m) o progettazione (f)

design (v) progettare

design department dipartimento o ufficio design

desk scrivania (f)

desk diary agenda (f) da tavolo

desk-top publishing (DTP) desktop publishing (m)

destination destinazione (f)

detail (n)
dettaglio (m)
detail (v)
dettagliare
detailed
dettagliato
detailed account resoconto (m) dettagliato
determine
determinare
devaluation
svalutazione (f)
devalue svalutare
develop *[build]*
costruire *o* sviluppare
develop *[plan]*
sviluppare
developing country
paese (m) in
via di sviluppo
development
sviluppo (m) *o*
progresso (m)
device
congegno (m)
diagram
diagramma (m)
dial (v) a number
formare *o*
comporre un numero
telefonico

dial direct
teleselezione (f)
dialling chiamata
(f) (telefonica)
dialling code pre-
fisso (m) telefonico
dialling tone segnale
(m) di linea libera
diary diario
dictate dettare
dictating machine
dittafono (m)
dictation dettatura (f)
differ dissentire
difference
differenza (f)
differences in price
differenze (fpl) di
prezzo
different diverso
differential (adj)
differenziale
differential tariffs
tariffe (fpl) dif-
ferenziali
digit cifra (f) *o*
numero (m)
dilution of equity
diluizione (f) della
partecipazione
azionaria

direct (adj) diretto
direct (adv)
direttamente
direct (v) dirigere
o guidare
direct cost costo
(m) diretto
direct debit addeb-
ito (m) diretto
direct mail vendita
(f) diretta tramite
corrispondenza
direct mailing
pubblicità (f) a
mezzo posta
direct selling
vendita (f) diretta
direct tax imposta
(f) diretta
direct taxation tas-
sazione (f) diretta
**direct-mail adver-
tising** pubblicità
(f) a mezzo posta
direction direzione
(f) o istruzione (f)
directions for use
istruzioni (fpl) per l'uso
directive direttiva (f)
director amminis-
tratore (m)

directory
annuario (m)
disburse pagare
disbursement
esborso (m) o
pagamento (m)
**discharge (n) [of
debt]** pagamento
(m) di un debito
**discharge (v)
[employee]**
licenziare
discharge a debt
estinguere un
debito
disclaimer
smentita (f)
disclose rivelare o
divulgare
**disclose a piece of
information**
divulgare un'infor-
mazione
disclosure
rivelazione (f) o
divulgazione (f)
**disclosure of confi-
dential information**
divulgazione (f) di
un'informazione
riservata

discontinue interrrompere

discount (n) sconto (m)

discount (v) vendere sotto costo

discount house [bank] banca (f) di sconto

discount house [shop] negozio (m) di vendita a prezzi ridotti

discount price prezzo (m) scontato

discount rate tasso (m) di sconto

discount store magazzino (m) a prezzi scontati

discountable scontabile

discounted cash flow (DCF) sconto (m) del valore attuale

discounter scontista (m)

discrepancy discrepanza (f)

discuss discutere

discussion discussione (f)

dishonour non onorare

dishonour a bill non onorare un effetto

disk disco (m)

disk drive unità (f) a dischi magnetici

diskette dischetto (m)

dismiss an employee licenziare un dipendente

dismissal licenziamento (m)

dispatch (n) [sending] spedizione (f)

dispatch (v) [send] spedire

dispatch department servizio (m) spedizioni

dispatch note bolla (f) di spedizione

display (n) esposizione (f) o mostra (f)

display (v) esporre

display case vetrinetta (f)

display material
materiale (m) da
esposizione
display pack con-
fezione (f) per
esposizione
display stand
banco (m) di
esposizione
display unit
video-unità
disposable da non
restituire o da
gettare
disposal vendita (f)
**dispose of excess
stock**
eliminare le scorte
in eccesso
dissolve risolvere o
dissolvere
**dissolve a partner-
ship** sciogliere
una società di
persone
**distress merchan-
dise** merci (fpl)
vendute sottocosto
distress sale ven-
dita (f) di merce
sottocosto

distributable profit
utili (mpl) dis-
tribuibili
distribute [goods]
distribuire
distribute [share]
distribuire
distribution
distribuzione (f)
**distribution chan-
nels** canali (mpl)
di distribuzione
distribution costs
costi (mpl) di
distribuzione
**distribution man-
ager** direttore
(m) delle
distribuzioni
**distribution net-
work** rete (f) di
distribuzione
distributor distri-
butore (m)
distributorship
concessione (f) di
vendita
diversification
diversificazione (f)
diversify
diversificare

dividend
dividendo (m)
dividend cover
rapporto (m) fra
utile e dividendo
dividend warrant
cedola (f) di
dividendo
dividend yield red-
dito (m) da dividendi
division *[part of a*
company] reparto (m)
division *[part of a*
group] divisione (f)
dock (n) bacino (m)
dock (v) *[remove*
money] decurtare
dock (v) *[ship]*
entrare in porto *o*
attraccare
docket elenco (m)
delle cause
doctor's certificate
certificato (m) medico
document
documento (m)
documentary
documentario (m)
documentary
evidence
documentazione (f)

documentary proof
prova (f) docu-
mentata
documentation
documentazione (f)
documents
documenti (mpl)
dollar dollaro (m)
dollar area
area (f) del
dollaro
dollar balance
bilancia (f) commer-
ciale in dollari
dollar crisis crisi
(f) del dollaro
domestic domestico
domestic market
mercato (m) interno
domestic produc-
tion produzione
(f) nazionale
domestic sales
vendite (fpl)
interne
domestic trade
commercio (m)
interno
domicile
domicilio (m)
door porta (f)

door-to-door a domicilio (m)
door-to-door sales-man venditore (m) a domicilio
door-to-door selling vendita (f) porta a porta
dossier dossier (m) o pratica (f)
dot-matrix printer stampante (f) a matrice d'aghi
double (adj) doppio
double (v) raddoppiare
double taxation doppia tassazione (f)
double taxation agreement sgravio (m) per doppia tassazione
double-book riservare una camera a due clienti
double-booking prenotazione (f) di una camera a due clienti
down discendente o giù

down payment versamento (m) d'acconto
down time tempo (m) improduttivo
down-market mercato (m) in ribasso
downside factor fattore (m) negativo
downtown (adv) in centro
downtown (n) centro (m) (di città)
downturn regresso (m)
downward discendente o giù
dozen dozzina (f)
draft (n) [money] tratta (f)
draft (n) [rough plan] bozza (f)
draft (v) abbozzare o redigere
draft a contract preparare lo schema di un contratto
draft a letter stendere la minuta (f) di una lettera

draft plan bozza (f) di un piano

draft project bozza (f) di un progetto

draw *[a cheque]* emettere un assegno

draw *[money]* prelevare

draw up redigere

draw up a contract stipulare un contratto

drawee trattario (m)

drawer traente (m)

drawing account conto (m) corrente

drive (n) *[campaign]* campagna (f)

drive (n) *[energy]* grinta (f)

drive (n) *[part of machine]* trasmissione (f)

drive (v) *[a car]* condurre o guidare

driver conducente (m)

drop (n) caduta (f) o ribasso (m)

drop (v) cadere o calare

drop in sales ribasso (m) delle vendite

due *[awaited]* atteso

due *[owing]* dovuto

dues *[orders]* ordinazioni (fpl) inevase

duly *[in time]* come previsto

duly *[legally]* regolarmente o dovutamente

dummy fittizio o falso

dummy pack confezione (f) finta

dump bin scaffale (m) per esposizione (in negozi)

dump goods on a market svendere merci sul mercato

dumping vendita (f) sottocosto

duplicate (n) duplicato (m)

duplicate (v) duplicare

duplicate an invoice fare il duplicato di una fattura
duplicate receipt *or* **duplicate of a receipt** ricevuta (f) in duplicato
duplication duplicazione (f)
durable goods beni (mpl) durevoli
duty *[tax]* dazio (m)
duty-free esente da dazio
duty-free shop 'duty free shop' o negozio (m) esente da tasse
duty-paid goods merce (f) con dazio pagato

Ee

e. & o.e. (errors and omissions excepted) Salvo errori e omissioni (S. E. & O)
early prossimo
earmark funds for a project accantonare fondi (mpl) per un progetto
earn *[interest]* fruttare
earn *[money]* guadagnare
earning capacity capacità (f) di guadagno
earnings *[profit]* utile (m) o profitto (m)
earnings *[salary]* guadagni (mpl)
earnings per share *or* **earnings yield** utile (m) per azione

easy facile
easy terms condizioni (fpl) moderate
economic [general] economico
economic [profitable] vantaggioso
economic cycle ciclo (m) economico
economic development sviluppo (m) economico
economic growth crescita (f) economica
economic indicators indicatori (mpl) economici
economic model modello (m) economico
economic planning programmazione (f) economica
economic trends congiuntura (f)
economical economico
economics [profitability] redditività (f)

economics [study] economia (f) o scienze (fpl) economiche
economies of scale economia (f) di massa
economist economista (mf)
economize economizzare
economy [saving] economia (f)
economy [system] economia (f)
economy class classe (f) turistica
ecu or ECU (= European currency unit) ecu (m) (Unità di Conto Europea)
effect (n) effetto (m)
effect (v) effettuare
effective effettivo
effective date data (f) di entrata in vigore
effective demand domanda (f) effettiva

effective yield
rendimento (m)
effettivo
effectiveness
efficacia (f)
efficiency
efficienza (f)
efficient efficiente
effort sforzo (m)
elasticity
elasticità (f)
elect eleggere
election elezione (f)
electronic mail
posta (f) elettronica
**electronic point of
sale (EPOS)** punto
(m) di vendita elet-
tronico
elevator *[goods]*
montacarichi (m)
elevator *[grain]*
silo (m)
**email (= electronic
mail)** posta (f)
elettronica
embargo (n)
embargo (m)
embargo (v) met-
tere l'em
bargo su

embark imbarcare
o imbarcarsi
embark on
imbarcarsi in
embarkation
imbarco (m)
embarkation card
carta (f) d'imbarco
embezzle appropri-
arsi indebitamente
embezzlement
appropriazione (f)
indebita
embezzler colpevole
(m) di appropri-
azione indebita
emergency
emergenza (f)
**emergency
reserves** riserve
(fpl) d'emergenza
employ impiegare *o*
assumere
employed *[in job]*
impiegato
employed *[money]*
investito
employed *[used]*
impiegato
employee
dipendente (m)

employer datore (m) di lavoro
employment impiego (m)
employment agency agenzia (f) di lavoro
employment bureau agenzia (f) di lavoro
empty (adj) vuoto
empty (v) vuotare
EMS (= European Monetary System) SME (Sistema Monetario Europeo)
encash incassare
encashment incasso (m)
enclose allegare
enclosure allegato (m)
end (n) fine (f) o termine (m)
end (v) finire o concludere
end of season sale svendite (fpl) di fine stagione
end product prodotto (m) finito

end user utente (m) finale
endorse a cheque girare un assegno
endorsee giratario (m)
endorsement [action] girata (f)
endorsement [on insurance] restrizione (f)
endorser girante (m)
energy [electricity] energia (f)
energy [human] energia (f) o dinamismo (m)
energy-saving (adj) che risparmia energia
enforce applicare
enforcement imposizione (f)
engaged [telephone] occupato
engaged tone segnale (m) di linea occupata
enquire (= inquire) chiedere informazioni

enquiry (= inquiry)
richiesta (f) di infor-
mazioni
enter [go in] entrare
enter [write in]
registrare
**enter into [discus-
sion]** prendere
parte in
entering
annotazione (f)
enterprise
impresa (f)
entitle conferire il
diritto
entitlement
diritto (m)
entrepot port
porto (m) di transito
entrepreneur
imprenditore (m)
entrepreneurial
imprenditoriale
entrust affidare
entry [going in]
entrata (f)
entry [writing]
scrittura (f)
contabile
entry visa visto
(m) d'ingresso

epos or EPOS
**(= electronic point
of sale)** punto (m)
di vendita
elettronico
equal (adj) uguale
equal (v)
uguagliare
equalization
equalizzazione (f)
equip equipaggiare
equipment
apparecchiatura (f)
equities azioni
(fpl) ordinarie
equity passivo (m)
patrimoniale
equity capital capi-
tale (m) effettivo
erode erodere
error errore (m)
error rate per-
centuale (f) d'errore
**errors and omis-
sions excepted (e. &
o.e.)** salvo errori e
omissioni (S.E & O)
escalate intensificare
escape clause
clausola (f) di
salvaguardia

escrow account
conto (m) a
garanzia
essential
indispensabile
establish stabilire
o istituire
establishment
[business] azienda
(f) commerciale
establishment
[staff] personale (m)
estimate (n) *[cal-*
culation]
valutazione (f)
estimate (n) *[quote]*
preventivo (m)
estimate (v) sti-
mare o valutare
estimated valutato
estimated figure
cifra (f) preventivata
estimated sales
vendite (fpl)
presunte
estimation
opinione (f)
EU (= European
Union) UE (Unione
(f) Europea)
euro euro (m)

Eurocheque
euroassegno (m)
Eurocurrency
euromoneta (f)
Eurodollar
eurodollaro (m)
Euromarket
euromercato (m)
European europeo
European Investment
Bank (EIB) Banca (f)
Europea per gli
Investimenti (BEI)
European Monetary
System (EMS)
Sistema (m) Monetario
Europeo (SME)
European Union
(EU) Unione (f)
Europea (UE)
evade evadere
evade tax sottrarsi
al pagamento
delle tasse
evaluate valutare
evaluate costs
valutare i costi
evaluation
valutazione (f)
evasion evasione
(f) d'imposta

ex coupon ex cedola (f)
ex dividend ex dividendo (m)
ex-directory che non compare nell' elenco telefonico
exact (adj) esatto
exact (v) esigere
exactly esattamente
examination [inspection] esame (f)
examination [test] esame (f)
examine esaminare
exceed sorpassare o superare
excellent eccellente
except eccetto o tranne
exceptional eccezionale o straordinario
exceptional items voci (fpl) straordinarie
excess eccesso
excess baggage bagaglio (m) in eccesso

excess capacity capacità (f) produttiva in eccesso
excess profits sovrapprofitti (mpl)
excessive eccessivo
excessive costs costi (mpl) eccessivi
exchange (n) [currency] cambio (m)
exchange (v) [currency] cambiare
exchange (v) [one thing for another] scambiare con
exchange control controlli (mpl) valutari
exchange rate tasso (m) di cambio
exchangeable scambiabile
Exchequer Ministero del Tesoro
excise (v) [cut out] tagliare
excise duty imposta (f) indiretta
Excise officer daziere (m)
exclude escludere

excluding escluso
exclusion
esclusione (f)
exclusion clause
clausola (f) di
esclusione
exclusive agreement
accordo (m)
in esclusiva
exclusive of escluso
exclusive of tax
tassa (f) esclusa
exclusivity
esclusività (f)
execute eseguire
execution
esecuzione (f)
executive (adj)
esecutivo
executive (n)
dirigente (m)
executive director
direttore (m)
esecutivo
exempt (adj) esente
exempt (v) esentare
exempt from tax
esente da
tassa
exemption
esenzione (f)

**exemption from
tax** esenzione (f)
da tassa
exercise (n)
esercizio (m)
exercise (v)
esercitare
exercise an option
esercitare
un'opzione
**exercise of an
option** esercizio
(m) di un'opzione
exhibit (v) esibire
exhibition espo-
sizione (f) o mostra (f)
exhibition hall sala
(f) esposizioni
exhibitor espositore
(m) o standista (m)
expand ampliare
expansion
allargamento (m)
expenditure
spese (fpl)
expense spesa (f)
o conto (m)
expense account
conto (m) spese
expenses
spese (fpl)

expensive costoso
experienced
esperto
expertise 'expert-
ise' (f) *o* perizia (f)
expiration
termine (m)
expire terminare *o*
scadere
expiry fine (f) *o*
scadenza (f)
expiry date data
(f) di scadenza
explain spiegare
explanation
spiegazione (f)
exploit sfruttare
explore esplorare
export (n)
esportazione (f)
export (v)
esportare
export department
reparto (m)
esportazioni
export duty dazio
(m) d'esportazione
export licence *or*
export permit
licenza (f) d'es-
portazione

export manager
direttore (m) del
reparto esportazioni
export trade
commercio (m)
d'esportazione
exporter
esportatore (m)
exporting (adj)
esportatore
exports
esportazioni (fpl)
exposure rischio
(m) finanziario
express (adj) *[fast]*
espresso
express (adj)
[stated clearly]
espresso
express (v) *[send*
fast] spedire per
espresso
express (v) *[state]*
esprimere
express delivery
spedizione (f) per
espresso
express letter
lettera (f) espresso
extend *[grant]*
accordare

extend *[make longer]* prolungare
extended credit credito (m) prorogato
extension *[making longer]* prolungamento (m)
extension *[telephone]* interno (m)
external *[foreign]* estero *o* straniero
external *[outside a company]* esterno
external account conto (m) estero (fuori l'area di sterlina)
external audit revisione (f) esterna
external auditor revisore (m) esterno
external trade commercio (m) estero
extra extra
extra charges spese (fpl) extra
extraordinary straordinario

extraordinary items voci (fpl) straordinarie
extras spese (fpl) supplementari

Ff

FAO (= for the attention of) all'attenzione di
face value valore (m) nominale
facilities servizi (mpl) *o* mezzi (mpl)
facility *[building]* edificio (m)
facility *[credit]* agevolazione (f)
facility *[ease]* agevolazione (f)
factor (n) *[influence]* fattore (m)

factor (n) *[person,*
company] agente
(m) di factoring *o*
società di factoring
factor (v) fare del
factoring
factoring
factoring (m)
factoring charges
costi (mpl) di
factoring
factors of produc-
tion fattori (mpl)
di produzione
factory fabbrica (f)
factory inspector
ispettore (m)
aziendale
factory outlet
punto (m) di ven-
dita diretta della
fabbrica
factory price prezzo
(m) di fabbrica
fail *[go bust]* fallire
fail *[not to do*
something]
non riuscire *o*
non fare
fail *[not to succeed]*
fallire

failing that se non
è possibile
failure in
successo (m)
fair (adj)
giusto *o* equo
fair dealing tratta-
mento (f) equo
fair price prezzi
(mpl) equi
fair trade commer-
cio (m) libero
fair trading com-
mercio (m) libero
fair wear and tear
normale usura
(f) e degrado (m)
fake (n)
imitazione (f)
fake (v) falsificare
faked documents
documenti (mpl) falsi
fall (n) caduta (f)
o crollo (m)
fall (v) *[go lower]*
cadere
fall (v) *[on a date]*
scadere
fall behind *[be in a*
worse position]
rimanere indietro

fall behind *[be late]*
essere in ritardo
(nel fare una cosa)
fall due essere
dovuto
fall off scendere *o*
diminuire
fall through fallire
o non arrivare a
compimento
falling in ribasso
false falso
false pretences mil-
lantato credito (m)
false weight peso
(m) contraffatto
falsification
falsificazione (f)
falsify falsificare
family company
ditta (f) a
conduzione familiare
fare tariffa (f)
farm out work
appaltare del lavoro
fast (adj) veloce
fast (adv) veloce-
mente *o* rapidamente
fast-selling items
articoli (mpl) che
vendono rapidamente

fault *[blame]*
colpa (f)
fault *[mechanical]*
difetto (m)
faulty equipment
apparecchiatura
(f) difettosa
favourable
favorevole
**favourable balance
of trade** bilancia
(f) commerciale
attiva
fax (n) fax (m)
fax (v) inviare
per fax
feasibility
fattibilità (f)
feasibility report
studio (m) della
fattibilità
fee *[admission]*
quota (f) d'iscrizione
fee *[for services]*
emolumento (m)
o compenso (m)
feedback
controreazione (f)
ferry traghetto (m)
fiddle (n) imbroglio
(m) *o* truffa (f)

fiddle (v) imbrogliare
field campo (m) *o*
area (f)
field sales manager
direttore (m)
vendite esterne
field work attività
(f) esterna di
ricerca e di studio
FIFO (= first in
first out) primo ad
entrare primo ad
uscire
figure cifra (f)
figures cifre (fpl) *o*
numeri (mpl)
file (n) *[computer]*
file (m) *o*
archivio (m)
file (n) *[documents]*
fascicolo (m)
file (v) *[request]*
inoltrare
file a patent appli-
cation inoltrare
una domanda di
brevetto
file documents
depositare documenti
filing *[action]*
schedatura (f)

filing cabinet
schedario (m)
filing card scheda (f)
fill a gap colmare
una lacuna (f)
final finale
final demand
domanda (f) finale
final discharge
quietanza (f) finale
final dividend divi-
dendo (m) finale
finalize completare
finance (n) finanza
(f) *o* attività (f)
finanziaria
finance (v)
finanziare
finance an opera-
tion finanziare
un'operazione
finance company
società (f) finanziaria
finance director
direttore (m) delle
finanze
finances
finanze (fpl)
financial
finanziario *o*
economico

financial assets
disponibilità (fpl)
finanziarie
financial crisis crisi
(f) finanziaria
financial institution
Istituto (m)
finanziario
financial position
posizione (f)
finanziaria
financial resources
risorse (fpl)
finanziarie
financial risk ris-
chio (m) finanziario
**financial settle-
ment** regolamento
(m) finanziario
financial year eser-
cizio (m) finanziario
financially
finanziariamente
financing finanzia-
mento (m)
fine (adv) *[very
good]* molto bene
fine (adv) *[very
small]* fine
fine (n) multa (f)
fine (v) multare

fine tuning per-
fetta sintonia (f)
finished finito
finished goods
prodotti (mpl)
finiti
fire (n) fuoco (m)
o incendio (m)
fire damage danno
(m) causato da
un incendio
fire insurance
assicurazione (f)
contro gli incendi
fire regulations
norme (fpl)
antincendio
fire risk rischio (m)
d'incendio
**fire-damaged
goods** merce (f)
danneggiata da
incendio
firm (adj) stabile o
solido
firm (n) ditta (f) o
azienda (f) o
impresa (f)
firm (v) consolidarsi
firm price prezzo
(m) stabile

first primo
first in first out
(FIFO) primo ad
entrare primo ad
uscire
first option prima
opzione (f)
first quarter primo
trimestre (m)
first-class prima
classe
fiscal fiscale
fiscal measures
provvedimenti
(mpl) fiscali
fittings
accessori (mpl)
fix *[arrange]* fissare
fix *[mend]* riparare
**fix a meeting for 3
p.m.** fissare
una riunione per le
3 del pomeriggio
fixed fisso o fissato
fixed assets immo-
bilizzi (mpl)
fixed costs costi
(mpl) fissi
fixed deposit
deposito (m)
vincolato

fixed exchange rate
tasso (m)
fisso di cambio
fixed income red-
dito (m) fisso
fixed interest
interesse (m) fisso
**fixed scale of
charges** tabella (f)
fissa dei prezzi
**fixed-interest
investments**
investimenti (mpl)
ad interessi fissi
**fixed-price agree-
ment** contratto
(m) a prezzo fisso
fixing fissaggio (m)
flat (adj) *[dull]*
piatto
flat (adj) *[fixed]*
fisso
flat (n) apparta-
mento (m)
flat rate importo
(m) fisso
flexibility
flessibilità (f)
flexible flessibile
flexible prices
prezzi (mpl) flessibili

flexible pricing policy politica (f)
dei prezzi flessibile
flight *[of money]*
fuga (f) (di denaro)
flight *[of plane]*
volo (m)
flight information
informazioni
(fpl) di volo
flight of capital
capitale (m) in fuga
flip chart blocco
(m) di fogli per
lavagna
float (n) *[money]*
anticipo (m)
float (n) *[of company]* lancio (m)
di una società
float (v) *[a currency]* far fluttuare
float a company
lanciare una società
floating fluttuante
floating exchange rates tasso
fluttuante di cambio
floating of a company lancio (m) di
una società

flood (n) inondazione (f)
flood (v) inondare
floor *[level]* piano (m)
floor *[surface]*
pavimento (m)
floor manager capo
(m) reparto
floor plan
planimetria (f)
floor space superficie (f) di pavimento
flop (n)
insuccesso (m)
flop (v) fare fiasco
flotation lancio
(m) di una società
flourish prosperare
flourishing fiorente
flourishing trade
attività (f) commerciale fiorente
flow (n) flusso (m)
flow (v) fluire
flow chart schema
(m) del ciclo
flow diagram
diagramma (m)
del ciclo di
lavorazione

fluctuate fluttuare
o oscillare
fluctuating
fluttuante
fluctuation
fluttuazione (f)
FOB or **f.o.b. (free on board)**
franco a bordo
follow seguire o
fare seguito
follow up aggiorna-
mento (m) o
sollecito (m)
follow-up letter
lettera (f) di
sollecito
for sale in vendita
forbid proibire
force majeure
causa (f) di forza
maggiore
force prices down
provocare la
diminuzione dei
prezzi
force prices up far
salire i prezzi
forced forzato
forced sale vendita
(f) coatta

forecast (n)
previsione (f)
forecast (v)
prevedere
forecasting attività
(f) previsionale
foreign straniero o
estero
foreign currency
divise (fpl) o
moneta (f) straniera
foreign exchange
[changing money] mercato
(m) dei cambi
foreign exchange
[currency]
divise (fpl) o valuta
(f) estera
foreign exchange broker agente
(m) in cambi
foreign exchange dealer operatore
(m) in cambi
foreign exchange market mercato
(m) dei cambi
**foreign invest-
ments** investimenti
(mpl) esteri

foreign money order ordine (m) di pagamento di valuta estera

foreign trade commercio (m) estero

forfeit (n) multa (f) o penalità (f)

forfeit (v) perdere (un diritto)

forfeit a deposit perdere un deposito

forfeiture perdita (f) (di un diritto)

forge falsificare

forgery *[action]* contraffazione (f)

forgery *[copy]* falso (m)

fork-lift truck carrello (m) elevatore (a forche)

form (n) modulo (m)

form (v) formare o comporre

form of words formulazione (f)

formal formale

formality formalità (f)

forward spedire

forward buying acquisto (m) a termine

forward contract contratto (m) a termine

forward market mercato (m) a termine

forward rate corso (m) per operazioni a termine

forward sales vendite (fpl) a termine

forwarding spedizione (f) o inoltro (m)

forwarding address indirizzo (m) d'inoltro

forwarding agent spedizioniere (m) (per via terra)

forwarding instructions istruzioni (fpl) per la spedizione

fourth quarter quarto trimestre (m)

fragile fragile
franchise (n)
concessione (f)
franchise (v)
concedere il diritto
di esclusiva
franchisee conces-
sionario (m)
franchiser
concedente (m)
franchising
concessione (f) di
vendita
franco senza spese
(fpl) o franco
frank (v) affrancare
franking machine
macchina (f)
affrancatrice
fraud frode (f)
fraudulent fraudo-
lento o disonesto
**fraudulent transac-
tion** operazione
(f) disonesta
fraudulently
disonestamente
free (adj) *[no pay-
ment]* gratis
free (adj) *[no
restrictions]* libero

free (adj) *[not
busy]* libero
free (adj) *[not
occupied]* libero
free (adv) *[no pay-
ment]* gratis o
gratuitamente
free (v) liberare
free delivery con-
segna (f) gratuita
free gift omaggio
(m) o dono (m)
**free market econ-
omy** economia (f)
di mercato libero
free of charge gra-
tuito o franco di
spese
free of duty franco
dogana (f)
free of tax esente
da tasse
**free on board
(f.o.b.)** franco a
bordo
free on rail franco
su rotaia
free port porto (m)
franco
free sample campi-
one (m) gratuito

free trade libero
scambio (m)
free trade area
zona (f) di libero
scambio
free trade zone
zona (f) di libero
scambio
free trial prova (f)
gratuita
free zone zona (f)
franca
freelance (n)
"freelance" o libero
professionista (m)
freeze (n) blocco
(m) (commerciale)
freeze (v) *[prices]*
congelare
freeze credits con-
gelare un credito
**freeze wages and
prices** bloccare
i salari e i prezzi
freight *[carriage]*
trasporto (m)
(via mare)
freight costs spese
(fpl) di trasporto
freight depot scalo
(m) merci

freight forward
porto (m) assegnato
freight plane aereo
(m) da carico
freight rates tar-
iffe (fpl) di nolo
freight train treno
(m) merci
freightage trasporto
(m) di merci
freighter *[plane]*
aereo (m) da
carico
freighter *[ship]*
nave (f) da carico
freightliner treno
(m) merci
frequent frequente
frozen congelato o
bloccato
frozen account
conto (m) congelato
frozen assets
cespiti (mpl)
congelati
frozen credits
crediti (mpl)
congelati
fulfil an order
evadere un'ordi-
nazione

fulfilment adempimento (m)
full pieno o intero
full discharge of a debt pieno scarico (m) di un debito
full payment pagamento (m) a saldo o pagamento totale
full price prezzo (m) intero
full refund rimborso (m) totale
full-scale (adj) in scala (f) naturale
full-time orario (m) pieno
full-time employment impiego (m) a tempo pieno
fund (n) fondo (m) o fondi (mpl)
fund (v) finanziare
funding (financing) finanziamento (m)
funding [of debt] consolidamento (m)
further to in seguito a

future delivery futura consegna (f)
futures contratti (mpl) a termine e a premio

Gg

gain (n) *[getting bigger]* aumento (m)
gain (n) *[increase in value]* guadagno (m)
gain (v) [become bigger] aumentare
gain (v) [get] ottenere
gap divario (m)
gap in the market apertura (f) sul mercato
GDP (= gross domestic product) prodotto (m) interno lordo (PIL)

gear ingranaggio (m)
gearing rapporto
(m) di indebitamento
general generale
general audit revi-
sione (f)
contabile periodica
general average
avaria (f) generale
general manager
direttore (m) generale
general meeting
assemblea (f) gen-
erale
general office uffi-
cio (m) pubblico
general post office
Amministrazione
Centrale delle
 Poste (UK)
general strike
sciopero (m)
generale
**gentleman's agree-
ment** accordo
(m) sulla parola (f)
genuine vero o aut-
entico
genuine purchaser
acquirente (m)
genuino

get procurarsi
get along cavarsela
**get back [something
lost]** avere indietro
get into debt
indebitarsi
get rid of something
liberarsi di qualcosa
**get round [a prob-
lem]** aggirare
get the sack essere
licenziato
gift regalo (m)
gift coupon buono
(m) premio
gift shop negozio (m)
per articoli da regalo
gift voucher buono
(m) premio
**gilt-edged securi-
ties** titoli (mpl) di
prim'ordine
gilts titoli (mpl) di
prim'ordine
giro account conto
corrente di
corrispondenza
**giro account num-
ber** numero (m)
di conto corrente di
corrispondenza

giro system (sistema di) giroconto (m)

give [as gift] regalare

give [pass] dare

give away regalare

glut (n) saturazione (f)

glut (v) saturare

GNP (= gross national product) prodotto (m) nazionale lordo (PNL)

go andare

go into business mettersi in affari

go-ahead (adj) intraprendente

go-slow sciopero (m) bianco

going andamento (m)

going rate tariffa (f) in vigore

gold card carta (f) di credito d'oro

good buono

good buy buon affare (m)

good management buona gestione (f)

good quality buona qualità (f)

good value (for money) conveniente

goods merce (f)

goods depot deposito (m) merci

goods in transit merce (f) in transito

goods train treno (m) merci

goodwill avviamento (m) commerciale

government (adj) governativo o del governo

government (n) governo (m)

government bonds titoli (mpl) di stato

government contractor fornitore (m) allo stato o statale

government stock titoli (mpl) di stato

government-backed con l'appoggio del governo

government-con-trolled a controllo statale

government-regu-lated a controllo statale

government-sponsored sponsorizzato dal governo

graded advertising rates tariffe (fpl) pubblicitarie differenziali

graded hotel albergo (m) selezionato

graded tax imposta (f) progressiva

gradual graduale

graduate trainee laureato (m) che fa tirocinio come dirigente

graduated graduato

graduated income tax imposta (f) progressiva sul reddito

gram *or* gramme grammo (m)

grand total totale (m) generale

grant (n) concessione (f) *o* borsa (f) di studio

grant (v) concedere *o* accordare

gratis gratis

grid griglia (f) *o* reticolo (m)

grid structure struttura a rete

gross (adj) lordo

gross (n) (= 144) grossa (f) (dodici dozzine)

gross (v) avere un ricavo lordo *o* incassare

gross domestic product (GDP) prodotto (m) interno lordo (PIL)

gross earnings guadagno (m) lordo

gross income reddito (m) lordo

gross margin margine (m) lordo

gross national product (GNP) prodotto (m) nazionale lordo (PNL)

gross profit utile (m) lordo

gross salary stipendio (m) lordo

gross tonnage tonnellaggio (m) lordo

gross weight peso (m) lordo

gross yield rendimento (m) lordo

group *[of businesses]* gruppo (m) industriale

group *[of people]* gruppo (m)

growth crescita (f)

growth index indice (m) di crescita

growth rate percentuale (f) di crescita

guarantee (n) garanzia (f)

guarantee (v) garantire

guarantee a debt garantire un debito

guaranteed minimum wage salario (m) minimo garantito

guarantor avallante (m)

guideline direttiva (f)

guild gilda (f) o corporazione (f)

Hh

haggle mercanteggiare

half (adj) mezzo

half (n) metà (f)

half a dozen ora

half-dozen mezza dozzina (f)

half-price sale saldo (m) a metà prezzo

half-year semestre (m)

half-yearly accounts contabilità (f) semestrale

half-yearly payment pagamento (m) semestrale

**half-yearly state-
ment** resoconto
(m) semestrale
hand in consegnare
o restituire
hand luggage
bagaglio (m) a mano
hand over passag-
gio (m) delle
consegne
handle (v) *[deal
with]* occuparsi di
handle (v) *[sell]*
commerciare
handling maneggio
(m) *o* gestione (f)
handling charge
spese (fpl) di con-
fezione, spedizione
handwriting
calligrafia (f)
handwritten
scritto a mano
handy maneggev-
ole *o* pratico
harbour porto (m)
harbour dues
diritti (mpl) portuali
harbour facilities
impianti (mpl)
portuali

hard bargain affare
(m) poco
vantaggioso
hard bargaining
trattative (fpl)
difficili
hard copy copia (f)
in chiaro
hard currency val-
uta (f) solida
hard disk hard
disk (m)
hard selling cam-
pagna (di vendita, di
pubblicità) aggressiva
harmonization
armonizzazione (f)
haulage tras
porto (m)
haulage contractor
trasportatore (m)
haulage costs
orhaulage rates
prezzo (m) del
trasporto
**head of depart-
ment** capo (m)
reparto
head office sede (f)
headquarters (HQ)
sede (f) centrale

heads of agreement
capi (mpl) d'intesa
health salute (f) *o*
sanità (f)
health insurance
assicurazione (f)
malattie
healthy profit buon
guadagno (m)
heavy *[important]*
grave
heavy *[weight]*
pesante
**heavy costs *or*
heavy expenditure**
forti costi (mpl) *o*
spese (fpl)
heavy equipment
apparecchiatura (f)
pesante
**heavy goods vehicle
(HGV)** veicolo (m)
per merci pesanti
heavy industry
industria (f) pesante
heavy machinery
macchinario (m)
pesante
hectare ettaro (m)
hedge (n) barriera
(f) *o* protezione (f)

hedging copertura (f)
**HGV (= heavy
goods vehicle)**
veicolo (m) per
merci pesanti
hidden asset attiv-
ità (fpl) occulte
hidden reserves
riserve (fpl) occulte
high interest inter-
esse (m) alto
high rent affitto
(m) alto
high taxation tas-
sazione (f) alta
high-quality di
qualità superiore
high-quality goods
prodotti (mpl)
di alta qualità
highest bidder
migliore
offerente (m)
**highly motivated
sales staff**
personale (m) di
vendita molto
motivato
highly qualified
altamente
qualificato

highly-geared com-pany azienda (f) con forte indebitamento

highly-paid altamente retribuito

highly-priced ad alto prezzo

hire (n) noleggio (m)

hire a car noleggiare un'automobile

hire car automobile (f) a noleggio

hire purchase (HP) acquisto (m) rateale

hire staff assumere personale

hire-purchase com-pany ditta (f) di vendita a rate

historic(al) cost costo (m) effettivo

historical figures cifre (fpl) effettive

hive off assegnare la produzione di qualcosa ad un'azienda consociata

hoard ammasso (m)

hoarding *[for posters]* tabellone (m)

hoarding *[of goods]* accaparramento (m)

hold (n) *[ship]* stiva (f)

hold (v) *[contain]* contenere

hold (v) *[keep]* tenere

hold a meeting or a discussion tenere una seduta

hold out for fare il braccio di ferro per

hold over posporre

hold the line please *or* **please hold** resti in linea per favore

hold up (v) *[delay]* trattenere

hold-up (n) *[delay]* ritardo (m)

holder *[person]* titolare (m)

holder *[thing]* contenitore (m) o sostegno (m)

holding company 'holding' (f) o società (f) controllante

holiday pay retribuzione (f) ferie
home address indirizzo (m) personale
home consumption consumo (m) interno o nazionale
home market mercato (m) nazionale
home sales vendite (fpl) nazionali o vendite sul mercato interno
homeward freight carico (m) di ritorno
homeward journey viaggio (m) di ritorno
homeworker lavoratore (m) a domicilio
honorarium onorario (m)
honour a bill onorare una cambiale
honour a signature onorare una firma
horizontal communication comunicazione (f) orizzontale

horizontal integration integrazione (f) orizzontale
hotel hotel (m) o albergo (m)
hotel accommodation ricettività (f) alberghi
hotel bill conto dell'albergo
hotel manager direttore (m) d'albergo
hotel staff personale (m) alberghiero
hour ora (f)
hourly orario
hourly rate retribuzione (f) a ore
hourly wage salario (m) orario
hourly-paid workers dipendenti (mpl) pagati a ore
house *[company]* ditta (f) o impresa (f)
house *[for family]* casa (f)
house insurance assicurazione (f) sulla casa

house magazine
rivista (f) aziendale
house-to-house a
domicilio *o* di
casa in casa
house-to-house
selling vendita (f)
a domicilio
HP (= hire pur-
chase) sistema (m)
di acquisti a rate
HQ (= headquar-
ters) sede centrale
hurry up affrettarsi
hype (n) montatura
(f) giornalistica
hype (v) fare un
grosso lancio
pubblicitario di
hypermarket iper-
mercato (m) li
illegal illegale
illegality illegalità (f)
illegally
illegalmente
illicit illecito
ILO (= International
Labour Organization)
Organizzazione
Internazionale del
Lavoro (OIL)

IMF (=
International
Monetary Fund)
Fondo Monetario
Internazionale
imitation imi-
tazione (f)
immediate
immediato
immediately imme-
diatamente
imperfect
imperfetto
imperfection
imperfezione (f)
implement (n)
strumento (m)
implement (v)
attuare *o* realizzare
implement an
agreement rendere
effettivo un accordo
implementation
attuazione (f)
import (n)
importazione (f)
import (v)
importare
import ban
divieto (m) di
importazione

import duty dazio (m) doganale
import levy prlievo (m) sulle impotazioni
import licence *or* **import permit** licenza (f) di importazione
import quota contingente (m) di importazione
import restrictions restrizioni (fpl) alle importazioni
import surcharge soprattassa (f) di importazione
import-export (adj importazioni-esportazioni
importance importanza (f)
important importante
importation importazione (f)
importer importatore (m)
importing (adj) importatore, importatrice

importing (n) importazione (f)
imports importazioni (fpl)
impose imporre
impulse impulso (m)
impulse buyer acquirente (mf) che compra per impulso
impulse purchase acquisto (m) fatto per impulso
in-house interno (alla ditta, allo stabilimento)
in-house training addestramento (m) interno (alla ditta)
incentive incentivo (m)
incentive bonus gratifica (f) di bilancio
incentive payments premio (m) d'operosità
incidental expenses spese (fpl) impreviste
include includere

inclusive incluso
inclusive charge
spesa (f)
compresa
inclusive of tax
comprese tasse (fpl)
income reddito (m)
income tax imposta
(f) sul reddito
incoming call tele-
fonata (f) in arrivo
incoming mail
posta (f) in arrivo
incompetent
incapace
incorporate *[a com-
pany]* costituire
incorporation cos-
tituzione (f)
incorrect scorretto
incorrectly
scorrettamente
increase (n)
aumento (m)
increase (n) *[higher
salary]* aumento (m)
increase (v)
aumentare
**increase (v) in
price** aumentare di
prezzo

increasing
crescente
increasing profits
utile (m) in
aumento
increment
incremento (m)
incremental
incrementativo
incremental cost
costo (m) marginale
incremental scale
scala (f)
incrementale
incur incorrere (in)
incur *[costs]*
sostenere spese
incur debts con-
trarre debiti
indebted indebitato
indebtedness
indebitamento (m)
indemnification
indennità (f) o
indennizzo (m)
indemnify risarcire
o indennizzare
**indemnify someone
for a loss** risarcire
qualcuno per una
perdita

indemnity garanzia (f) *o* assicurazione (f)
independent indipendente
independent company azienda (f) autonoma
index (n) *[alphabetical]* indice (m)
index (n) *[of prices]* indice (m)
index (v) elencare
index card scheda (f)
index number indice (m) economico
index-linked indicizzato
indexation *or* **index-linking** indicizzazione (f)
indicator indicatore (m)
indirect indiretto
indirect labour costs costi (mpl) indiretti del lavoro
indirect tax imposte (fpl) indirette
indirect taxation tassazione (f) indiretta

induction inserimento (m) in un nuovo lavoro
induction course *or* **induction training** corso (m) introduttivo
industrial industriale
industrial accident infortunio (m) sul lavoro
industrial arbitration tribunal tribunale (m) di arbitrato industriale
industrial capacity capacità (f) industriale
industrial centre centro (m) industriale
industrial design disegno (m) industriale
industrial disputes vertenza (f) operaia
industrial espionage spionaggio (m) industriale
industrial estate zona (f) industriale

industrial expansion espansione (f) industriale
industrial processes processi (mpl) industriali
industrial relations relazioni (fpl) industriali
industrial tribunal tribunale (m) del lavoro
industrialist industriale (m)
industrialization industrializzazione (f)
industrialize industrializzare
industrialized societies paesi (mpl) industrializzati
industry [companies] industria (f)
industry [general] industria (f)
inefficiency inefficienza (f)
inefficient inefficiente
inflated currency moneta (f) inflazionata

inflated prices prezzi (mpl) inflazionati
inflation inflazione (f)
inflationary inflazionistico
influence (n) influenza (f)
influence (v) influenzare
inform informare
information informazione (f)
information bureau ufficio (m) informazioni
information officer impiegato (m) addetto alle informazioni
infrastructure infrastruttura (f)
infringe infrangere
infringe a patent usurpare un brevetto
infringement of customs regulations violazione (f) dei regolamenti doganali

infringement of patent usurpazione (f) di brevetto
initial (adj) iniziale
initial (v) siglare
initial capital capitale (m) d'apporto
initiate iniziare
initiate discussions iniziare un dibattito (m)
initiative iniziativa (f)
inland interno o del territorio nazionale
innovate innovare
innovation innovazione (f)
innovative innovativo
innovator innovatore (m)
input (v) information immettere informazioni nel computer
input tax IVA (Imposta sul Valore Aggiunto)
inquire chiedere informazioni
inquiry richiesta (f)

insider persona (f) che dispone di informazioni riservate
insider dealing compravendita (f) di azioni da parte degli stessi amministratori della Società
insolvency insolvenza (f)
insolvent insolvente
inspect esaminare
inspection ispezione (f)
instalment rata (f)
instant (adj) [current] corrente
instant (adj) [immediate] immediato o istantaneo
instant credit credito (m) immediato
institute (n) istituto (m)
institute (v) istituire
institution O istituzione (f)
institutional istituzionale

institutional investors investitori (mpl) istituzionali

instruction istruzione (f)

instrument [device] strumento (m)

instrument [document] documento (m) o strumento (m)

insufficient funds [US] fondi (mpl) insufficienti

insurable assicurabile

insurance assicurazione (f)

insurance agent agente (m) di assicurazione

insurance broker mediatore (m) assicurativo

insurance claim richiesta (f) di indennizzo assicurativo

insurance company compagnia (f) di assicurazione

insurance contract contratto (m) di assicurazione

insurance cover copertura (f) assicurativa

insurance policy polizza (f) di assicurazione

insurance premium premio (m) di assicurazione

insurance rates tariffe (fpl) di assicurazione

insurance salesman venditore (m) di assicurazioni

insure assicurare

insurer assicuratore (m)

intangible intangibile

intangible assets attività (fpl) immateriali

interest (n) [investment] partecipazione (f)

interest (n) [paid on investment] interesse (m)

interest (v) interessare

interest charges
addebiti (mpl)
per interessi
interest rate tasso
(m) d'interesse
interest-bearing
deposits depositi
(mpl) fruttiferi
interest-free credit
credito (m)
esente da interessi
interface (n)
interfaccia (f)
interface (v) fun-
gere da interfaccia
interim dividend
dividendo (m) in
acconto
interim payment
pagamento (m)
provvisiorio
interim report
relazione (f) provvisoria
intermediary inter-
mediario (m)
internal [inside a
company] interno
internal [inside a
country] interno
internal audit revi-
sione (f) interna

internal auditor
revisore (m)
interno
internal telephone
telefono (m)
interno
international
internazionale
international call
telefonata (f)
internazionale
international direct
dialling telese-
lezione (f) inter-
nazionale
International
Labour Organization
ILO) Organizzazione
Internazionale del
Lavoro (OIL)
international law
diritto (m)
internazionale
International
Monetary Fund
(IMF) Fondo
Monetario
Internazionale (FMI)
international trade
commercio (m)
internazionale

interpret
interpretare
interpreter
interprete (mf)
intervention price
prezzo (m)
d'intervento
interview (n)
intervista (f)
interview (n)
[for a job]
intervista (f) o
colloquio (m)
interview (v)
intervistare
interview (v) *[for a*
job] avere un
colloquio con
interviewee
intervistato (m)
interviewer
intervistatore (m)
introduce
introdurre o
presentare
introduction *[bring-*
ing into use]
introduzione (m)
introduction *[let-*
ter] lettera (f) di
presentazione

introductory offer
offerta (f) di propa-
ganda
invalid inabile o
privo di validità
invalidate invalidare
invalidation
annullamento (m)
invalidity inabilità
(f) o invalidità (f)
inventory (n) *[list*
of contents]
inventario (m)
inventory (n)
[stock] inventario
(m) o scorte (fpl) o
stock (m)
inventory (v)
inventariare o fare
l'inventario
inventory control
controllo (m) di
magazzino
invest investire
investigate
investigare
investigation
analisi (f) o
indagine (f)
investment investi-
mento (m)

investment income
reddito (m) da
investimenti
investor
investitore (m)
invisible assets
beni (mpl) invisibili
invisible earnings
proventi (mpl)
da partite invisibili
invisible trade com-
mercio (m) invisibile
invitation invito (m)
invite invitare
invoice (n) fattura (f)
invoice (v)
fatturare
invoice number
numero (m) di fattura
invoice value
prezzo (m) di fattura
invoicing fat-
turazione (f)
**invoicing depart-
ment** ufficio (m)
addetto alla
fatturazione
IOU (= I owe you)
riconoscimento (m)
scritto di un debito
o pagherò (m)

irrecoverable debt
debito (m)
inesigibile
irredeemable bond
obbligazione
(f) irredimibile
irregular irregolare
irregularities
irregolarità (fpl)
irrevocable
irrevocabile
**irrevocable accept-
ance** effetto
(m) accettato
irrevocabilmente
**irrevocable letter
of credit** lettera
(f) di credito
irrevocabile
issue (n) *[maga-
zine]* numero (m)
issue (n) *[of
shares]* rilascio (m)
o emissione (f)
issue (v) *[shares]*
emettere
**issue a letter of
credit** aprire una
lettera di credito
issue instructions
diramare istruzioni

issuing bank banca (f) d'emissione
item [information] voce (f)
item [on agenda] argomento (m) o questione (f)
item [thing for sale] articolo (m)
itemize specificare o dettagliare
itemized account conto (m) dettagliato
itemized invoice fattura (f) dettagliata
itinerary itinerario (m)

Jj

job [employment] impiego (m) o lavoro (m)

job [piece of work] lavoro (m)
job analysis analisi (f) delle mansioni
job application domanda (f) di lavoro
job cuts riduzione (f) di posti lavorativi
job description descrizione (f) dei compiti
job satisfaction soddisfazione (f) sul lavoro
job security sicurezza (f) del posto di lavoro
job specification specificazione (f) delle mansioni
job title denominazione (f) della mansione
join unire
joint congiunto o unito
joint account conto (m) congiunto
joint discussions discussione (f) collettiva

joint management condirezione (f)
joint managing director condirettore (m)
joint owner comproprietario (m)
joint ownership comproprietà (f)
joint signatory firmatario (m) congiunto
joint venture 'joint venture' (f) o associazione (f) in partecipazione
jointly in comune
journal *[accounts book]* libro (m) giornale
journal *[magazine]* rivista (f) o periodico (m)
journey order ordine trasmesso dal dettagliante al fornitore tramite commesso viaggiatore
judge (n) giudice (m) o magistrato (m)
judge (v) giudicare

judgement *or* **judgment** verdetto (m) o decisione (f)
judgment debtor debitore (m) riconosciuto da tribunale
judicial processes procedimenti (mpl) legali
jump the queue passare in testa ad una coda
junior (adj) junior o giovane
junior clerk apprendista (m)
junior executive or junior manager dirigente (m) di grado inferiore
junior partner socio di minore importanza (più recente)
junk bonds obbligazioni (fpl) 'cartastraccia'
junk mail opuscoli (mpl) pubblicitari
jurisdiction giurisdizione (f)

Kk

keen competition
concorrenza (f)
accanita
keen demand forte
richiesta (f)
keen prices prezzi
(mpl) concorrenziali
keep a promise
mantenere una
promessa
keep back
trattenere
keep up tenere su
**keep up with the
demand** stare al
passo con la richiesta
**key (adj) *[impor-
tant]*** chiave
key *[on keyboard]*
tasto (m)
key *[to door]*
chiave (f)
key industry indus-
tria (f) chiave/di base
**key personnel *or*
key staff**
personale-chiave

key post posto (m)
chiave
keyboard (n)
tastiera (f)
keyboard (v)
digitare
keyboarder
operatore (m) su
tastiera
keyboarding
immissione (f)
mediante tastiera
kilo *or* kilogram
chilo (m) o
chilogrammo (m)
**knock down (v)
*[price]*** ridurre o
abbassare
**knock off *[reduce
price]***
abbassare
o ridurre il prezzo di
**knock off *[stop
work]*** cessare di
lavorare
knock-on effect
effetto (m) a
catena
knockdown prices
riduzione (f) di
prezzi

krona *[currency used in Sweden]* corona (f) (svedese)
krone *[currency used in Denmark and Norway]* corona (danese, norvegese)

Ll

label (n) etichetta (f)
label (v) etichettare
labelling etichet-tatura (f)
labour lavoro (m)
labour costs costo (m) della manodopera
labour disputes vertenza (f) di lavoro
labour force forza (f) lavoro
lack of funds man-canza (f) di fondi

land (n) terra (f) o terreno (m)
land (v) *[of plane]* atterrare
land (v) *[passengers, cargo]* sbarcare
land goods at a port scaricare merce in un porto
landed costs costi (mpl) fondiari
landing card carta (f) di sbarco
landing charges spese (fpl) di scarico (da nave)
landlord locatore (m)
lapse (v) scadere
laser printer stam-pante (f) laser
last in first out (LIFO) ultimo a entrare, primo a uscire
last quarter ultimo trimestre (m)
late (adv) tardi o in ritardo
late-night open-ing aprire fino a notte tarda

latest recentissimo
launch (n) lancio (m)
launch (v) lanciare
launching lancio (m)
launching costs costi (mpl) di lancio
launching date data (f) del lancio
launder (money) riciclare
law *[rule]* legge (f)
law *[study]* diritto (m)
law courts tribunale (m)
law of diminishing returns legge (f) del rendimento decrescente
law of supply and demand legge (f) dell'offerta e della domanda
lawful legittimo
lawful trade commercio (m) legittimo
lawsuit causa (f)
lawyer avvocato (m)

lay off workers licenziare personale (per mancanza di attività)
LBO (= leveraged buyout) finanziamento (m) per l'acquisto del pacchetto azionario contro garanzia delle attività finanziarie
L/C (= letter of credit) lettera (f) di credito
lead time intervallo (m) (fra ordinazione e consegna)
leaflet volantino (m)
leakage dispersione (f)
lease (n) affitto (m)
lease (v) *[of landlord]* affittare o dare in affitto
lease (v) *[of tenant]* affittare o tenere in affitto
lease back praticare il leasing (m) immobiliare

lease equipment
affittare *[impianti]*
lease-back leasing
(m) immobiliare
leasing 'leasing' (m)
leave (n) congedo (m)
leave (v) *[go away]*
partire o lasciare
leave (v) *[resign]*
abbandonare o
lasciare
leave of absence
aspettativa (f) o
congedo (m)
autorizzato
ledger libro (m)
mastro
left *[not right]*
sinistro
left luggage office
ufficio (m)
deposito bagagli
legal *[according to
law]* legale
legal *[referring to
law]* giuridico
legal advice con-
sulenza (f) legale
legal adviser
consulente (m)
legale

legal costs *or* **legal
charges** spese (fpl)
legali
legal currency
moneta (f) legale
legal department
ufficio (m)
legale
legal expenses
spese (fpl) legali
legal proceedings
vie (fpl) legali
legal status stato
(m) giuridico
legal tender mon-
eta (f) a corso
legale
legislation
legislazione (f)
lend prestare
lender prestatore (m)
lending prestito (m)
lending limit limite
(m) del prestito
lessee affittuario (m)
lessor locatore (m)
let (n) affitto (m)
let (v) affittare
let an office
affittare un negozio
letter lettera (f)

letter of application richiesta (f) di iscrizione

letter of appointment lettera (f) di assunzione

letter of complaint lettera (f) di reclamo

letter of credit (L/C) lettera (f) di credito

letter of intent lettera (f) di intenti

letter of reference lettera (f) di referenze

letters of administration nomina (f) di amministratore giudiziario

letters patent brevetto (m)

letting agency agenzia (f) immobiliare

level (n) livello (m)

level off *or* **level out** stabilizzarsi

leverage leva (f) finanziaria

leveraged buyout (LBO) finanziamento (m) per l'acquisto del pacchetto azionario contro garanzia delle attività societarie

levy (n) imposta (f)

levy (v) imporre (una tassa)

liabilities passività (fpl)

liability responsabilità (f) o obbligo (m)

liable for responsabile per

liable to passibile di

licence licenza (f)

license autorizzare

licensee concessionario (m)

licensing concessione (f) di licenze

lien privilegio (m)

life assurance assicurazione (f) sulla vita

life insurance assicurazione (f) sulla vita

life interest
usufrutto (m) *o* rendita (f) vitalizia
LIFO (= last in first out) metodo
(m) LIFO (ultimo a entrare, primo a uscire)
lift (n) ascensore (m)
lift (v) *[remove]*
togliere
lift an embargo
togliere l'embargo
limit (n) limite (m)
limit (v) limitare
limitation
restrizione (f)
limited limitato
limited (liability) company (Ltd)
società (f) di capitali a responsabilità limitata
limited liability
responsabilità (f) limitata
limited market
mercato (m) limitato
limited partnership
società (f) in accomandita semplice

line (n) linea (f)
line management
linea (f) gerarchica
line organization
organizzazione
(f) gerarchica
line printer stampante (f) lineare
liquid assets
liquidità (fpl)
liquidate a company mettere in
liquidazione una
società
liquidate stock
mettere in
liquidazione scorte
di magazzino
liquidation liquidazione (f)
liquidator liquidatore (m)
liquidity liquidità (f)
liquidity crisis
crisi (f) di
mancanza di
liquidità
lira *[currency used in Turkey]* lira (f)
(turca)
list (n) lista (f)

list (n) [catalogue]
listino (m) o
catalogo (m)
list (v) elencare
list price prezzo
(m) di listino
litre litro (m)
Lloyd's register
Registro (m) dei
Lloyd (di classifi-
cazione delle navi)
load (n) carico (m)
load (v) caricare
**load (v) [computer
program]** caricare
**load a lorry or a
ship** caricare un
camion o una nave
load factor
coefficiente (m) di
carico
load line linea (f)
di carico
loading bay area
(f) di carico
loading ramp
rampa (f) di carico
loan (n) prestito
(m) o mutuo (m)
loan (v) prestare o
dare in prestito

loan capital capi-
tale (m) mutuato
loan stock capitale
(m) obbligazionario
local locale/del
luogo
local call tele-
fonata (f) urbana
local government
ente (m) locale
local labour man-
odopera (m) locale
lock (n) serratura (f)
lock (v) chiudere a
chiave
**lock up a shop or
an office** chiudere
a chiave un negozio
o un ufficio
lock up capital
investire capitali
lock-up premises
immobile (m)
con chiusura di
sicurezza
log (v) registrare
log calls registrare
chiamate
logo logogramma (m)
long lungo o per
molto tempo

long credit credito
(m) a lungo termine
long-dated bill
effetto (m) a lunga
scadenza
long-distance flight
volo (m) a lunga
percorrenza
long-haul flight volo
(m) a lungo raggio
long-range a lunga
scadenza
long-standing di
vecchia data
**long-standing
agreement** accordo
(m) di lunga data
long-term a lungo
termine
long-term debts
debiti (mpl) a
lungo termine
long-term forecast
previsione (f) a
lungo termine
**long-term liabili-
ties** passività (fpl)
a lungo termine
long-term loan
mutuo (m) a lunga
scadenza

long-term planning
pianificazione
(f) a lunga scadenza
loose sciolto
lorry camion (m)
lorry driver
camionista (m)
lorry-load carico
(di camion)
**lose *[fall to a lower
level]*** cadere
lose an order
perdere
un'ordinazione
lose money
perdere denaro
loss *[not a profit]*
perdita (f)
loss *[of something]*
perdita (f)
loss of an order
perdita (f) di
un'ordinazione
loss of customers
perdita (f) di
clientela
loss-leader articolo
(m) di richiamo per
la clientela
lot *[of items]* par-
tita (f) (di merci)

low (adj) basso o
scadente
low (n) basso
livello (m)
low sales vendite
(fpl) basse
low-grade di qual-
ità inferiore
low-level di livello
inferiore
low-quality di
qualità inferiore
lower (adj) inferi-
ore o più basso
lower (v)
abbassare
lower prices
abbassare i prezzi
lowering calo (m)
**Ltd (= limited com-
pany)** a respons-
abilità limitata
luggage bagaglio (m)
lump sum importo
(m) forfettario
luxury goods arti-
coli (mpl) di lusso

Mm

machine
macchina (f)
macro-economics
macroeconomia (f)
magazine rivista (f)
magazine insert
fascicolo (m) sup-
plementare (in una
rivista)
magazine mailing
invio (m) di riviste
per posta
**magnetic tape *or*
mag tape** nastro
(m) magnetico
**mail (n) *[letters sent
or received]*** posta (f)
**mail (n) *[postal
system]*** posta (f)
mail (v) spedire
per posta
mail shot campagna
(f) promozionale a
mezzo posta
mail-order ordi-
nazioni (fpl) per
corrispondenza

**mail-order busi-
ness** *or* **mail-order
firm** *or* **mail-order**
società (f) di
vendita per cor-
rispondenza
**mail-order cata-
logue** catalogo (m)
di vendita per cor-
rispondenza
mailing invio (m)
(per posta)
mailing list elenco
(m) di indirizzi
mailing piece
materiale (m) pro-
mozionale preparato
specificatamente per
l'invio (per posta)
mailing shot
campagna (f)
promozionale a
mezzo posta
main principale
main building
edificio (m)
principale
main office sede
(f) centrale *o*
direzione (f)
centrale

maintain *[keep at
same level]*
mantenere
maintain *[keep
going]* tenere in
efficienza
maintenance *[keep-
ing in working
order]* manuten-
zione (f)
maintenance *[keep-
ing things going]*
mantenimento (m)
**maintenance of
contacts** manteni-
mento (m) di
contatti
**maintenance of
supplies** manteni-
mento (m) delle
provvigioni
major maggiore *o*
importante
major shareholder
azionista (m)
principale
majority
maggioranza (f)
**majority share-
holder** azionista
(m) di maggioranza

make good [a defect or loss] indennizzare o risarcire
make money fare soldi
make out [invoice] compilare
make provision for provvedere a
make up for compensare
make-ready time periodo (m) di avviamento
maladministration cattiva amministrazione (f)
man (n) uomo (m)
man (v) fornire il personale (necessario)
man-hour ora (f) lavorativa
manage amministrare o gestire
manage property amministrare un patrimonio
manage to riuscire a
manageable trattabile o controllabile

management [action] gestione (f)
management [managers] direzione (f)
management accounts conti (mpl) gestione
management buyout (MBO) acquisto (m) di una società da parte dei suoi stessi dirigenti
management consultant consulente (m) di direzione aziendale
management course corso (m) in amministrazione
management team quadri (mpl) direttivi
management techniques tecniche (fpl) gestionali
management trainee apprendista (m) in direzione aziendale
management training addestramento (m) dei dirigenti

manager *[of branch orshop]* direttore (m), direttrice (f)
manager *[of department]* direttore (m), direttrice (f)
managerial direttivo o gestionale
managerial staff personale (m) dirigente
managing director (MD) amministratore delegato
mandate mandato (m)
manifest manifesto (m)
manned aperto
manning organico (m)
manning levels livello (m) di organico
manpower manodopera (f)
manpower forecasting previsione (f) della necessità di manodopera

manpower planning programmazione (f) delle assunzioni di manodopera
manpower requirements esigenza (f) di manodopera
manpower shortage carenza (f) di manodopera
manual (adj) manuale
manual (n) manuale (m)
manual work lavoro (m) manuale
manual worker manovale (m)
manufacture (n) lavorazione (f) o fabbricazione (f)
manufacture (v) produrre o fabbricare
manufactured goods manufatti (mpl)

manufacturer
produttore (m) *o*
fabbricante (m)
**manufacturer's rec-
ommended price
(MRP)** prezzo (m) di
fabbrica consigliato
manufacturing
manifatturiero
**manufacturing
capacity** capacità
(f) di produzione
**manufacturing
costs** costi (mpl)
di produzione
**manufacturing over-
heads** spese (fpl)
generali di produzione
margin *[profit]*
margine (m)
margin of error mar-
gine (m) di errore
marginal marginale
marginal cost
costo (m) marginale
marginal pricing
determinazione (f)
marginale del prezzo
marine marittimo
marine insurance
assicurazione (f)
marittima

marine underwriter
assicuratore
(m) marittimo
maritime marittimo
o navale
maritime law
diritto (m) della
navigazione
maritime lawyer
avvocato (m) che
si occupa del diritto
della navigazione
maritime trade
commercio (m)
marittimo
mark (n)
impronta (f)
mark (v) notare
mark down abbas-
sare il prezzo (di
articoli)
mark up aumentare
il prezzo (di articoli)
mark-down
diminuzione (f) di
prezzo
mark-up *[action]*
aumento (m) di
prezzo
**mark-up *[profit
margin]*** margine
(m) *o* utile lordo

marker pen evidenziatore (m)
market (n) *[place]* mercato (m)
market (n) *[possible sales]* mercato (m)
market (n) *[where a product might sell]* mercato (m)
market (v) vendere *o* commercializzare
market analysis analisi (f) di mercato
market analyst analista (m) di mercato
market capitalization capitalizzazione (f) di mercato
market economist economista (mf) di mercato
market forces forze (fpl) di mercato
market forecast previsioni (fpl) di mercato
market leader prodotto-guida (m) del mercato *o* azienda (f) primaria sul mercato

market opportunities possibilità (fpl) di mercato
market penetration penetrazione (f) di mercato
market price prezzo (m) di mercato
market rate prezzo (m) di mercato
market research ricerca (f) di mercato
market share quota (f) di mercato
market trends tendenza (f) di mercato
market value valore (m) di mercato
marketable commerciabile
marketing marketing (m)
marketing agreement accordo (m) di marketing
marketing department servizio (m) di marketing
marketing division reparto (m) marketing

marketing manager direttore di marketing

marketing strategy strategia (f) di marketing

marketing techniques tecniche (fpl) di marketing

marketplace [in town] (piazza (f) del) mercato (m)

marketplace [place where something is sold] mercato (m)

mass [of people] massa (f)

mass [of things] massa (f) o grande quantità (f)

mass market product prodotto (m) per il mercato di massa

mass marketing marketing (m) di massa

mass media mass-media (mpl) o mezzi (mpl) di comunicazione di massa

mass production produzione (f) in serie

mass-produce produrre in serie

mass-produce cars produrre automobili in serie

Master's degree in Business Administration (MBA) master (m) in gestione d'impresa

materials control controllo (m) dei materiali

materials handling movimentazione (f) dei materiali

maternity leave congedo (m) per maternità

matter (n) [problem] faccenda (f) o problema (f)

matter (n) [to be discussed] argomento (m) o questione (f)

matter (v) avere importanza

mature (v) scadere
mature economy
economia (f) matura
maturity date data
(f) di scadenza
maximization mas-
simizzazione (f)
maximize mas-
simizzare
maximum (adj)
massimo
maximum (n)
massimo (m)
maximum price
prezzo (m) massimo
MBA (= Master in
Business
Administration)
master (m) in
gestione d'impresa
MBO (= manage-
ment buyout)
acquisto (m)
di una società da
parte dei suoi stessi
dirigenti
MD (= managing
director)
direttore generale
mean (adj) medio
mean (n) media (f)

mean annual
increase aumento
(m) medio annuale
means *[money]*
mezzi (mpl)
means *[ways]*
mezzi (mpl) o
strumenti (mpl)
means test accer-
tamento (m)
patrimoniale
measurement of
profitability
misura (f) della
redditività
measurements
misure (fpl)
media coverage
diffusione (f) nei
mass-media
median valore (m)
mediano
mediate mediare
mediation
mediazione (f)
mediator
mediatore (m)
medium (adj)
medio o di mezzo
medium (n)
mezzo (m)

medium-sized di medie dimensioni

medium-term a medio termine

meet *[be satisfactory]* soddisfare

meet *[expenses]* far fronte *[a una spesa]*

meet *[someone]* incontrare

meet a deadline rispettare una scadenza

meet a demand andare incontro ad una richiesta

meet a target raggiungere un obiettivo

meeting riunione (f)

meeting place luogo (m) d'incontro

member *[of a group]* socio (m)

membership *[all members]* gli iscritti (mpl)

membership *[being a member]* iscrizione (f)

memo memorandum (m)

memorandum memorandum (m)

memory *[computer]* memoria (f)

merchandise (n) merce (f)

merchandize (v) commerciare

merchandize a product esercitare il commercio di un prodotto

merchandizer commerciante (m)

merchandizing attività (f) promozionale

merchant mercante (m)

merchant bank 'merchant bank' (f) o banca (f) mercantile

merchant navy marina (f) mercantile

merchant ship *or* **merchant vessel** nave (f) mercantile

merge incorporare
merger fusione (f)
merit merito (n)
merit award *or*
merit bonus pre-
mio (m) di merito
message
messaggio (m)
messenger
fattorino (m)
micro-economics
microeconomia (f)
microcomputer
microelaboratore (m)
mid-month accounts
contabilità (f) di
metà mese
mid-week metà
settimana (f)
middle management
quadri (mpl) intermedi
middle-sized com-
pany società (f)
di medie dimensioni
middleman inter-
mediario (m)
million milione (m)
millionaire miliar-
dario (m)
minimum (adj)
minimo

minimum (n)
minimo (m)
minimum dividend
dividendo
(m) minimo
minimum payment
pagamento (m)
minimo
minimum wage
salario (m) minimo
minor shareholders
azionista (m)
di secondaria
importanza
minority
minoranza (f)
minority share-
holder azionista
(m) di minoranza
minus meno *o*
negativo
minus factor fat-
tore (m) negativo
minute (n) *[time]*
minuto (m)
minute (v)
verbalizzare *o* met-
tere a verbale
minutes (n) *[of*
meeting] verbale
(m) (di assemblea)

misappropriate appropriarsi indebitamente

misappropriation appropriazione (f) indebita

miscalculate fare male i propri calcoli

miscalculation calcolo (m) sbagliato

miscellaneous miscellaneo o vario

miscellaneous items articoli (mpl) diversi

mismanage dirigere male

mismanagement cattiva amministrazione (f)

miss [not to hit] mancare

miss [not to meet] mancare

miss [train, plane] perdere

miss a target mancare il bersaglio

miss an instalment non pagare una rata

mistake errore (m)

misunderstanding malinteso (m)

mixed [different sorts] misto

mixed [neither good nor bad] misto

mixed economy economia (f) di tipo misto

mobility mobilità (f)

mobilize mobilizzare

mobilize capital mobilizzare capitali

mock-up modello (m) in scala

mode modo (m)

mode of payment modalità (fpl) di pagamento

model (n) [person] indossatrice (f)

model (n) [small copy] modello (m)

model (n) [style of product] modello (m)

model (v) [clothes] presentare (un modello)

model agreement accordo-tipo (m)

modem modem (m)
moderate (adj)
moderato
moderate (v)
moderare
monetary monetario
monetary base
base (f) monetaria
monetary unit
unità (f) monetaria
money denaro (m)
money changer
cambiavalute (m)
money markets
mercati (mpl)
monetari
money order vaglia
(m) (mandato
di pagamento)
money rates tassi
(mpl) monetari
money supply
disponibilità (f) di
capitali
money up front
soldi (mpl) in anticipo
money-making
redditizio
money-making
plan progetto (m)
redditizio

moneylender
finanziatore (m) o
chi fa prestiti
monitor (n) [screen]
monitor (m)
monitor (v)
controllare
monopolization
monopolizzazione (f)
monopolize
monopolizzare
monopoly
monopolio (m)
month mese (m)
month end fine (f)
del mese
month-end
accounts contabil-
ità (f) di fine mese
monthly (adj)
mensile
monthly (adv)
mensilmente
monthly payments
pagamenti
(mpl) mensili
monthly state-
ment resoconto
(m) mensile
moonlight (v)
lavorare al nero

moonlighter (n)
lavoratore (m) al nero
moonlighting (n)
lavoro (m) nero
moratorium
moratoria (f)
mortgage (n)
ipoteca (f)
mortgage (v)
ipotecare
**mortgage pay-
ments** pagamenti
(mpl) ipotecari
mortgagee credi-
tore (m) ipotecario
**mortgager ormort-
gagor** debitore
(m) ipotecario
**most-favoured
nation** nazione (f)
più favorita
motivated motivato
motivation moti-
vazione (f)
motor insurance
assicurazione (f) auto
mount up aumentare
mounting in
aumento
move [be sold]
vendersi

**move [house,
office]** traslocare
move [propose]
proporre
movement
movimento (m)
**movements of capi-
tal** movimenti
(m) di capitali
**MRP (= manufac-
turer's recom-
mended price)**
prezzo (m) con-
sigliato di fabbrica
**multicurrency
operation** oper-
azione (f) a denomi-
nazione valutaria
multipla
multilateral
multilaterale
**multilateral agree-
ment** accordo
(m) multilaterale
multilateral trade
commercio (m)
multilaterale
multinational (n)
multinazionale (f)
multiple (adj)
multiplo

multiple entry visa
visto (m)
consolare multiplo
multiple ownership
proprietà (f) multipla
multiple store
negozio (m) apparte-
nente ad una catena
multiplication
moltiplicazione (f)
multiply moltiplicare
mutual (adj)
mutuo o reciproco
mutual (insurance)
company società (f)
mutua (di assicu-
razioni)

Nn

national nazionale
national advertising
pubblicità (f) su tutto
il territorio nazionale
nationalization
nazionalizzazione (f)

nationalized indus-
try industria (f)
statalizzata
nationwide di
dimensioni nazionali
natural resources
risorse (fpl) naturali
natural wastage
numero di lavoratori
(mpl) che abbando-
nano l'attività per
pensionamento
near letter-quality
(NLQ) ad alta
definizione
necessary necessario
negative cash flow
reddito (m)
societario negativo
neglected business
attività (f) trascurata
neglected shares
azioni (fpl) trascurate
negligence
negligenza (f)
negligent negligente
negligible
trascurabile
negotiable
trattabile o
negoziabile

negotiable instrument strumento (m) negoziabile

negotiate negoziare *o* trattare

negotiation negoziato (m) *o* trattativa (f)

negotiator negoziatore (m)

net (adj) netto

net (v) ricavare al netto

net assets *or* **net worth** valore (m) patrimoniale netto

net earnings *or* **net income** utili (mpl) netti

net income *or* **net salary** reddito (m) netto

net loss perdita (f) netta

net margin margine (m) netto

net price prezzo (m) netto

net profit utile (m) netto

net receipts incassi (mpl) netti

net sales ricavi (mpl) netti

net weight peso (m) netto

net yield rendimento (m) netto

network (n) rete (f) *o* sistema (m)

network (v) *[computers]* collegare in rete

news agency agenzia (f) di stampa

newspaper giornale (m)

niche nicchia (f)

night notte (f)

night rate tariffa (f) notturna

night shift turno (m) di notte

nil nulla (m) *o* zero (m)

nil return ricavo (m) nullo

NLQ (= near letter-quality) ad alta definizione

no-claims bonus premio (m) agli assicurati che non hanno denunciato sinistri

**no-strike agree-
ment** *or* **no-strike
clause** accordo (m)
o clausola (f)
che stabilisce il divi-
eto di sciopero
nominal capital cap-
itale (m) nominale
nominal ledger
mastro (m) nominale
nominal rent
affitto (m) nominale
nominal value val-
ore (m) nominale
nominee can-
didato (m)
nominee account
conto (m) di
prestanome
non profit-making
senza scopo di lucro
non-delivery man-
cata consegna (f)
**non-executive
director** direttore
(m) senza poteri
esecutivi
**non-negotiable
instrument** stru-
mento (m) non
negoziabile

non-payment *[of a
debt]* omesso
pagamento (m) di
un debito
**non-recurring
items** articoli (mpl)
non ricorrenti
**non-refundable
deposit** deposito
(m) non rim-
borsabile
**non-returnable
packing** imballo
(m) a perdere
non-stop senza
scalo *o* ininterrotto
non-taxable income
reddito (m)
non imponibile
nonfeasance reato
(m) di
omissione
norm norma (f)
notary public
notaio (m)
note (n) nota (f)
note (v) *[details]*
notare
note of hand
pagherò (m)
cambiario

notice *[piece of information]*
avviso (m)
notice *[that worker is leaving his job]* preavviso (m)
notice *[time allowed]*
preavviso (m)
notice *[warning that a contract is going to end]*
preavviso (m)
notification
notificazione (f)
notify notificare
null nullo
number (n) *[figure]*
numero (m)
number (v) numerare
numbered account
conto (m) numerato
numeric *or* **numerical** numerico
numeric keypad
tastierino (m)
numerico

Oo

objective (adj) obiettivo *o* oggettivo
objective (n)
obiettivo (m)
obligation *[debt]*
debito (m)
obligation *[duty]*
dovere (m) *o*
impegno (m)
obsolescence
invecchiamento (m)
obsolescent
obsolescente
obsolete antiquato
obtain ottenere
obtainable conseguibile *o* ottenibile
occupancy
occupazione (f)
occupancy rate
percentuale (f) di
occupazione
occupant occupante
(m) *o* chi occupa
occupational
occupazionale *o*
professionale

occupational acci-dent incidente (m) professionale

odd *[not a pair]* spaiato

odd *[not even]* dispari

odd numbers numeri (mpl) dispari

off *[away from work]* assente

off *[cancelled]* annullato

off *[reduced by]* con sconto di

off the record ufficiosamente

off-peak non di punta

off-season fuori stagione

off-the-job training corsi (mpl) di addestramento esterni (al posto di lavoro)

offer (n) offerta (f)

offer (v) *[to buy]* offrire o proporre

offer (v) *[to sell]* offrire (in vendita)

offer for sale offerta (f) di vendita

offer price prezzo (m) d'offerta

office ufficio (m)

office equipment attrezzatura (f) per ufficio

office furniture arredamento (m) per ufficio

office hours orario (m) d'ufficio

office security sistema (m) di sorveglianza dell'ufficio

office space area (f) uffici

office staff personale (m) d'ufficio

office stationery cancelleria (f) d'ufficio

offices to let affitansi uffici (mpl)

official (adj) ufficiale

official (n) funzionario (m)

official receiver liquidatore (m)

official return reddito (m) ufficiale
officialese linguaggio (m) burocratico
offload scaricare
offshore offshore o all'estero
oil *[cooking]* olio (m)
oil *[petroleum]* petrolio (m)
oil price prezzo (m) del petrolio
oil-exporting countries paesi (mpl) esportatori di petrolio
oil-producing countries paesi (mpl) produttori di petrolio
old vecchio
old-established di vecchia istituzione (f)
old-fashioned antiquato
ombudsman difensore (m) civico
omission omissione (f)
omit trascurare o omettere
on a short-term basis a breve termine

on account in acconto
on agreed terms secondo i termini convenuti
on an annual basis annualmente
on an average in media
on approval salvo vista e verifica
on behalf of per conto di
on board a bordo
on business per affari
on condition that a condizione che
on credit a credito
on favourable terms a condizioni (fpl) vantaggiose
on line *or* **online** in linea
on order (che è stato) ordinato
on request su richiesta
on sale in vendita
on the increase in aumento

on time puntuale
on-the-job training addestramento (m) sul lavoro
one-off unico
one-off item articolo (m) unico
one-sided parziale
one-sided agreement accordo (m) parziale
one-way fare biglietto (m) di andata
one-way trade commercio (m) a senso unico
OPEC (= Organization of Petroleum Exporting Countries) Organizzazione (f) dei paesi esportatori di petrolio
open (adj) *[not closed]* aperto
open (v) *[begin]* iniziare
open (v) *[start new business]* aprire
open a bank account aprire un conto bancario

open a line of credit aprire una linea di credito
open a meeting aprire una seduta
open account conto (m) aperto
open an account aprire un conto
open cheque assegno (m) non sbarrato
open credit credito (m) aperto
open market mercato (m) libero
open negotiations aprire trattative
open ticket biglietto (m) aperto (senza data di ritorno)
open to offers aperto ad offerte
open-ended agreement accordo (m) aperto
open-plan office ufficio (m) a pianta aperta
opening (adj) iniziale o d'apertura

opening (n)
apertura (f)
opening balance
bilancio (m)
d'apertura
opening bid offerta
(f) d'apertura
opening hours
orario (m)
d'apertura
opening price prezzo
(m) d'apertura
opening stock
rimanenze (fpl)
iniziali
opening time orario
(m) d'apertura
operate funzionare
operating (n) fun-
zionamento (m)
operating budget
budget (m)
operativo
operating costs *or*
operating expenses
costi (mpl) d'esercizio
o spese (fpl)
d'esercizio
operating manual
manuale (m)
operativo

operating profit
utile (m)
d'esercizio
operating system
sistema (m)
operativo
operation
operazione (f)
operational
operativo
operational budget
budget (m) di
gestione
operational costs
costi (mpl) di
gestione
operative (adj)
operativo
operative (n)
operatore (m)
operator
operatore (m)
opinion poll
sondaggio (m)
d'opinione
opportunity
opportunità (f)
option to purchase
opzione (f) per
l'acquisto
optional facoltativo

optional extras
spese (fpl)
supplementari
order (n) [certain
way] ordine (m)
order (n) [for goods]
ordinazione (f)
order (n) [instruc-
tion] ordine (m)
order (n) [money]
mandato (m) di paga-
mento o vaglia (m)
order (v) [goods]
ordinare
order (v) [put in
order] mettere in
ordine
order book registro
(m) delle ordinazioni
order fulfilment
evasione (f) di
un'ordinazione
order number
numero (m)
d'ordinazione
order picking
selezione (f) delle
ordinazioni
order processing
elaborazione (f)
delle ordinazioni

order: on order
essere stato
ordinato
ordinary ordinario
ordinary shares
azioni (fpl) ordinarie
organization [insti-
tution] organiz-
zazione (f)
organization [way
of arranging] orga-
nizzazione (f)
organization and
methods organiz-
zazione (f) e
metodo (m)
organization chart
organigramma (m)
Organization of
Petroleum
Exporting
Countries (OPEC)
Organizzazione (f)
dei paesi esportatori
di petrolio
organizational
organizzativo
organize organizzare
origin origine (f)
original (adj)
originario

original (n)
originale (m)
OS (= outsize) di
taglia forte
out of control fuori
controllo
out of date non
attuale
out of pocket
rimetterci
out of stock
esaurito
out of work
disoccupato
out-of-pocket
expenses piccole
spese (fpl)
outbid offrire un
prezzo superiore
outgoing in uscita
outgoing mail
posta (f) in partenza
outgoings spese (fpl)
outlay esborso (m)
outlet sbocco (m)
output (n) *[com-*
puter] output (m) o
dati (mpl) di
emissione
output (n) *[goods]*
produzione (f)

output (v) *[com-*
puter] emettere
output tax IVA
outright assoluto
outside esteriore
outside director
direttore esterno
outside line linea
(f) esterna
outside office
hours fuori orario
d'ufficio
outsize (OS) di
taglia forte
outstanding
[exceptional]
straordinario
outstanding
[unpaid] non pagato
outstanding debts
debiti (mpl) insoluti
outstanding orders
ordinazioni
(fpl) da evadere
overall totale
overall plan piano
(m) globale
overbook prenotare
più (stanze, posti
ecc.) di quanti siano
disponibili

overbooking
prenotazione (f) di
più (stanze, posti,
ecc.) di quanti
siano disponibili
overcapacity
capacità (f) in
eccedenza
overcharge (n)
prezzo (m) eccessivo
overcharge (v) far
pagare troppo
overdraft
scoperto (di c/c)
overdraft facility
facilitazioni (fpl)
di scoperto
overdraw emettere
allo scoperto
overdrawn account
conto (m) scoperto
overdue scaduto
overestimate (v)
sopravvalutare
overhead budget
budget (m) generale
**overhead costs or
expenses** spese
(fpl) generali
overheads
spese (fpl) generali

overmanning
personale (m) in
eccedenza
overpayment paga-
mento (m) in più
overproduce
produrre in eccesso
overproduction
produzione (f) in
eccesso
overseas (adj)
all'estero
overseas (n) l'es-
tero (m) o i paesi
stranieri
overseas markets
mercati (mpl) esteri
overseas trade
commercio (m)
estero
overspend
spendere oltre le
proprie possibilità
**overspend one's
budget** spendere
oltre il proprio
budget
overstock (v) satu-
rare di prodotti
overstocks sovrac-
carico (m) di scorte

overtime lavoro (m) straordinario
overtime ban blocco (m) del lavoro straordinario
overtime pay compenso (m) per lavoro straordinario
overvalue sopravvalutare
overweight: to be overweight di peso eccedente
owe essere debitore
owing dovuto o a debito
owing to a causa di
own (v) possedere
own brand goods prodotti (mpl) con marchio proprio
own label goods prodotti (mpl) con etichetta propria
owner proprietario (m)
ownership proprietà (f)

Pp

p & p (= postage and packing) spese (fpl) postali e imballo
PA (= personal assistant) segretaria (f) personale
pack (n) pacco (m)
pack (v) imballare o impacchettare
pack goods into cartons imballare le merci
pack of envelopes pacchetto (m) di buste
package [of goods] pacco (m)
package [of services] contratto (m) globale
package deal pacchetto (m) rivendicativo
packaging [action] imballaggio (m)

packaging [mate-rial] materiale (m) d'imballaggio

packaging material materiale (m) d'imballaggio

packer impacchet-tatore (m)

packet pacchetto (m)

packet of cigarettes pacchetto (m) di sigarette

packing [action] imballaggio (m)

packing [material] materiali (mpl) di imballaggio

packing case cassa (f) da imballaggio

packing charges spese (f) d'imballo

packing list or **packing slip** distinta (f) d'imballaggio

paid [for work] pagato o remunerato

paid [invoice] pagato

pallet paletta (f)

palletize palettiz-zare o trasportare a mezzo di palette

panel pannello (m)

panic buying incetta (f) in previsione di aumento dei prezzi

paper bag sac-chetto (m) di carta

paper feed alimen-tatore (m) di fogli

paper loss perdita (f) sulla carta

paper profit utili (mpl) ipotetici

paperclip graffetta (f)

papers incarta-menti (mpl)

paperwork lavoro (m) d'ufficio

par pari

par value valore (m) nominale

parcel (n) pacco (m)

parcel (v) impacchettare

parcel post servizio (m) pacchi postali

parent company
società (f)
controllante
parity parità (f)
part (n) parte (f)
part exchange per-
muta (f) come
pagamento parziale
part-owner com-
proprietario (m)
part-ownership
comproprietà (f)
part-time orario
(m) ridotto
part-time work *or*
part-time employ-
ment lavoro (m) a
orario ridotto
part-timer lavoratore
(m) a orario ridotto
partial loss perdita
(f) parziale
partial payment
pagamento (m)
parziale
particulars
dettagli (mpl)
partner socio (m) *o*
compagno/a
partnership società
(f) di persone

party parte (f)
[legale]
patent brevetto (m)
patent agent agente
(m) di brevetti
patent an invention
brevettare
un'invenzione
patent applied for
or **patent**
pending brevetto
(m) richiesto o in
attesa di brevetto
patented
brevettato
pay (n) *[salary]*
paga (f) o
retribuzione (f) o
stipendio (m)
pay (v) *[bill]*
pagare o saldare
pay (v) *[worker]*
pagare o remunerare
pay a bill pagare
un conto
pay a dividend
pagare un dividendo
pay an invoice
pagare una fattura
pay back
rimborsare

pay by cheque
pagare con un
assegno
pay by credit card
pagare con
carta di credito
pay cash pagare in
contanti
pay cheque assegno
(m) dello stipendio
pay desk banco
(m) dei pagamenti
pay in advance
pagare
anticipatamente
pay in instalments
pagare a rate
pay interest pagare
gli interessi
pay money down
pagare in contanti
pay off *[debt]*
estinguere (un
debito)
pay off *[worker]*
liquidare
pay out sborsare
pay phone telefono
(m) a gettoni
pay rise aumento
(m) salariale

pay up pagare
payable pagabile
**payable at sixty
days** pagabile a
sessanta giorni
payable in advance
pagabile
anticipatamente
payable on delivery
pagabile alla
consegna
payable on demand
pagabile su richiesta
payback recupero
(m) dell'investimento
payback clause
clausola (f)
di recupero
dell'investimento
payback period peri-
odo (m) di recupero
payee
beneficiario (m)
payer chi paga
paying (adj)
redditizio
paying (n) paga-
mento (m)
paying-in slip
distinta (f) di
versamento

payload carico (m) utile
payment pagamento (m)
payment by cheque pagamento (m) tramite assegno
payment by results pagamento (m) in base al lavoro effettuato
payment in cash pagamento (m) in contanti
payment in kind pagamento (m) in natura
payment on account pagamento (m) in acconto
PC (= personal computer) personal computer (m) o elaboratore (m) ad uso personale
P/E ratio (= price/earnings ratio) rapporto (m) corso/utili
peak (n) valore (m) massimo
peak (v) raggiungere un punto massimo o culminare
peak output livello (m) massimo di produzione
peak period periodo (m) di massima attività
peg prices bloccare i prezzi
penalize penalizzare
penalty penale (f) o multa (f)
penalty clause clausola (f) di penalità
pending pendente
penetrate a market realizzare la penetrazione di un mercato
pension pensione (f)
pension fund fondo (m) pensioni
pension scheme piano (m) pensioni
per per o per mezzo
per annum all'anno

per capita pro-capite
per cent per cento
per day al giorno
per head per persona
per hour all'ora
per week alla
settimana
per year all'anno
percentage
percentuale (f)
**percentage dis-
count** sconto (m)
percentuale
**percentage
increase** aumento
(m) percentuale
percentage point
punto (m)
percentuale
performance
prestazione (f)
performance rating
valutazione (f)
della prestazione
period periodo (m)
period of notice
periodo (m) di
preavviso
period of validity
periodo (m) di
validità

periodic *or* **periodical (adj)** periodico
periodical (n)
pubblicazione (f)
periodica
peripherals
periferiche (fpl)
perishable deperibile
perishable goods *or*
items *or* **cargo**
merci (fpl) *o* articoli
(mpl) *o* derrate (fpl)
deperibili
perishables merci
(fpl) deperibili
permission
autorizzazione (f)
permit (n)
permesso (m)
permit (v) autoriz-
zare (qualcuno a
fare qualcosa)
personal personale
personal allowances
detrazioni (fpl)
personali
personal assets
attivo (m) mobiliare
**personal assistant
(PA)** segretaria (f)
personale

personal computer (PC) personal computer (m) *o* elaboratore (m) ad uso personale
personal income reddito (m) personale
personalized personalizzato
personalized briefcase ventiquattrore (f) personalizzata
personalized cheques assegni (mpl) personalizzati
personnel personale (m)
personnel department ufficio (m) del personale
personnel management direzione (f) del personale
personnel manager capo (m) del personale
petty di scarsa importanza
petty cash piccola cassa (f)

petty cash box scatola (f) per la piccola cassa
petty expenses piccole spese (fpl)
phase in introdurre gradualmente
phase out eliminare gradualmente
phoenix syndrome sindrome (f) della fenice
phone (n) telefono (m)
phone (v) telefonare
phone back ritelefonare
phone call chiamata (f) telefonica
phone card carta (f) di credito telefonica
phone number numero (m) di telefono *o* numero telefonico
photocopier fotocopiatrice (f)
photocopy (n) fotocopia (f)

photocopy (v)
fotocopiare
photocopying
fotocopiatura (f)
**photocopying
bureau** ufficio (m)
dove si fanno
fotocopie
picking list lista
(f) di selezione
pie chart grafico
(m) a settori
piece pezzo (m)
piece rate ret-
ribuzione (f) a cottimo
piecework lavoro
(m) a cottimo
**pilferage *or* pilfer-
ing** furto (m) di
scarsa entità
pilot (adj) pilota
pilot (n) *[person]*
pilota (m)
pilot scheme prog-
etto (m) pilota
pioneer (n)
pioniere (m)
pioneer (v) fare da
pioniere in
**place (n) *[in a com-
petition]*** posto (m)

place (n) *[in a text]*
segno (m)
place (n) *[job]*
posto (m) o
impiego (m)
**place (n) *[situa-
tion]*** posto (m) o
luogo (m)
place (v) posare o
mettere
place an order fare
un'ordinazione
place of work
posto (m) di lavoro
plaintiff
querelante (m)
plan (n) *[drawing]*
pianta (f)
plan (n) *[project]*
piano (m) o
progetto (m)
plan (v) progettare
o organizzare
plan investments
pianificare
investimenti
plane aereo (m)
planner
pianificatore (m)
planning
pianificazione (f)

plant (n) [factory]
fabbrica (f) o
stabilimento (m)
plant (n) [machinery] impianti (mpl)
plant-hire firm
ditta (f) di noleggio
impianti
**platform [railway
station]** binario (m)
**PLC or plc (= Public
Limited Company)**
Società di capitali a
sottoscrizione
pubblica (SpA)
plug (n) [electric]
spina (f) elettrica
plug (v) [block]
tappare
plug (v) [publicize]
pubblicizzare
plus positivo
plus factor fattore
(m) positivo
pocket (n) tasca (f)
pocket (v) incassare
**pocket calculator
or pocket diary**
calcolatrice (f) tas-
cabile o agenda (f)
tascabile

point punto (m)
**point of sale (p.o.s.
or POS)** punto
(m) di vendita
point of sale material (POS material)
materiale (m) per
punto di vendita
**policy [plan of
action]** politica (f)
policy [insurance]
polizza (f)
pool resources
mettere insieme le
risorse
poor quality qual-
ità (f) scadente
poor service
servizio (m)
scadente
popular popolare
popular prices
prezzi (mpl) popolari
port [computer]
porta (f) [di
computer]
port [harbour]
porto (m)
port authority
autorità (fpl)
portuali

port charges *or*
port dues diritti
(mpl) di porto
port of call porto
(m) di scalo
port of embarka-
tion porto (m)
d'imbarco
port of registry
porto (m)
d'armamento
portable portatile
portfolio *[file]*
cartella (f) *o*
portfolio (m)
portfolio *[of shares]*
portafoglio (m)
portfolio manage-
ment gestione (f)
del portafoglio
p.o.s. *or* POS (=
point of sale)
punto (m) di vendita
POS material
(point of sale
material) materiale
(m) per punto
di vendita
position *[job]*
impiego (m) *o*
lavoro (m)

position *[state of*
affairs] posizione
(f) *o* situazione (f)
positive positivo
positive cash flow
flusso (m) di
cassa positivo
possess possedere
possibility
possibilità (f)
possible possibile
post (n) *[job]*
posto (m) di lavoro
o impiego (m)
post (n) *[letters]*
posta (f)
post (n) *[system]*
posta (f) *o*
servizio (m) postale
post (v)
spedire per posta
post an entry reg-
istrare una voce
(contabile)
post free
franco posta
postage spesa (f)
postale
postage and pack-
ing (p & p) spese
postali e imballo

postage paid
porto pagato
postal postale
postal charges or
postal rates
[peso]
spese (fpl) postali
postal order vaglia
(m) postale
postcode codice
(m) d'avviamento
postale
postdate postdatare
poste restante
fermoposta (m)
postpaid affran-
catura (f) pagata
postpone differire
o rinviare
postponement
dilazione (f) o
rinvio (m)
potential (adj)
potenziale
potential (n)
potenziale (m)
potential cus-
tomers clienti
(mpl) eventuali
potential market
mercato (m)
potenziale

pound *[money]*
sterlina (f)
pound *[weight:*
0.45kg] libbra (f)
[peso]
pound sterling
lira sterlina
power of attorney
procura (f)
PR (= public rela-
tions) pubbliche
relazioni
pre-empt
acquistare con
diritto di prelazione
pre-financing pre-
finanziamento (m)
prefer preferire
preference
preferenza (f)
preference shares
azioni (fpl) privilegiate
preferential
preferenziale
preferential credi-
tor creditore (m)
privilegiato
preferential duty
orpreferential
tariff dazio (m)
preferenziale

preferred creditor creditore (m) privilegiato

premises locali (mpl)

premium *[extra charge]* maggiorazione (f)

premium *[insurance]* premio (m) di assicurazione

premium *[on lease]* importo (m) aggiuntivo

premium offer offerta (f) premio

premium quality qualità (f) extra

prepack *or* **prepackage** preconfezionare

prepaid pagato in anticipo

prepay pagare in anticipo

prepayment pagamento (m) anticipato

present (adj) *[being there]* presente

present (adj) *[now]* attuale

present (n) *[gift]* regalo (m)

present (v) *[give]* regalare o offrire

present (v) *[show a document]* presentare

present a bill for acceptance presentare un effetto (m) per l'accettazione

present a bill for payment presentare un effetto (m) per il pagamento

present value valore (m) attuale

presentation *[exhibition]* presentazione (f)

presentation *[showing a document]* presentazione (f)

press stampa (f)

press conference conferenza (f) stampa

press release comunicato (m) stampa

prestige prestigio (m)

prestige product
prodotto (m) di
prestigio
pretax profit utile
(m) al lordo
delle imposte
prevent prevenire
prevention
prevenzione (f)
preventive
preventivo
previous precedente
price (n) prezzo (m)
price (v) stabilire il
prezzo
price ceiling tetto
(m) dei prezzi
price control
contollo (m) dei
prezzi
price controls con-
trolli (mpl) dei prezzi
price differential
disparità (f) dei
prezzi
price ex quay
prezzi (mpl) franco
banchina
price ex warehouse
prezzi (mpl) franco
magazzino

price ex works
prezzo (m) franco
stabilimento
price label
cartellino (m) del
prezzo
price list listino
(m) prezzi
price range gamma
(f) dei prezzi
price reductions
diminuzione (f) dei
prezzi
price stability sta-
bilità (f) dei prezzi
price tag cartellino
(m) del prezzo
price ticket
cartellino (m) del
prezzo
price war guerra
(f) dei prezzi
price-cutting war
guerra (f) della
diminuzione dei
prezzi
price-sensitive
product prodotto
(m) sensibile ai
cambiamenti di
prezzo

price/earnings
ratio (P/E ratio)
rapporto (m)
corso/utili
pricing
determinazione (f)
del prezzo
pricing policy
politica (f) della
determinazione dei
prezzi
primary primario
primary industry
industria (f)
primaria
prime primo *o* di
prima qualità
prime cost costi
(mpl) diretti
prime rate tasso
(m) di base
principal (adj)
principale
principal (n)
[money] capitale (m)
principal (n) *[per-
son]* capo (m) *o*
direttore (m),
direttrice (f)
principle
principio (m)

print out stampare
printer *[company]*
tipografia (f)
printer *[machine]*
stampante (f)
printout
stampato (m)
prior precedente
private privato
private enterprise
iniziativa (f) privata
**private limited
company** società
(f) a responsabilità
limitata (Srl)
private ownership
proprietà (f) privata
private property
proprietà (f) privata
private sector set-
tore (m) privato
privatization
privatizzazione (f)
privatize privatizzare
pro forma (invoice)
(fattura) proforma
pro rata prorata *o*
proporzionale
probation prova (f)
probationary
probatorio

problem
problema (m)
problem area area
(f) problematica
problem solver
persona (f) che
risolve problemi
problem solving
risoluzione (f) di
problemi
procedure
procedura (f)
proceed procedere
process (n)
processo (m)
process (v) [deal with] trattare
process (v) [raw materials]
lavorare o trattare
process figures
elaborare cifre
processing of information or of statistics elaborazione (f) delle
informazioni o delle
statistiche
produce (n) [food]
prodotti (mpl)
agricoli

produce (v) [bring out] produrre o
presentare
produce (v) [interest] fruttare o
rendere
produce (v) [make]
produrre o fabbricare
producer
produttore (m)
product
prodotto (m)
product advertising
pubblicità (f)
di un prodotto
product cycle vita
(f) ciclica di un
prodotto
product design
progettazione (f)
del prodotto
product development sviluppo
(m) del prodotto
product engineer
responsabile (m)
di un prodotto
product line linea
(f) di prodotti
product mix gamma
(f) di prodotti

production *[making]* produzione (f)
production *[showing]* presentazione (f)
production costs costi (mpl) di produzione
production department ufficio (m) produzioni
production line catena (f) di montaggio
production manager direttore (m) di produzione
production standards standard (m) di produzione
production targets obiettivi (mpl) di produzione
production unit complesso (m) produttivo
productive produttivo
productive discussions discussione (f) produttiva
productivity produttività (f)
productivity agreement accordo (m) sulla produttività
productivity bonus premio (m) di produttività
professional (adj) *[expert]* professionale
professional (n) *[expert]* professionista (m) o esperto (m)
professional qualifications qualifiche (fpl) professionali
profit profitto (m) o utile (m)
profit after tax utile (m) al netto delle imposte
profit and loss account conto (m) profitti e perdite
profit before tax utile (m) al lordo delle imposte
profit centre centro (m) di profitto
profit margin margine (m) di utile

profit-making a scopo di lucro
profit-oriented company società (f) orientata al profitto
profit-sharing compartecipazione (f) agli utili
profitability *[making a profit]* redditività (f)
profitability *[ratio of profit to cost]* coefficiente (m) di redditività
profitable remunerativo *o* proficuo *o* redditizio
program a computer programmare un computer
programme *or* **program** programma (m)
programming language linguaggio (m) di programmazione
progress (n) progresso (m)
progress (v) avanzare *o* fare progressi

progress chaser addetto (m) al controllo dell'avanzamento
progress payments pagamento (m) progressivo
progress report relazione (f) sull'avanzamento
progressive taxation imposte (fpl) progressive
prohibitive proibitivo
project *[plan]* progetto (m)
project analysis analisi (f) del progetto
project manager direttore (m) del progetto
projected progettato
projected sales vendite (fpl) previste
promise (n) promessa (f)
promise (v) promettere

promissory note
pagherò (m)
promote *[advertise]*
promuovere
**promote *[give bet-*
*ter job]*** promuovere
**promote a
corporate image**
promuovere un'im-
magine aziendale
**promote a new
product**
pubblicizzare un
nuovo prodotto
**promotion *[public-*
*ity]*** promozione (f)
**promotion *[to*
*better job]***
promozione (f)
promotion budget
budget (m) per le
spese di promozione
**promotion of a
product**
promozione (f) di un
prodotto
promotional
promozionale
promotional budget
stanziamento (m)
promozionale
prompt sollecito

prompt payment
pagamento (m) in
contanti
prompt service
servizio (m) sollecito
proof prova (f)
proportion
proporzione (f)
proportional
proporzionale
**proposal *[insur-*
*ance]*** proposta (f)
(di assicurazione)
**proposal *[sugges-*
*tion]*** proposta (f)
propose *[a motion]*
proporre
**propose to *[do*
*something]*** intendere
**proprietary com-
pany *[US]*** società
(f) controllante
proprietor
proprietario (m)
proprietress
proprietaria (f)
prosecute perseguire
(legalmente)
**prosecution
*[legal action]***
procedimento (m)
giudiziario

prosecution *[party in legal action]*
parte (f) querelante
prosecution counsel avvocato (m) della parte querelante
prospective probabile
prospective buyer possibile acquirente (m)
prospects prospettive (fpl)
prospectus prospetto (m)
protective protettivo
protective tariff tariffa (f) protezionistica
protest (n) *[against something]* protesta (f)
protest (n) *[official document]* protesto (m) (per mancato pagamento)
protest (v) *[against something]* protestare contro qualcosa
protest a bill protestare una cambiale

protest strike sciopero (m) di protesta
provide provvedere
provide for provvedere a
provided that *or* **providing** a patto che
provision *[condition]* condizione (f) o clausola (f)
provision *[money put aside]* accantonamento (m) o riserva (f)
provisional provvisorio
provisional budget budget (m) provvisorio
provisional forecast of sales previsione (f) delle vendite provvisoria
proviso clausola (f) condizionale
proxy *[deed]* procura (f) o delega (f)
proxy *[person]* mandatario (m)
proxy vote voto (m) per delega

public (adj) pubblico
public finance
finanza (f) pubblica
public funds fondi
(mpl) pubblici
public holiday
festa (f) nazionale
public image immag-
ine (f) pubblica
Public Limited
Company (Plc)
società (f) di capi-
tali a sottoscrizione
pubblica
public opinion
opinione (f) pubblica
public relations
(PR) pubbliche
relazioni (fpl)
public relations
department ufficio
(m) delle pubbliche
relazioni
public relations man
addetto (m) alle
pubbliche relazioni
public relations
officer dirigente
(m) delle pubbliche
relazioni
public sector set-
tore (m) pubblico
public transport
trasporti (mpl)
pubblici
publicity
pubblicità (f)
publicity budget
budget (m)
pubblicitario
publicity campaign
campagna (f)
pubblicitaria
publicity depart-
ment ufficio (m)
della pubblicità
publicity expendi-
ture spese (f)
pubblicitarie
publicity manager
direttore (m) della
pubblicità
publicize
pubblicizzare
purchase (n)
acquisto (m)
purchase (v)
acquistare o
comperare
purchase ledger
libro (m) mastro
degli acquisti
purchase order
ordine (m) d'acquisto

purchase price
prezzo (m)
d'acquisto
purchase tax
imposta (f) generale
sugli acquisti
purchaser
compratore (m)
purchasing
acquisto (m)
**purchasing depart-
ment** ufficio
(m) acquisti
**purchasing man-
ager** direttore (m)
dell'ufficio acquisti
purchasing power
potere (m)
d'acquisto
put (v) [place]
mettere
put back [later]
posticipare
put in writing met-
tere per iscritto
put money down
dare soldi come
anticipo

Qq

qty (= quantity)
quantità (f) (q)
qualified [skilled]
abile o
qualificato
**qualified [with
reservations]**
con riserve o
condizionato
qualify as qualificarsi
quality qualità (f)
quality control
controllo (m) di
qualità
quality controller
controllore (m)
della qualità
quality label
marchio (m) di
qualità
quantity quantità (f)
quantity discount
sconto (m) sul
quantitativo
quarter [25%]
quarto (m)

quarter *[three months]* trimestre
quarter day primo giorno (m) del trimestre
quarterly (adj) trimestrale
quarterly (adv) trimestralmente
quay molo (m)
quorum numero (m) minimo legale
quota quota (f)
quotation *[estimate of cost]* quotazione (f)
quote (n) *[estimate of cost]* quotazione (f)
quote (v) *[a reference number]* quotare
quote (v) *[estimate costs]* indicare un prezzo o quotare
quoted company società (f) quotata in Borsa
quoted shares azioni (fpl) quotate

Rr

R&D (= research and development) RS (ricerca e sviluppo)
racketeer organizzatore (m) di attività illegali
racketeering attività (f) illegale
rail ferrovia (f)
rail transport trasporto (m) ferroviario
railroad *[US]* ferrovia (f)
railway *[GB]* ferrovia (f)
railway station stazione (f) ferroviaria
raise (v) *[a question]* sollevare
raise (v) *[increase]* aumentare
raise (v) *[obtain money]* raccogliere fondi

raise an invoice
emettere una fattura
rally (n) ripresa (f)
rally (v) rafforzarsi
random accidentale
o casuale
random check
sondaggio (m)
random error
errore (m) casuale
random sample
campione (m)
casuale
random sampling
campionatura (f)
casuale
range (n) *[series of
items]* gamma (f)
range (n) *[varia-
tion]* variazioni
(fpl) o scala (f)
range (v) variare o
estendersi
rate (n) *[amount]*
tasso (m)
rate (n) *[price]*
quota (f) o tariffa
(f) o tasso (m)
rate of exchange
tasso (m) di cambio
rate of inflation
tasso (m) d'inflazione

rate of production
tasso (m) di
produzione
rate of return indice
(m) di rendimento
ratification ratifica (f)
ratify ratificare
rating quotazione (f)
ratio rapporto (m)
rationalization
razionalizzazione (f)
rationalize razion-
alizzare
raw materials
materie (fpl) prime
re-elect rieleggere
re-election
rielezione (f)
re-employ riassumere
re-employment
riassunzione (f)
re-export (n)
riesportazione (f)
re-export (v)
riesportare
reach *[arrive]*
raggiungere
reach *[come to]*
arrivare a
reach a decision
arrivare ad una
decisione

reach an agreement giungere ad un accordo
readjust riadattare
readjustment riassestamento (m)
ready pronto
ready cash pronta cassa (f)
real reale
real estate proprietà (f) immobiliare
real income or real wages reddito (m) effettivo
real-time system sistema (m) in tempo reale
realizable assets attivo (m) esigibile o cespiti (mpl) realizzabili
realization of assets realizzazione (f) di cespiti
realize [sell for money] realizzare
realize [understand] capire o rendersi conto di
realize a project or a plan realizzare un progetto o un piano

realize property or assets realizzare beni o cespiti
reapplication nuova domanda (f)
reappoint ricollocare
reappointment ricollocamento (m)
reassess fare una nuova stima
reassessment nuovo accertamento (m)
rebate [money back] rimborso (m)
rebate [price reduction] riduzione (f) o sconto (m)
receipt [paper] ricevuta (f)
receipt [receiving] ricevimento (m)
receipt book registro (m) delle ricevute
receipts entrate (fpl)
receivable da ricevere
receivables effetti (mpl) attivi
receive ricevere
receiver [liquidator] liquidatore (m)
receiving ricevente

reception
portineria (f)
reception clerk
portiere (f)
reception desk
portineria (f) o banco
(m) d'albergo
receptionist
receptionist (m)
recession
recessione (f)
reciprocal mutuo o
reciproco
**reciprocal agree-
ment** accordo (m)
bilaterale
reciprocal trade
commercio (m)
bilaterale
reciprocity
scambio (m)
recognition
riconoscimento (m)
recognize a union
riconoscere un
sindacato
**recommend [say
something is good]**
raccomandare
**recommend [sug-
gest action]**
consigliare

recommendation
raccomandazione (f)
reconcile
riconciliare
reconciliation
riconciliazione (f)
**reconciliation of
accounts** riconcili-
azione (f) dei conti
**record (n) [better
than before]**
primato (m)
**record (n) [for per-
sonnel]** archivi (mpl)
**record (n) [of what
has happened]**
rapporto (m)
record (v) registrare
**record sales or
record losses or
record profits** ven-
dite (fpl) record o
perdite (fpl) record
o utili (mpl) record
record-breaking
da primato
recorded delivery
raccomandata (f) con
ricevuta di ritorno
records documen-
tazione (f) o
archivio (m)

**recoup one's
losses** rifarsi delle
perdite
recover [get better]
riprendersi
**recover [get
something back]**
ricuperare
recoverable
recuperabile
**recovery [getting
better]** ripresa (f)
**recovery [getting
something back]**
ricupero (m)
rectification
rettifica (f)
rectify correggere
recurrent ricorrente
recycle riciclare
recycled paper
carta (f) riciclata
red tape lungag-
gine (f) burocratica
redeem estinguere
redeem a bond
rimborsare un'ob-
bligazione
redeem a debt
estinguere un debito
redeem a pledge
riscattare un pegno

redeemable redimibile
**redemption [of a
loan]** riscatto (m)
(di un prestito)
redemption date
data (f) di rimborso
redevelop adibire
ad altro uso
redevelopment
progetto (m) edilizio
di ricostruzione
redistribute
ridistribuire
reduce ridurre
reduce a price
ridurre un prezzo
reduce expenditure
ridurre le spese
reduced rate tasso
(m) ridotto
reduction ribasso (m)
redundancy cassa
(f) integrazione
redundant in cassa
integrazione
**refer [pass to some-
one]** sottoporre
refer [to item]
riferirsi o fare
riferimento a
**reference [dealing
with]** riferimento (m)

reference *[person who reports]* persona che è chiamata a dare referenza
reference *[report on person]* referenze (fpl) *o* attestato (m)
reference number numero (m) di riferimento
refinancing of a loan rifinanziamento (m) di un prestito
refresher course corso (m) d'aggiornamento
refund (n) rimborso (m)
refund (v) rimborsare
refundable rimborsabile
refundable deposit caparra (f) rimborsabile
refunding of a loan conversione (f) di un prestito
refusal rifiuto (m)

refuse (v) rifiutare
regarding riguardante
regardless of senza tener conto di
regional regionale
register (n) *[large book]* registro (m) *o* libro (m) contabile
register (n) *[official list]* registro (m)
register (v) *[at hotel]* firmare il registro
register (v) *[in official list]* iscriversi
register (v) *[letter]* fare una lettera raccomandata
register a company iscrivere una società
register a property iscrivere al catasto una proprietà immobiliare
register a trademark depositare un marchio di fabbrica
register of directors registro (m) degli amministratori

register of shareholders registro (m) degli azionisti o registro (m) delle azioni

registered (adj) registrato

registered letter raccomandata (f)

registered office sede (f) legale

registered trademark marchio (m) di fabbrica depositato

registrar ufficiale (m) di stato civile

Registrar of Companies Conservatore (m) del Registro delle Società

registration registrazione (f)

registration fee tassa (f) di registrazione

registration form modulo (m) d'iscrizione

registration number numero (m) di matricola

registry registrazione (f)

registry office anagrafe (f)

regular [always at same time] consueto o fisso

regular [ordinary] regolare o normale

regular customer cliente (mf) abituale

regular income reddito (m) fisso

regular size formato (m) normale

regular staff personale (m) di ruolo

regulate [adjust] regolare

regulate [by law] regolarizzare

regulation regolamento (m)

regulations regolamenti (mpl) o disposizioni (fpl)

reimbursement rimborso (m)

reimbursement of expenses rimborso (m) delle spese

reimport (n)
reimportazione (f)
reimport (v)
reimportare
reimportation
reimportazione (f)
reinsurance
riassicurazione (f)
reinsure
riassicurare
reinsurer
riassicuratore (m)
reinvest reinvestire
reinvestment
reinvestimento (m)
reject (n) scarto (m)
reject (v) rifiutare
o respingere
rejection rifiuto (m)
relating to relativo a
relations
relazioni (fpl)
release (n)
rilascio (m)
release (v) *[free]*
liberare
release (v) *[make
public]* rilasciare
release (v) *[put on
the market]*
mettere in vendita

release dues liquid-
are gli ordini arretrati
relevant relativo
reliability
attendibilità (f)
reliable attendibile
remain *[be left]*
restare
remain *[stay]* restare
remind rammentare
reminder
sollecito (m)
remit (n)
competenza (f)
remit (v)
rimettere
remit by cheque
inviare rimessa a
mezzo assegno
remittance
rimessa (f)
remote control
telecomando (m)
removal *[sacking
someone]* desti-
tuzione (f)
removal *[to new
house]* trasloco (m)
remove rimuovere
remunerate
retribuire

remuneration
retribuzione (f)
render an account
presentare un conto
renew rinnovare
**renew a bill of
exchange** *or* **renew
a lease** rinnovare
una cambiale *o*
rinnovare un
contratto d'affitto
**renew a subscrip-
tion** rinnovare un
abbonamento
renewal rinnovo (m)
renewal notice
avviso (m) di rinnovo
renewal of a lease *or*
of a subscription *or*
of a bill rinnovo (m)
di un contratto d'af-
fitto *o* un abbona-
mento *o* una cambiale
renewal premium
premio (m) di rinnovo
rent (n) affitto (m)
rent (v) *[pay money
for]* prendere in
affitto
rent collector esat-
tore (m) di affitti

rent control blocco
(m) degli affitti
rent tribunal
sindacato (m) degli
inquilini
rent-free esente da
canone d'affitto
rental affitto (m)
rental income red-
dito (m) da affittanze
renunciation
rinuncia (f)
reorder (n) nuova
ordinazione (f)
reorder (v) riordinare
reorder level livello
(m) di riordinazione
reorganization
riorganizzazione (f)
reorganize
riorganizzare
**rep (= representa-
tive)** rappresen-
tante (m)
repair (n)
riparazione (m)
repair (v)
aggiustare *o* riparare
repay ripagare
repayable
rimborsabile

repayment
rimborso (m)
repeat replica (f)
repeat an order
ripetere un'
ordinazione
repeat order
ordinazione (f)
rinnovata
replace sostituire
replacement [item]
sostituzione (f)
replacement [person] sostituto (m)
o rimpiazzo (m)
replacement value
valore (m) di
sostituzione
reply (n) risposta (f)
reply (v) rispondere
reply coupon
coupon (m) con
risposta pagata
report (n)
rapporto (m)
report (v) riferire
report (v) [go to a place] presentarsi
report a loss
dichiarare una
perdita

report for an interview presentarsi
per un colloquio di
lavoro
**report on the
progress of the work
or of the negotiations**
relazionare sull'anda-
mento di un lavoro o
dei negoziati
report to someone
dover rispondere a
qualcuno
repossess
recuperare
represent
rappresentare
representative (adj)
rappresentativo
representative [company] ufficio (m) di
rappresentanza
representative [person] rappresentante
(m) di commercio
repudiate ripudiare
repudiate an agreement rifiutare un
accordo
request (n)
richiesta (f)

request (v) richiedere o domandare

request: on request su richiesta

require *[demand]* richiedere

require *[need]* aver bisogno di

requirements richieste (fpl)

resale rivendita (f)

resale price prezzo (m) di rivendita

rescind rescindere

research (n) ricerca (f)

research (v) documentarsi su *o* fare ricerche

research and development (R & D) ricerca (f) e sviluppo (m) (RS)

research programme programma (m) di ricerca

research worker ricercatore (m), ricercatrice (f)

researcher ricercatore (m), ricercatrice (f)

reservation prenotazione (f)

reserve (n) *[money]* fondo (m)

reserve (n) *[supplies]* riserva (f)

reserve (v) riservare

reserve a room *or* a table *or* a seat riservare una camera *o* un tavolo *o* un posto

reserve currency valuta (f) di riserva

reserve price prezzo (m) minimo

reserves riserve (fpl)

residence residenza (f)

residence permit permesso (m) di soggiorno

resident (adj) residente

resident (n) residente (m) *o* abitante (m)

resign dimettersi

resignation dimissioni (fpl)

resolution
risoluzione (f)
resolve decidere
resources risorse (fpl)
respect (v)
rispettare
response reazione (f)
responsibilities
responsabilità (fpl)
responsibility
responsabilità (f)
responsible (for)
responsabile di
**responsible to some-
one** che deve rispon-
dere a qualcuno
restock rifornire
restocking
rifornimento (m)
restraint
restrizione (f)
restraint of trade
limitazione (f) agli
scambi commerciali
restrict limitare
restrict credit
limitare il credito
restriction
restrizione (f)
restrictive
restrittivo

**restrictive prac-
tices** pratiche (fpl)
restrittive
restructure ristrut-
turare
restructuring
ristrutturazione (f)
**restructuring of a
loan** rifinanzia-
mento (m) (di un
prestito)
**restructuring of
the company** rior-
ganizzazione (f) di
una società
result *[general]*
risultato (m)
result from derivare
result in avere
come risultato
**results *[company's
profit orloss]***
risultati (mpl)
resume riprendere
**resume negotia-
tions** riprendere le
trattative
retail (n) vendita
(f) al dettaglio
retail (v) *[goods]*
vendere al dettaglio

retail (v) *[sell for a price]* vendersi a

retail dealer dettagliante (m)

retail goods merce per la vendita al dettaglio

retail outlets punto (m) di vendita al dettaglio

retail price prezzo (m) al dettaglio

retail price index Indice (m) dei prezzi al dettaglio

retailer dettagliante (m)

retailing vendita (f) al dettaglio

retire *[from one's job]* andare in pensione

retirement pensionamento (m)

retirement age età (f) della pensione

retiring uscente

retrain riaddestrare

retraining riaddestramento (m)

retrenchment riduzione (f) delle spese

retrieval reperimento (m)

retrieval system sistema (m) di recupero delle informazioni

retrieve reperire

retroactive retroattivo

retroactive pay rise aumento (m) di paga retroattivo

return (n) *[declaration]* dichiarazione (f)

return (n) *[going back]* ritorno (m)

return (n) *[profit]* profitto (m) *o* guadagno (m)

return (n) *[sending back]* restituzione (f)

return (v) *[declare]* dichiarare

return (v) *[send back]* respingere *o* mandare indietro

return a letter to sender rimandare una lettera al mittente

return address
indirizzo (m) del
mittente
return on
investment (ROI)
reddito (m) sugli
investimenti
returnable
restituibile
returned empties
vuoti (mpl) a rendere
returns [profits]
incassi (mpl)
returns [unsold
goods] merce (f)
non venduta
revaluation
rivalutazione (f)
revalue rivalutare
revenue reddito (m)
revenue accounts
conto (m) delle
entrate
revenue from
advertising
ricavo (m) dalla
pubblicità
reversal
inversione (f)
reverse (adj)
inverso

reverse (v) invertire
reverse charge call
telefonata (f) a
carico del ricevente
reverse takeover
acquisizione (f)
di controllo inversa
reverse the charges
addebitare una tele-
fonata al ricevente
revise riesaminare
revoke revocare
revolving credit
credito (m) rinnov-
abile automatica-
mente
revolving credit credito (m) rinnovabile
automaticamente
rider clausola (f)
addizionale
right (adj) [not
left] destro
right (adj) [not
wrong] corretto
right (n) [legal
title] diritto (m)
right of veto diritto
(m) di veto
right of way diritto
(m) di precedenza

right-hand man
uomo (m) di fiducia
rightful giusto
rightful claimant pretendente (m) di diritto
rightful owner proprietario (m) legittimo
rights issue emissione (f) di diritti
rise (n) *[increase]*
aumento (m)
rise (n) *[salary]*
aumento (m)
rise (v) aumentare
risk (n) rischio (m)
risk (v) *[money]*
rischiare
risk capital capitale (m) di rischio
risk premium premio (m) di rischio
risk-free investment investimento (m) privo di rischio
risky rischioso
rival company società (f) rivale
road strada (f)
road haulage
trasporto (m) su
strada (di merci)

road haulier
trasportatore (m) su
strada
road tax tassa (f)
di circolazione
road transport
trasporto (m) su
strada
rock-bottom prices
prezzo (m) ridottissimo
ROI (= return on investment) reddito
(m) sugli investimenti
roll on/roll off ferry roll on/roll
off o traghetto (m)
per automezzi
rolling plan piano
(m) continuo
room *[general]*
stanza (f)
room *[hotel]*
camera (f)
room *[space]*
spazio (m)
room reservations
prenotazioni (fpl) di
camera
room service servizio
(m) in camera

rough approssimativo
rough calculation calcolo (m) approssimativo
rough draft bozza (f)
rough estimate valutazione (f) approssimativa
round down arrotondare diminuendo
round up arrotondare aumentando
routine (adj) abituale
routine (n) routine (f) o ordinaria amministrazione (f)
routine call telefonata (f) di routine
routine work lavoro (m) di routine
royalty diritto (m) di concessione
rubber check *[US]* assegno (m) a vuoto
rule (n) norma (f)
rule (v) *[be in force]* essere in vigore
rule (v) *[give decision]* decretare
ruling (adj) corrente

ruling (n) decreto (m)
run (n) *[regular route]* percorso (m)
run (n) *[work routine]* serie (f) o sequela (f)
run (v) *[be in force]* essere valido o entrare in vigore
run (v) *[buses, trains]* fare servizio
run (v) *[manage]* dirigere
run (v) *[work machine]* far funzionare
run a risk correre un rischio
run into debt contrarre debiti
run out of esaurire
running (n) *[of machine]* marcia (f) o funzionamento (m)
running costs *or* **running expenses** spese (fpl) d'esercizio o costi (mpl) di gestione di un'azienda

running total
totale (m) corrente
rush (n) ressa (f)
rush (v) affrettarsi
rush hour ora (f) di
punta
rush job lavoro (m)
urgente
rush order ordi-
nazione (f) urgente

Ss

sack someone
licenziare qualcuno
safe (adj) sicuro o
prudente
safe (n)
cassaforte (f)
safe deposit
deposito (m)
in cassetta di
sicurezza
safe investment
investimento (m)
sicuro

safeguard
salvaguardia (f)
safety sicurezza (f)
safety measures
misure (fpl) di
sicurezza
safety precautions
misure (fpl) di
sicurezza
safety regulations
norme (fpl) di
sicurezza
salaried stipendiato
salary stipendio (m)
salary cheque
assegno (m) dello
stipendio
salary review
revisione (f) dello
stipendio
sale (n) *[at a low
price]* saldo (m)
sale (n) *[selling]*
vendita (f)
sale by auction
vendita (f) all'asta
sale *or* return ven-
duto con possibilità
di resa
saleability
vendibilità (f)

saleable vendibile
sales vendite (fpl)
o fatturato (m)
sales analysis analisi (f) delle vendite
sales book libro (m) vendite
sales budget previsione (f) di vendita
sales campaign campagna (f) di vendite
sales chart grafico (m) delle vendite
sales clerk addetto (m) alle vendite
sales conference raduno (m) dei venditori
sales curve curva (f) delle vendite
sales department ufficio (m) vendite
sales executive dirigente (m) delle vendite **sales figures** volume (m) d'affari
sales force forza (f) vendita o personale (m) addetto alle vendite

sales forecast previsione (f) di vendita
sales ledger partitario (m) delle vendite
sales ledger clerk impiegato (m) addetto al partitario delle vendite
sales literature materiale (m) illustrativo delle vendite
sales manager direttore (m) commerciale
sales people venditori (mpl)
sales pitch imbonimento (m)
sales promotion promozione (f) delle vendite
sales receipt ricevuta (f) (di vendita)
sales representative rappresentante (m)
sales revenue fatturato (m)
sales target obiettivo (m) di vendita

sales tax imposta (f) sul volume di affari

sales team personale (m) addetto alle vendite

sales volume volume (m) delle vendite

salesman *[in shop]* commesso (m)

salesman *[representative]* rappresentante (m) (di commercio)

salvage (n) *[action]* recupero (m)

salvage (n) *[things saved]* materiale (m) di recupero

salvage (v) salvare o recuperare

salvage vessel nave (f) di salvataggio

sample (n) *[group]* campione (m)

sample (n) *[part]* campione (m) o saggio (m)

sample (v) *[ask questions]* fare un sondaggio

sample (v) *[test]* campionare

sampling *[statistics]* campionamento (m)

sampling *[testing]* campionamento (m)

satisfaction soddisfazione (f)

satisfy *[customer]* soddisfare

satisfy a demand soddisfare una richiesta

saturate saturare

saturate the market rendere saturo il mercato

saturation saturazione (f)

save (v) *[money]* risparmiare

save (v) *[not waste]* risparmiare o economizzare

save (v) *[on computer]* salvare su disco

save on economizzare

save up mettere da parte denaro

savings
risparmi (mpl)
savings account
conto (m) di
risparmio
scale *[system]*
scala (f)
scale down ridurre
proporzionalmente
scale of charges
tariffa (f)
scale up aumentare
proporzionalmente
scarcity value val-
ore alto dettato
dalla scarsità di
fornitura
scheduled flight
volo (m) di linea
scheduling
elencazione (f)
screen candidates
selezionare candidati
scrip documento
(m) provvisorio
scrip issue emis-
sione (f) di certificati
azionari provvisori
seal (n) sigillo (m)
seal (v) *[attach a
seal]* sigillare

seal (v) *[envelope]*
chiudere *o* incollare
sealed envelope
busta (f) chiusa
sealed tenders
offerta (f) in busta
chiusa
season *[time for
something]* stagione
(f) *o* periodo (m)
season *[time of
year]* stagione (f)
season ticket
tessera (f) (di
abbonamento
ferroviario)
seasonal sta-
gionale *o* periodico
**seasonal adjust-
ments** adattamento
(m) stagionale
seasonal demand
richiesta (f)
stagionale
seasonal variations
variazioni (fpl)
stagionali
**seasonally
adjusted figures**
cifre (fpl) desta-
gionalizzate

second (adj) secondo
second (v) *[member
of staff]* trasferire o
distaccare
second quarter secondo trimestre (m)
second-class seconda classe (sui
mezzi di trasporto)
o seconda categoria
(di merci)
secondary industry
industria (f)
secondaria
secondhand usato
o di seconda mano
seconds prodotti
(mpl) di seconda
qualità
secret (adj) segreto
secret (n)
segreto (m)
secretarial college
scuola (f) per segretarie d'azienda
secretary segretaria/o (fm)
secretary *[company
official]* segretario
(m) del consiglio di
amministrazione

secretary *[government minister]*
ministro (m)
sector settore (m)
secure funds
procurarsi fondi
secure investment
investimento (m)
garantito
secure job lavoro
(m) stabile
secured creditor
creditore (m)
privilegiato
secured debts debiti (mpl) privilegiati
secured loan
mutuo (m) garantito
securities titoli (mpl)
security *[being
safe]* sicurezza (f)
security *[guarantee]* garanzia (f)
security guard
guardia (f) giurata
security of employment sicurezza (f)
dell'impiego
security of tenure
sicurezza (f) di
possesso

see-safe vendita (f) con possibilità di resa

seize sequestrare

seizure sequestro (m)

selection selezione (f)

selection procedure procedura (f) di selezione

self-employed che lavora in proprio

self-financing (adj) che può autofinanziarsi

self-financing (n) autofinanzia-mento (m)

self-regulation autoregolazione (f)

self-regulatory autoregolatore

sell vendere

sell forward vendere a termine

sell off svendere

sell out *[all stock]* vendere tutto

sell out *[sell one's business]* vendere (un impresa)

sell-by date data (f) di scadenza

seller venditore (m)

seller's market mercato (m) favorev-ole ai venditori

selling (n) vendita (f)

selling price prezzo (m) di vendita

semi-finished prod-ucts prodotti (mpl) semilavorati

semi-skilled work-ers lavoratori (mpl) parzialmente qualificati

send inviare

send a package by airmail spedire un pacco per via aerea

send a package by surface mail spedire un pacco per posta ordinaria

send a shipment by sea mandare un carico per mare

send an invoice by post spedire una fattura (per posta)

sender mittente (m)

senior anziano o piu vecchio

senior manager *or*
senior executive
dirigente (m) in
capo *o* direttore (m)
senior partner
socio (m) anziano
separate (adj) sep-
arato
separate (v) separare
sequester *or*
sequestrate
sequestrare
sequestration
sequestro (m)
sequestrator
sequestratario (m)
serial number
numero (m) di serie
serve servire
serve a customer
servire un cliente
service (n) *[busi-*
ness which helps]
società (f) di servizi
service (n) *[dealing*
with customers]
servizio (m)
service (n) *[of*
machine]
revisione (f) *o*
manutenzione (f)

service (n) *[regular*
working] servizio (m)
service (n) *[work-*
ing for a company]
servizio (m)
service (v) *[a*
machine] revisionare
service a debt
pagare un debito
service centre cen-
tro (m) assistenza
service charge per-
centuale (f) per il
servizio
service department
ufficio (m) assistenza
service manual
manuale (m) di
manutenzione
set (adj) fisso
set (n) serie (f)
set (v) fissare
set against
contrapporre
set price prezzo
(m) stabilito
set targets fissare
obiettivi
set up a company
costituire una
società (f)

set up in business
mettersi in affari
setback battuta (f)
d'arresto
settle *[an invoice]*
liquidare o pagare
una fattura
settle *[arrange
things]* sistemare
settle a claim
definire una domanda
d'indennizzo
settle an account
saldare un conto
settlement *[agree-
ment]* accordo (m)
settlement *[payment]*
pagamento (m)
setup *[company]*
organizzazione (f)
setup *[organization]*
organizzazione (f)
share (n) *[in a com-
pany]* azione (f)
share (v) *[divide
among]* spartire o
dividere
share (v) *[use with
someone]* dividere
share an office
spartire un ufficio

share capital capi-
tale (m) sociale
share certificate
certificato (m)
azionario
share issue emis-
sione (f) azionaria
shareholder
azionista (m)
shareholding
partecipazione (f)
azionaria
sharp practice
pratica (f)
spregiudicata
sheet of paper
foglio (m) di carta
shelf scaffale (m)
shelf filler persona
addetta al riforni-
mento degli scaffali
**shelf life of a prod-
uct** periodo (m)
medio di perma-
nenza di un prodotto
shell company
società (f) esistente
solo di nome
shelter riparo (m)
shelve accantonare
o differire

shelving *[postponing]*
accantonamento (m)
shelving *[shelves]*
scaffalatura (f)
shift (n) *[change]*
cambiamento (m)
shift (n) *[team of
workers]* turno (m)
(di lavoro)
shift key tasto (m)
delle maiuscole
shift work lavoro
(m) con turni
ship (n) nave (f)
ship (v) trasportare
o spedire
ship broker agente
(m) marittimo
shipment trasporto
(m) marittimo
shipper spedizion-
iere (m) marittimo
shipping spedizione
(f) marittima
shipping agent
spedizioniere (m)
marittimo
shipping charges *or*
shipping costs costi
(mpl) per la spedi-
zione marittima

shipping clerk
impiegato (m) di
spedizioniere
shipping company
società (f) di
navigazione
shipping instruc-
tions istruzioni (fpl)
per la spedizione
shipping line linea
(f) di navigazione
shipping note bolla
(f) di spedizione
shop negozio (m)
shop around con-
frontare i prezzi
shop assistant
commesso/a (mf)
di negozio
shop window
vetrina (f)
shop-soiled arti-
colo (m) sciupato
per prolungata
esposizione
shopkeeper
negoziante (m)
shoplifter taccheg-
giatore (m)
shoplifting
taccheggiare

shopper acquirente (mf) *o* cliente (mf)

shopping *[action]* spesa (f)

shopping *[goods bought]* acquisti (mpl)

shopping arcade galleria (f) (con negozi) *o* centro (m) commerciale

shopping centre centro (m) commerciale

shopping mall galleria (f) (con negozi) *o* centro (m) commerciale

shopping precinct zona (f) commerciale

short credit credito (m) a breve termine

short of a meno di

short-dated bills effetti (mpl) a breve termine

short-term (adj) a breve *o* a breve termine

short-term contract contratto (m) a breve termine

short-term credit credito (m) a breve

short-term debts indebitamento (m) a breve

short-term loan mutuo (m) a breve scadenza

shortage scarsità (f)

shortfall ammanco (m)

shortlist (n) lista (f) ristretta (di candidati)

shortlist (v) iscrivere qualcuno in una rosa di candidati

show (n) *[exhibition]* mostra (f)

show (v) mostrare

show a profit indicare un profitto

showcase bacheca (f)

showroom sala (f) di esposizione

shrink-wrapped imballato con metodo termocontrattile

shrink-wrapping imballaggio (m) termocontrattile

shrinkage restring-imento (m) *o* deprezzamento (m)
shut (adj) chiuso
shut (v) chiudere
side lato (m)
sideline attività (f) secondaria
sight vista (f)
sight draft tratta (f) a vista
sign (n) insegna (f)
sign (v) firmare
sign a cheque firmare un assegno
sign a contract firmare un contratto
signatory firmatario (m)
signature firma (f)
simple interest interesse (m) semplice
single singolo
Single European Market Mercato Europeo Unico
sister company società (f) sorella
sister ship nave (f) gemella

sit-down protest protesta (f) con occupazione
sit-down strike sciopero (m) con occupazione
site luogo (m)
site engineer ingegnere (m) edile
sitting tenant affittuario (m) occupante
situated situato
situation *[place]* posizione (f) *o* collocazione (f)
situation *[state of affairs]* situazione (f)
situations vacant offerte (fpl) d'impiego
size dimensione (f)
skeleton staff personale (m) ridotto al minimo
skill abilità (f) tecnica
skilled specializzato
skilled labour or skilled workers manodopera (f) qualificata

slack lento o
stagnante
slash prices *or*
credit terms
tagliare i prezzi o le
condizioni di credito
sleeping partner
socio (m)
accomandante
slip (n) *[mistake]*
errore (m)
slip (n) *[piece of*
paper] foglietto (m)
slow lento
slow down
rallentare
slow payer paga-
tore (m) tardivo
slowdown rallenta-
mento (m)
slump (n) *[depres-*
sion] crollo (m)
o crisi (f) economica
slump (n) *[rapid fall]*
brusca caduta (f)
slump (v) crollare
o subire una forte
flessione
slump in sales dis-
cesa (f) delle vendite
small piccolo

small ads piccoli
annunci (mpl)
small businesses
piccole imprese (fpl)
small businessman
piccolo affarista/uomo
d'affari
small change mon-
eta (f) spicciola
small-scale in
scala (f) ridotta
small-scale enter-
prise iniziativa
(f) su scala ridotta
soar salire alle
stelle
social sociale
social costs costi
(mpl) sociali
social security
previdenza (f)
sociale
society *[club]*
associazione (f) o
circolo (m)
society *[general]*
società (f)
socio-economic
groups gruppi
(mpl) socioeco-
nomici

soft currency
valuta (f) debole
soft loan prestito
(m) agevolato
soft sell tecnica (f)
di vendita basata
sulla persuasione
software
software (m)
sole solo *o* unico
sole agency rapp-
resentanza (f)
esclusiva
sole agent
rappresentante (m)
esclusivo
sole owner unico
proprietario (m)
sole trader com-
merciante (m) in
proprio
solicit orders
sollecitare un'ordi-
nazione
solicitor procura-
tore (m) legale
solution soluzione (f)
solve a problem
risolvere un problema
solvency
solvibilità (f)

solvent (adj)
solvente
source of income
fonte (f) di reddito
spare part pezzo
(m) di ricambio
spare time tempo
(m) libero
special speciale
**special drawing
rights (SDRs)**
diritti (mpl) speciali
di prelievo (DSP)
special offer
offerta (f) speciale
specialist special-
ista (m)
specialization spe-
cializzazione (f)
specialize essere
specializzato
specification
specifica (f)
specify specificare
speech of thanks
discorso (m) di
ringraziamento
spend *[money]*
spendere
spend *[time]* pas-
sare il tempo a

spending money
denaro (m) per le
piccole spese
spending power
potere (m) d'acquisto
spinoff sotto-
prodotto (m)
spoil rovinare o
viziare
sponsor (n) sponsor
(m) o garante (m)
sponsor (v) garan-
tire o sponsorizzare
o patrocinare
sponsorship spon-
sorizzazione (f) o
avallo (m)
spot *[place]* posto
(m) o luogo (m)
spot cash pagamento
(m) in contanti
spot price prezzo
(m) per merce
pronta
spot purchase tran-
sazione (f) a pronti
spread a risk ripar-
tire un rischio
spreadsheet *[com-
puter]* foglio (m) di
calcolo elettronico

stability stabilità (f)
stabilization stabi-
lizzazione (f)
stabilize stabilizzare
stable fermo o stabile
stable currency
moneta (f) stabile
stable economy
economia (f) solida
**stable exchange
rate** tasso (m) di
cambio stabile
stable prices prezzi
(mpl) stabili
staff (n)
personale (m)
staff (v) fornire di
personale
staff appointment
nomina (f) del
personale
staff meeting assem-
blea (f) del personale
stage (n) stadio (m)
stage (v) *[organize]*
organizzare
stage a recovery
riprendersi
staged payments
pagamenti (mpl)
scaglionati

stagger scaglionare
stagnant stagnante
stagnation
ristagno (m)
stamp (n) [device]
timbro (m)
stamp (n) [post]
francobollo (m)
stamp (v) [letter]
affrancare o mettere
francobolli
stamp (v) [mark]
timbrare
stamp duty
imposta (f) di bollo
**stand (n) [at exhi-
bition]** stand (m)
stand down ritirare
la propria candi-
datura
stand security for
avallare
**stand surety for
someone** garantire
per qualcuno
standard (adj)
standard
standard (n)
norma (f)
standard letter
lettera (f) standard

**standard rate (of
tax)** aliquota (f)
d'imposta base
standardization
standardizzazione (f)
standardize
standardizzare
**standby arrange-
ments** accordo (m)
creditizio di sostegno
standby credit cred-
ito (m) di appoggio
standby ticket
biglietto (m) aereo
privo di preno-
tazione
standing legitti-
mazione (f)
standing order
ordine (m)
permanente
staple (n) punto
(m) metallico
staple (v)
cucire con punti
metallici o graffare
staple industry
industria (f) di base
**staple papers
together** graffare
insieme fogli

staple product prodotti (mpl) essenziali
stapler cucitrice (f) o graffatrice (f)
start (n) avvio (m)
start (v) iniziare o cominciare
start-up avviamento (m)
start-up costs spese (fpl) di avviamento
starting (adj) iniziale
starting date data (f) d'inizio
starting point punto (m) di partenza
starting salary stipendio (m) iniziale
state (n) [condition] condizione (f) o stato (m)
state (n) [country] stato (m) o nazione (f)
state (v) dichiarare o precisare
state-of-the-art all'avanguardia
statement rendiconto (m)

statement of account estratto (m) conto
statement of expenses rendiconto (m) delle spese
station [train] stazione (f)
statistical statistico
statistical analysis analisi (f) statistica
statistician esperto (m) di statistica
statistics statistica (f)
status condizione (f) sociale
status inquiry informazioni (fpl) commerciali
status symbol simbolo (m) di successo
statute of limitations prescrizione (f)
statutory statutario
statutory holiday giorno (m) festivo legale
stay (n) [time] permanenza (f)
stay (v) fermarsi

stay of execution
sospensiva (f)
steadiness
saldezza (f)
sterling lira (f)
sterlina
stevedore stivatore
(m) o scaricatore
(m) (di porto)
stiff competition
concorrenza (f) dura
stimulate the econ-
omy stimolare
l'economia
stimulus stimolo (m)
stipulat e stipulare
stipulation
stipula (f)
stock (adj) *[nor-*
mal] standard o
usuale
stock (n) *[goods]*
stock (m) o
scorte (fpl)
stock (v) *[goods]*
rifornire o tenere
stock code codice
(m) di magazzino
stock control
controllo (m) delle
scorte

stock controller
persona (f) addetta
al controllo delle
scorte
stock exchange Borsa
(f) o Borsa Valori
stock level livello
(m) delle scorte
stock list
inventario (m)
stock market mer-
cato (m) azionario
stock market valu-
ation valutazione
(f) del mercato
azionario
stock of raw mate-
rials riserva (f) di
materia prima
stock size misura (f)
o taglia (f) standard
stock turnover
rotazione (f) delle
scorte
stock up
immagazzinare
stock valuation
valutazione (f) delle
scorte
stockbroker agente
(m) di cambio

stockbroking mediazione (f) di cambio
stockist
rivenditore (m)
stocklist
inventario (m)
stockpile (n)
scorta (f) (di
materie prime)
stockpile (v)
costruire riserve *o*
stoccare
stockroom
magazzino (m)
stocktaking
inventario (m)
stocktaking sale
saldi (mpl) per
inventario
stop (n) stop (m) *o*
fine (f) *o* arresto (m)
stop (v) *[doing
something]* cessare
o finire
stop a cheque
bloccare un assegno
stop an account
bloccare un conto
stop payments
sospendere i
pagamenti

stoppage *[act of stopping]* sospensione (f)
stoppage of payments sospensione
(f) dei pagamenti
storage (n) *[computer]* memoria (f)
storage (n) *[cost]*
spese (fpl) di
immagazzinamento
storage (n) *[in warehouse]* magazzinaggio
(m) *o* deposito (m)
storage capacity
capienza (f) di
magazzino
storage facilities
impianti (m) di
magazzinaggio
storage unit
impianto (m) di
magazzinaggio
store (n) *[items
kept]* riserva (f)
store (n) *[large shop]*
negozio (m) *o* grande
magazzino (m)
store (n) *[place
where goods are
kept]* deposito (m)
o magazzino (m)

store (v) *[keep for future]* mettere in serbo

store (v) *[keep in warehouse]* immagazzinare

storeroom magazzino (m)

storm damage danni (mpl) causati da un temporale

straight line depreciation ammortamento (m) a quote costanti

strategic strategico

strategic planning pianificazione (f) strategica

strategy strategia (f)

street directory guida (f) stradale

strike (n) sciopero (m)

strike (v) scioperare

striker scioperante (m)

strong forte

strong currency divisa (f) forte

structural strutturale

structural adjustment correzione (f) strutturale

structural unemployment disoccupazione (f) strutturale

structure (n) struttura (f)

structure (v) *[arrange]* strutturare

study (n) studio (m)

study (v) studiare

sub judice in contenzioso

subcontract (n) subappalto (m)

subcontract (v) dare in subappalto

subcontractor subappaltatore (m)

subject to soggetto a

sublease (n) subaffitto (m)

sublease (v) subaffittare

sublessee subaffittuario (m)

sublessor subaffittante (m)

sublet subaffittare

subsidiary (adj)
sussidiario
subsidiary (n)
filiale (f)
subsidiary company affiliata (f)
subsidize
sovvenzionare
subsidy sussidio (m)
o sovvenzione (f)
subtotal totale (m)
parziale
subvention
sovvenzione (f)
succeed *[do as planned]* riuscire
succeed *[do well]*
riuscire o avere
successo
succeed *[follow someone]*
succedere
success successo (m)
successful di
successo
successful bidder
miglior offerente (m)
sue citare o
intentare causa
suffer damage
subire un danno

sufficient sufficiente
sum *[of money]*
somma (f)
sum *[total]*
totale (m)
summons citazione
(f) in giudizio
sundries articoli
(mpl) vari
sundry items
partite (fpl) varie
superior (adj) *[better quality]* superiore
superior (n) *[person]* superiore (m)
supermarket
supermercato (m)
superstore grande
supermercato (m) o
ipermercato (m)
supervise
sorvegliare
supervision
supervisione (f) o
vigilanza (f)
supervisor
supervisore (m)
supervisory ispettivo o di supervisione
supplementary
supplementare

supplier fornitore (m)
supply (n) *[action]*
fornitura (f)
supply (n) *[stock of goods]* provvista (f)
supply (v) fornire
o approvvigionare
supply and demand
offerta (f) e
domanda (f)
supply price prezzo
(m) d'offerta
**supply side eco-
nomics** economia
(f) dell'offerta
support price
prezzo (m) di
sostegno
surcharge
sovrapprezzo (m)
surety (n) *[person]*
garante (m)
surety (n) *[secu-
rity]* garanzia (f)
surface mail posta
(f) ordinaria
surface transport
trasporto (m) di
superficie
surplus surplus
(m) o sovrappiù (m)

surrender (n)
[insurance policy]
riscatto (m)
surrender (v) *[insur-
ance]* riscattare
surrender a policy
riscattare una polizza
surrender value
valore (m) di riscatto
survey (n) *[exami-
nation]* indagine (f)
o studio (m)
survey (n) *[general
report]* quadro (m)
generale
survey (v)
[inspect] esaminare
o ispezionare
surveyor perito (m)
suspend sospendere
suspension
sospensione (f)
**suspension of
deliveries** ces-
sazione (f) delle
consegne
**suspension of pay-
ments** sospensione
(f) dei pagamenti
swap (n) scambio (m)
swap (v) scambiare

swatch ritaglio (m)
(di campioni)
switch (v) *[change]*
cambiare
switch over to
passare a
switchboard
centralino (m)
swop (= swap)
scambiare
sympathy strike
sciopero (m) di
solidarietà
synergy sinergia (f)
system sistema (m)
systems analysis
analisi (f) dei sistemi
systems analyst
analista (m)
dei sistemi

Tt

tabulate tabulare
tabulation
tabulazione (f)

tabulator
tabulatore (m)
tachograph
tachigrafo (m)
tacit agreement
tacito accordo (m)
tacit approval tac-
ito consenso (m)
take (n) *[money*
received] incasso (m)
take (v) *[need]*
volere *o* richiedere
take (v) *[receive*
money] guadagnare
take a call pren-
dere una telefonata
take a risk correre
un rischio
take action agire
take legal action
intentare azione legale
take legal advice
ricorrere a con-
sulenza legale
take note pren-
dere nota
take off *[deduct]*
dedurre *o* fare uno
sconto di
take off *[plane]*
decollare

take off *[rise fast]*
decollare
take on freight
prendere un carico
(m) a bordo
take on more staff
assumere altro
personale
take out a policy
sottoscrivere una
polizza
take over *[from
someone else]* suc-
cedere **take place**
avere luogo
**take someone to
court** portare qual-
cuno in tribunale
take stock fare
l'inventario
take the initiative
prendere l'iniziativa
**take the soft
option** scegliere la
strada più facile
take time off work
prendersi giorni di
ferie
take up an option
esercitare il diritto
d'opzione

takeover acqui-
sizione (f) di controllo
takeover bid
offerta (f) pubblica
d'acquisto
takeover target
obiettivo (m) di
rilevamento
takings incassi (mpl)
tangible tangibile
tangible assets
beni (mpl) reali
tanker petroliera (f)
tare tara (f)
target (n)
obiettivo (m)
target (v) stabilire
come obiettivo
target market mer-
cato (m) prescelto
tariff *[price]*
tariffa (f)
tariff barriers bar-
riere (fpl) tariffarie
tax (n) tassa (f) o
imposta (f)
tax (v) tassare o
gravare d'imposta
tax adjustments
adeguamento (m)
fiscale

tax allowance
riduzione (f)
d'imposta
tax assessment
accertamento (m)
fiscale
tax avoidance
evasione (f) fiscale
tax code codice
(m) fiscale
tax collection
riscossione (f) delle
imposte
tax collector esat-
tore (m) delle imposte
tax concession con-
cessione (f) fiscale
tax consultant con-
sulente (m) fiscale
tax credit credito
(m) d'imposta
**tax deducted at
source** imposta (f)
trattenuta alla fonte
tax deductions
*[taken from salary
to pay tax]*
detrazioni (fpl)
d'imposta
tax evasion eva-
sione (f) fiscale

tax exemption
esenzione (f) fiscale
tax form modulo
(m) delle tasse
tax haven rifugio
(m) fiscale
tax inspector ispet-
tore (m) delle tasse
tax loophole sot-
terfugio (m) fiscale
tax offence
infrazione (f) fiscale
tax paid imposta
(f) pagata
tax rate aliquota
(f) d'imposta
tax reductions
riduzioni (fpl)
d'imposta
tax relief
agevolazione (f)
fiscale
**tax return *or* tax
declaration** denun-
cia (f) dei redditi
tax shelter scappa-
toia (f) fiscale
tax system sistema
(m) tributario
tax year anno (m)
fiscale

tax-deductible detraibile dal reddito imponibile

tax-exempt esentasse

tax-free esente da tasse

taxable tassabile

taxable income reddito (m) imponibile

taxation tassazione (f)

taxpayer contribuente (m)

telephone (n) telefono (m)

telephone (v) telefonare

telephone book elenco (m) telefonico

telephone call chiamata (f) telefonica

telephone directory elenco (m) telefonico

telephone exchange centralino (m) telefonico

telephone line linea (f) telefonica

telephone number numero (m) telefonico o numero di telefono

telephone subscriber abbonato (m) al telefono

telephone switchboard centralino (m) telefonico

telephonist telefonista (mf)

telesales vendite (fpl) per telefono

telex (n) telescrivente (f) o telex (m)

teller sportellista (m)

temp (n) segretaria (f) temporanea

temp agency agenzia (f) che fornisce personale temporaneo

temporary employment lavoro (m) a contratto a termine

temporary staff personale (m) avventizio

tenancy *[agreement]* contratto (m) di locazione
tenancy *[period]* locazione (f)
tenant inquilino (m)
tender (n) *[offer to work]* licitazione (f) o offerta (f) d'appalto
tender for a contract fare offerta per un contratto d'appalto
tenderer offerente (m)
tendering licitazione (f)
tenure *[right]* diritto (m) di possesso
tenure *[time]* durata (f) in carica
term *[part of academic year]* trimestre (m) scolastico
term *[time of validity]* periodo (m) o durata (f)
term insurance assicurazione (f) temporanea
term loan prestito (m) a termine

terminal (adj) *[at the end]* terminale
terminal (n) *[airport]* terminal (m)
terminal bonus premio (m) (d'assicurazione) finale
terminate terminare
terminate an agreement rescindere un accordo
termination termine (m)
termination clause clausola (f) di rescissione
terms condizioni (fpl)
terms of employment condizioni (fpl) di impiego
terms of payment condizioni (fpl) di pagamento
terms of reference termini (mpl) stabiliti
terms of sale condizioni (fpl) di vendita
territory *[of salesman]* territorio (m)

tertiary industry
industria (f) terziaria
tertiary sector set-
tore (m) terziario
test (n) prova (f)
test (v) provare
theft furto (m)
third party terza
persona (f)
third quarter terzo
trimestre (m)
**third-party insur-
ance** assicurazione
(f) per danni verso
terzi
threshold soglia (f)
**threshold agree-
ment** accordo (m)
di indicizzazione
threshold price
prezzo (m)
d'entrata
throughput
produttività (f)
tie-up *[link]*
collegamento (m)
tight money
denaro (m) scarso
tighten up on
restringere
till (n) cassa (f)

**time and motion
study** studio (m) dei
tempi e dei movimenti
time deposit depos-
ito (m) a termine
time limit termine
(m) ultimo
time limitation
perenzione (f)
time rate tariffa (f)
a tempo
time scale scala (f)
temporale
time: on time pun-
tuale *o* in orario
timetable (n)
[appointments]
programma (m)
timetable (n) *[trains,
etc.]* orario (m)
timetable (v) pro-
grammare
timing scelta (f) del
momento opportuno
tip (n) *[advice]* informazione (f) riservata
tip (n) *[money]*
mancia (f)
tip (v) *[give
money]* dare la
mancia a

tip (v) *[say what might happen]* pronosticare

TIR (= Transports Internationaux Routiers) Trasporto Internazionale su Strada

token simbolo (m)

token charge costo (m) simbolico

token payment pagamento (m) simbolico

toll pedaggio (m)

toll free *[US]* esente da pedaggio

toll free number *[US]* servizio (m) telefonico gratuito

ton tonnellata (f)

tonnage tonnellaggio (m)

tonne tonnellata (f)

tool up attrezzare (una fabbrica)

top (adj) più alto o migliore

top (n) *[highest point]* cima (f) o vetta (f)

top (n) *[upper surface]* parte (f) superiore

top (v) *[go higher than]* superare

top management direzione (f) al vertice

top quality qualità (f) superiore

top-selling che è in testa alle vendite

total (adj) totale o globale

total (n) totale (m)

total (v) ammontare a

total amount importo (m) totale

total assets totale (m) delle attività

total cost costo (m) totale

total expenditure spesa (f) totale

total income reddito (m) totale

total invoice value valore (m) totale della fattura

total output produzione (f) totale

total revenue reddito (m) complessivo
track record curricolo (m)
trade (n) *[business]* commercio (m)
trade (v) commerciare *o* trafficare
trade agreement trattato (m) commerciale
trade association associazione (f) commerciale
trade cycle ciclo (m) economico
trade deficit *or* **trade gap** deficit (m) della bilancia commerciale
trade description descrizione (f) commerciale
trade directory annuario (m) commerciale
trade discount sconto (m) ai rivenditori
trade fair fiera (f) campionaria

trade in *[buy and sell]* commerciare in *o* trafficare in
trade in *[give in old item for new]* farsi ritirare l'usato
trade journal giornale (m) di categoria
trade magazine rivista (f) di categoria
trade mission missione (f) commerciale
trade price prezzo (m) al rivenditore
trade terms sconti (mpl) al rivenditore
trade union sindacato (m)
trade unionist sindacalista (m)
trade-in *[old item in exchange]* permuta (f)
trade-in price prezzo (m) di permuta
trademark or trade name marchio (m)
trader commerciante (m)
trading commerciale

trading company
società (f)
commerciale
trading loss perdita
(f) d'esercizio
trading partner
partner (m)
commerciale
trading profit utile
(m) d'esercizio
train (n) treno (m)
train (v) *[learn]*
fare pratica
train (v) *[teach]*
istruire
trainee
tirocinante (m)
traineeship
apprendistato (m)
training for-
mazione (f)
training levy
contributo (m) azien-
dale per l'addestra-
mento
training officer fun-
zionario (m) addetto
all'addestramento
transact business
fare affari

transaction
transazione (f)
transfer (n)
trasferimento (m)
transfer (v) *[move
to new place]*
trasferire
transfer of funds
trasferimento (m) di
capitali
transferable
trasferibile
**transferred charge
call** telefonata (f) a
carico del ricevente
transit transito (m)
transit lounge sala
(f) transiti
transit visa visto
(m) consolare di
transito
translate tradurre
translation
traduzione (f)
translation bureau
ufficio (m) traduzioni
translator traduttore
(m), traduttrice (f)
transport (n)
trasporto (m)

transport (v)
trasportare
transport facilities
servizi (mpl) di
trasporto
treasury tesoreria (f)
treble triplo
trend andamento (m)
trial [court case]
processo (m)
trial [test of product] prova (f)
trial and error
metodo (m) per
tentativi
trial balance bilancio (m) di verifica
trial period periodo
(m) di prova
trial sample campione (m) di prova
triple (adj) triplo
triple (v)
triplicare
triplicate: in triplicate in triplice copia
troubleshooter
mediatore (m)
truck [lorry]
camion (m)

truck [railway wagon]
carro (m) merci
trucker
camionista (m)
trucking trasporto
(m) mediante
autocarro
true copy copia (f)
autentica
trust company
società (f) fiduciaria
turn down rifiutare
turn over (v) [make sales] avere un giro
d'affari di
turnkey operation
operazione (f) chiavi
in mano
turnkey operator
costruttore (m)
chiavi in mano
turnover [of staff]
ricambio (m)
turnover [of stock]
movimento (m)
turnover [sales]
volume (m) d'affari
turnover tax
imposta (f) sul
volume d'affari

turnround [goods sold] rotazione (f)
turnround [making profitable] inversione (f) di tendenza
turnround [of plane] rotazione (f)

Uu

unaccounted for inspiegato
unaudited non verificato
unaudited accounts contabilità (f) non sottoposta a revisione contabile
unauthorized expenditure spesa (f) non autorizzata
unavailability non disponibilità (f)
unavailable non disponibile
unchanged immutato

unchecked figures cifre (fpl) non verificate
unclaimed baggage bagagli (mpl) non reclamati
unconditional incondizionato
unconfirmed non confermato
undated non datato
undelivered non consegnato
under [according to] secondo
under [less than] meno di o inferiore
under construction in costruzione
under contract sotto contratto
under control sotto controllo
under new management sotto nuova gestione
undercharge far pagare meno
undercut a rival vendere a minor prezzo di un concorrente

underdeveloped countries paesi (mpl) sottosviluppati

underequipped con attrezzatura insufficiente

underpaid malpagato

undersell vendere sotto costo

undersigned sottoscritto

underspend spendere meno

understand capire

understanding intesa (f)

undertake intraprendere

undertaking [company] azienda (f) o impresa (f)

undertaking [promise] compito (m) o impegno (m)

underwrite [guarantee] garantire

underwrite [pay costs] finanziare

underwriting syndicate gruppo (m) di collocamento

undischarged bankrupt fallito (m) non riabilitato

uneconomic rent affitto (m) non redditizio

unemployed disoccupato

unemployment disoccupazione (f)

unemployment pay sussidio (m) di disoccupazione

unfair ingiusto

unfair competition concorrenza (f) sleale

unfair dismissal licenziamento (m) ingiusto

unfavourable sfavorevole

unfavourable exchange rate tasso (m) di cambio sfavorevole

unfulfilled order ordinazione (f) inevasa

unilateral unilaterale

union sindacato (m)
union recognition
riconoscimento (m)
sindacale
**unique selling
point** *or* **proposition
(USP)** proposta (f)
unica di vendita
unit *[in unit trust]*
azione (f)
unit *[item]* unità (f)
unit cost costo (m)
unitario
unit price prezzo
(m) unitario
unit trust fondo (m)
comune di
investimento
unlimited liability
responsabilità (f)
illimitata
unload *[get rid of]*
disfarsi di
unload *[goods]*
scaricare
unobtainable non
ottenibile
unofficial
non ufficiale *o*
ufficioso
unpaid non pagato

unpaid invoices
fatture (fpl)
insolute
unsealed envelope
busta (f) aperta
unsecured creditor
creditore (m) non
garantito
unskilled non
specializzato
unsold invenduto
unsubsidized senza
sovvenzioni
unsuccessful che
non ha successo
up front anticipato
up to fino a *o*
conforme a
up to date *[complete]* aggiornato
up to date *[modern]* moderno *o*
attuale
up-market rivolto a
una fascia alta del
mercato
update (n) aggiornamento (m)
update (v)
aggiornare *o* mettere al corrente

upset price prezzo (m) d'apertura
upturn miglioramento (m)
upward trend tendenza (f) al rialzo
urgent urgente
use (n) uso (m)
use (v) usare
use up spare capacity impiegare la capacità produttiva inutilizzata
useful utile
user utente (m)
user-friendly facile da usare o accessibile
USP (= unique selling point or proposition) proposta (f) unica di vendita
usual solito o abituale
utilization utilizzazione (f)

Vv

vacancy [for job] posto (m) vacante
vacant vacante
vacate lasciar vuoto
valid valido
validity validità (f)
valuation valutazione (f)
value (n) valore (m)
value (v) valutare
value added tax (VAT) imposta sul valore aggiunto (IVA)
valuer stimatore (m)
van furgone (m)
variable costs costi (mpl) variabili
variance variazione (f)
variation variazione (f)
VAT (= value added tax) imposta sul valore aggiunto (IVA)
VAT declaration dichiarazione (f) IVA

VAT inspector
ispettore (m) IVA
VAT invoice fattura
con IVA
vehicle veicolo (m)
vendor venditore (m)
venture (n) *[business]*
affare (m) rischioso
venture (v) *[risk]*
rischiare
venture capital cap-
itale (m) di rischio
venue luogo (m) di
ritrovo
verbal verbale
verbal agreement
accordo (m) verbale
verification
verifica (f)
verify verificare
**vertical communi-
cation** comuni-
cazione (f) verticale
**vertical integra-
tion** integrazione
(f) verticale
vested interest interessi (mpl) costituiti
veto a decision porre
il veto a una decisione
via via o tramite

viable realizzabile
VIP lounge sala (f)
per VIP
visa visto (m)
consolare
visible imports
importazioni (fpl)
visibili
visible trade par-
tite (fpl) visibili
void (adj) *[not
valid]* nullo
void (v) invalidare
o annullare
volume volume (m)
volume discount
sconto (m) sul
quantitativo
volume of sales
volume (m) delle
vendite
**volume of trade or
volume of business**
volume (m) degli
scambi commerciali
**voluntary liquida-
tion** liquidazione
(f) volontaria
**voluntary redun-
dancy** cassa (f) inte-
grazione volontaria

vote of thanks
ringraziamento (m)
voucher *[document from an auditor]*
pezza (f) giustificativa
voucher *[paper given instead of money]* buono (m)

Ww

wage salario (m)
wage claim rivendicazione (f) salariale
wage freeze congelamento (m) salariale
wage levels livelli (mpl) salariali
wage negotiations negoziato (m) salariale
wage scale scala (f) retributiva
waive rinunciare
waive a payment rinunciare ad un pagamento

waiver *[of right]*
rinuncia (f)
waiver clause clausola (f) di recessione
warehouse (n) magazzino (m)
warehouse (v) immagazzinare
warehouseman magazziniere (m)
warehousing magazzinaggio (m)
warrant (n) *[document]* autorizzazione (f)
warrant (v) *[guarantee]* garantire
warrant (v) *[justify]* giustificare
warranty (n) garanzia (f)
wastage spreco (m)
waste (n) spreco (m)
waste (v) (use too much) sprecare
waybill lettera (f) di vettura
weak market mercato (m) fiacco

wear and tear deterioramento (m) naturale

week settimana (f)

weekly settimanale

weigh pesare

weighbridge pesa a ponte (f)

weight peso (m)

weight limit limite (m) di peso

weighted average media (f) ponderata

weighted index indice (m) ponderato

weighting ponderazione (f)

well-paid job lavoro (m) ben pagato

wharf molo (m)

white knight 'cavaliere (m) bianco'

whole-life insurance assicurazione (f) sulla vita

wholesale (adv) all'ingrosso

wholesale dealer commerciante (m) all'ingrosso

wholesale discount sconto (m) all'ingrosso

wholesale price index indice (m) dei prezzi all'ingrosso

wholesaler commerciante (m) all'ingrosso

wildcat strike sciopero (m) selvaggio

win a contract vincere un contratto

wind up *[a company]* mettere in liquidazione

wind up *[a meeting]* dichiarare sciolta una riunione

winding up liquidazione (f) o scioglimento (m)

window finestra (f)

window display esposizione (f) in vetrina

withdraw *[an offer]* ritirare

withdraw *[money]* prelevare

withdraw a takeover bid ritrattare un'offerta di rilevamento

withdrawal *[of money]* ritiro (m)
withholding tax ritenuta (f) d'acconto
witness (n) testimone (m)
witness (v) *[a document]* firmare come testimone
witness an agreement firmare un accordo come testimone
word-processing videoscrittura (f)
wording dicitura (f)
work (n) lavoro (m)
work (v) lavorare
work in progress lavori in corso
work permit permesso (m) di lavoro
work-to-rule sciopero (m) bianco
worker lavoratore (m), lavoratrice (f)
worker director lavoratore che fa parte del consiglio di amministrazione e che agisce come portavoce del personale

workforce forza (f) lavoro
working (adj) attivo
working capital capitale (m) d'esercizio
working conditions condizioni (fpl) di lavoro
working party commissione (f) di studio
workshop officina (f)
workstation *[at computer]* posto (m) di lavoro
world mondo (m)
world market mercato (m) mondiale
worldwide (adj) mondiale
worldwide (adv) in tutto il mondo
worth (n) *[value]* valore (m)
worth: be worth valere
worthless privo di valore
wrap up *[discussion]* concludere

wrap up *[goods]*
impaccare
wrapper confezion-
atore (m)
wrapping involucro
(m) *o* imballaggio (m)
wrapping paper carta
(f) da imballaggio
wreck (n) *[company]*
impresa (f) fallita
wreck (n) *[ship]*
nave (f) naufragata
wreck (v) *[ruin]*
distruggere
writ mandato (m)
write scrivere
write down *[assets]*
ridurre il valore
write off *[debt]*
annullare
write out redigere
write out a cheque
compilare un assegno
write-off *[loss]*
svalutazione (f)
writedown *[of asset]*
svalutazione (f)
writing scrittura (f)
written agreement
accordo (m) scritto
wrong sbagliato

wrongful dismissal
licenziamento (m)
ingiustificato

Xx Yy Zz

year anno (m)
year end fine (f)
esercizio
yearly payment
pagamento (m)
annuale
yellow pages
Pagine Gialle (fpl)
**yield (n) *[on invest-
ment]*** rendita (f)
yield (v) *[interest]*
rendere
zero zero (m)
zero-rated aliquota
(f) nulla
zip code *[US]*
codice (m) d'avvia-
mento postale

Italiano-Inglese
Italian-English

Aa

abbandonare *[lasciare]* abandon; leave

abbassare lower (v)

abbassare *[ridurre il prezzo]* knock down *or* knock off *or* reduce price

abbassare i prezzi lower prices

abbassare il prezzo (di articoli) mark down

abbonato (m) al telefono telephone subscriber

abbozzare *[redigere]* draft (v)

abile *[qualificato]* qualified *[skilled]*

abilità (f) *[capacità]* capacity *or* ability

abilità (f) tecnica skill

abitante (m) *[residente]* inhabitant *or* resident (n)

abituale (solito) usual *or* routine

abolire i controlli (mpl) decontrol

abolizione (f) della regolamentazione deregulation

accantonamento (m) shelving *or* postponing

accantonamento (m) *[riserva]* provision *or* money put aside

accantonamento (m) al fondo di ammortamento allowance for depreciation

accantonare (differire) shelve

accantonare *[accumulare]* accumulate

accantonare fondi (mpl) per un progetto earmark funds for a project

accaparramento (m) hoarding *[of goods]*

accaparramento (m) *[monopolio]* corner (n) *or* monopoly

accaparrarsi il mercato (m) corner the market
accertamento (m) dei danni assessment of damages
accertamento (m) fiscale tax assessment
accertamento (m) patrimoniale means test
accertare [stabilire il valore] assess
accertare i danni assess damages
accessibile [facile da usare] user-friendly
accessori (mpl) fittings
accettabile [soddisfacente] acceptable
accettar accept (v)
accettar accept (v) or agree
accettare di fare qualcosa agree to do something
accettare una cambiale accept a bill
accettazione (f) acceptance
accettazione (f) di un'offerta acceptance of an offer
accidentale [casuale] random
accomodamento (m) composition [with creditors]
accomodamento (m) [accordo] adjustment
acconsentire a fare qualcosa agree to do something
acconto (m) deposit (n) [paid in advance]
accont : in acconto on account
accordare [cedere] allow or give
accordare [concedere] grant (v)
accordo (m) settlement or agreement
accord : essere d'accordo con agree with [be of the same opinion]
accordo (m) [accomodamento] adjustment

accordo (m) [intesa] arrangement *or* compromise

accordo (m) aperto open-ended agreement

accordo (m) bilaterale reciprocal agreement

accordo (m) creditizio di sostegno standby arrangements

accordo (m) di indicizzazione threshold agreement

accordo (m) di lunga data long-standing agreement

accordo (m) di marketing marketing agreement

accordo (m) in esclusiva exclusive agreement

accordo (m) multilaterale multilateral agreement

accordo (m) parziale one-sided agreement

accordo (m) scritto written agreement

accordo (m) sulla parola (f) gentleman's agreement

accordo (m) sulla produttività productivity agreement

accordo (m) verbale verbal agreement

accord -tipo (m) model agreement

accreditare (un conto) credit (v)

accumulare accumulate

accumularsi [maturare] accrue

accurato [preciso] accurate

accusa (f) charge (n) *[in court]*

accusare ricevuta di una lettera acknowledge receipt of a letter

accusato (m) defendant

acquirente (m) [cliente] shopper

acquirente (m) genuino genuine purchaser

acquisizione (f)
[acquisto] acquisition
**acquisizione (f) di
controllo contestata**
contested takeover
**acquisizione (f) di
controllo inversa**
reverse takeover
acquistare *[comper-
are]* purchase (v)
acquisti (mpl)
shopping *[goods
bought]*
acquisto (m) pur-
chase (n); purcha-
sing *or* buying
**acquisto (m) a ter-
mine** forward buying
**acquisto (m) cen-
tralizzato** central
purchasing
**acquisto (m) di una
società da parte dei
suoi stessi diri-
genti** management
buyout (MBO)
**acquisto (m) fatto
per impulso**
impulse purchase
**acquisto (m) in
massa** bulk buying

**acquisto (m) per
contanti** cash
purchase
**acquisto (m)
rateale** hire
purchase (HP)
acquisto (m) *[acqui-
sizione]* acquisition
or purchase
ad alta definizione
near letter-quality (NLQ)
ad valorem ad valorem
**adattamento (m)
stagionale** sea-
sonal adjustments
adattare *[adeguare]*
adjust
**addebitare un
acquisto** charge a
purchase
addebitare un conto
debit an account
**addebitare una tele-
fonata al ricevente**
reverse the charges
**addebiti (mpl) per
interessi** interest
charges
addebito (m) debit (n)
**addebito (m)
diretto** direct debit

**addestramento (m)
dei dirigenti** man-
agement training
**addestramento (m)
interno (alla ditta)**
in-house training
**addestramento (m)
sul lavoro** on-the-job
training
**addetto (m) al con-
trollo dell'avanza-
mento** progress chaser
**addetto (m) alle
pubbliche relazioni**
public relations man
**addetto (m) alle
vendite** sales clerk
**addetto (m)
commerciale**
commercial attaché
**addizionale (supple-
mentare)** additional
addizione (f) addi-
tion *[calculation]*
**adeguamento (m)
fiscale** tax
adjustments
adeguare *[adattare]*
adjust
**adeguato *[suffi-
ciente]*** adequate

adempimento (m)
fulfilment
**adempimento (m) di
un contratto** com-
pletion of a contract
adibire ad altro uso
redevelop
aereo (m) plane
aereo (m) da carico
freight plane
**aeroplano (m) a nol-
eggio** charter plane
aeroporto (m) airport
affare (m) busi-
ness *[discussion]*
**affare (m) *[occa-
sione]*** bargain (n)
[cheaper than usual]
**affare (m) *[oper-
azione]*** deal (n)
**affare (m) poco
vantaggioso** hard
bargain
**affare (m) ris-
chioso** venture (n)
or risky deal
affari (mpl) busi-
ness *[commerce]*
affari: fare affari
do business *or*
transact business

affermare claim
(v) *or* suggest
affermativo
affirmative
affidare entrust
**affidare fondi ad un
progetto** commit
funds to a project
affiliata (f) sub-
sidiary company
affiliato *[associato]*
affiliated
**affitansi uffici
(mpl)** offices to let
affittare *[impianti]*
lease equipment
affittar let (v)
**affittare *[dare in
affitto]*** lease out
(v) *[of landlord]*
**affittare *[tenere in
affitto]*** lease (v)
[of tenant]
affittare un negozio
let an office
affitto (m) lease (n)
affitto (m) rent
affitto (m) alto
high rent
**affitto (m) nomi-
nale** nominal rent

**affitto (m) non
redditizio**
uneconomic rent
affittuario (m) lessee
**affittuario (m)
occupante** sitting
tenant
affrancar frank (v)
**affrancare *[mettere
francobolli]*** stamp
(v) a letter
**affrancatura (f)
pagata** postpaid
affrettarsi hurry up
agenda (f)
appointments book
**agenda (f) da
tavolo** desk diary
**agenda (f) tasca-
bile** pocket diary
agente (m) agent
[working in an agency]
**agente (m) *[rapp-
resentante]*** agent
or representative
**agente (m)
commissionario**
commission agent
**agente (m) di
assicurazione**
insurance agent

agente (m) di brevetti patent agent

agente (m) di cambio stockbroker

agente (m) di factoring factor (n) *[person]*

agente (m) doganale customs broker

agente (m) in cambi foreign exchange broker

agente (m) marittimo ship broker

agente (m) del credere del credere agent

agenzia (f) agency

agenzia (f) che fornisce personale temporaneo temp agency

agenzia (f) di lavoro employment agency *or* employment bureau

agenzia (f) di stampa news agency

agenzia (f) immobiliare letting agency

agenzia (f) per il recupero dei crediti debt collection agency

agenzia (f) per reperimento di referenze credit agency

agenzia (f) di pubblicità advertising agency

agevolazione (f) concession *[reduction]*

agevolazione (f) fiscale tax relief

agevolazioni (fpl) creditizie credit facilities

aggiornamento (m) update (n)

aggiornamento (m) *[sollecito]* follow up

aggiornare *[mettere al corrente]* update *or* bring up to date

aggiornare *[rimandare]* adjourn

aggiornare una riunione adjourn a meeting

aggiornato up to date *[complete]*

aggirare get round *[a problem]*

aggiudicare un con-tratto a qualcuno award a contract to someone

aggiudicazione (f) *[giudizio]* adjudication

aggiungere *[som-mare]* add

aggiungere il 10% per il servizio add on 10% for service

aggiunta (f) addi-tion *[thing added]*

aggiustare *[riparare]* repair (v)

agire act (v) *or* do something *or* take action

agricolo *o* **agrario** agricultural

aiuto (m) *[assis-tenza]* assistance

aiuto (m) *[appog-gio]* backing

al giorno per day

alla settimana per week

albergo (m) *[hotel]* hotel

albergo (m) sele-zionato graded hotel

alimentatore (m) di fogli paper feed

alimentazione (f) continua continuous feed

aliquota (f) d'im-posta tax rate

aliquota (f) d'im-posta base stan-dard rate (of tax)

all'anno per year *or* per annum

all'avanguardia state-of-the-art

all'estero abroad *or* overseas

all'estero *[off-shore]* offshore

all'ingrosso wholesale (adv)

all'ora per hour

allargamento (m) expansion

allegare enclose

allegato (m) enclosure

altamente qualificato highly qualified

altamente ret-ribuito highly-paid

alternativa (f)
alternative (n)
alternativo alter-
native (adj)
altezza: essere
all'altezza cope *or*
be up to
americano
American (adj)
Americano, -ana
American (n)
ammanco (m)
shortfall
ammasso (m) hoard
ammettere admit
or agree
amministrare
[gestire] manage
amministrare un
patrimonio manage
property
amministrativo
administrative
amministratore
(m) director
amministratore
(m) di società
company director
amministratore (m)
delegato *[direttore*
generale] managing
director (MD)

amministrazione
(f) *[gestione]*
administration
ammissione (f)
admission
ammontare (m)
[importo] amount
[of money]
ammontare a
amount to *or*
total (v)
ammortamento
(m) amortization
or depreciation
ammortamento
(m) a quote
costanti straight
line depreciation
ammortamento
(m) accelerato
accelerated
depreciation
ammortare o
ammortizzare
amortize *or*
depreciate
ampliare expand
anagrafe (f)
registry office
analisi (f) analysis
analisi (f) dei costi
cost analysis

analisi (f) dei sistemi systems analysis

analisi (f) del prog-etto project analysis

analisi (f) delle man-sioni job analysis

analisi (f) delle ven-dite sales analysis

analisi (f) di mer-cato market analysis

analisi (f) preven-tiva della conve-nienza dei costi cost-benefit analysis

analisi (f) statistica statistical analysis

analista (m) dei costi cost accountant

analista (m) dei sistemi systems analyst

analista (m) di mercato market analyst

analizzare analyse *or* analyze

analizzare il poten-ziale del mercato analyse the market potential

andamento (m) trend

andare go

andare in pensione retire *[from one's job]*

andare incontro ad una richiesta meet a demand

anno (m) year

anno (m) di base base year

anno (m) fiscale tax year

anno (m) solare calendar year

annotazione (f) entering

annuale *[annuo]* annual

annualmente annually *or* on an annual basis

annuario (m) directory

annuario (m) com-merciale commer-cial directory *or* trade directory

annullamento (m) invalidation

annullare *[cancel-lare]* cancel

annullare *[invali-dare]* void (v)

annullare un assegno cancel a cheque

annullare un contratto cancel a contract

annullato cancelled *or* off

annunci (mpl) economici (su giornale) classified ads *or* classified advertisements

annunciare announce

annuncio (m) announcement

annuncio (m) pubblicitario [pubblicità] advertisement

annuo [annuale] annual

anticipato advance (adj) *or* up front

anticipazione (f) su un conto advance on account

anticipo (m) advance (n) *[loan]*

anticipo (m) in contanti cash advance

antiquato obsolete *or* old-fashioned

anziano [piu vecchio] senior

aperto open (adj)

aperto ad offerte open to offers

apertura (f) opening (n)

apertura: d'apertura [iniziale] opening (adj) *or* initial

apertura (f) sul mercato gap in the market

appaltare lavoro farm out work

apparecchiatura (f) equipment

apparecchiatura (f) d'ufficio business equipment

apparecchiatura (f) difettosa faulty equipment

apparecchiatura (f) pesante heavy equipment

appartamento (m) flat (n)

appartenere a
belong to
appellare *[ricorrere in appello]* appeal
(v) *[against a decision]*
appello (m) *[ricorso]* appeal (n)
[against a decision]
appendice (f)
appendix
applicare enforce
appoggio (m) *[aiuto]* backing
apportare bring in
apporto (m) di capitali contribution of
capital
apprendista (m)
junior clerk
apprendista (m) in direzione aziendale
management trainee
apprendistato (m)
traineeship
apprezzamento (m)
appreciation *[how good something is]*
apprezzare appreciate *[how good something is]*

appropriarsi indebitamente embezzle
or misappropriate
appropriazione (f) indebita embezzlement
or misappropriation
approssimativamente approximately
approssimativo
approximate *or* rough
approvare approve
or agree
approvare: far approvare carry *or*
approve in a vote
approvare i termini di un contratto
approve the terms
of a contract
approvvigionare *[fornire]* supply (v)
appuntamento (m)
appointment
[meeting]
aprire open (v)
[start new business]
aprire fino a notte tarda late-night
opening
aprire trattative
open negotiations

aprire un conto
open an account
aprire un conto
bancario open a
bank account
aprire una lettera
di credito issue a
letter of credit
aprire una linea di
credito open a line
of credit
aprire una seduta
open a meeting
arbitrare una
vertenza arbitrate
in a dispute
arbitrato (m)
arbitration
arbitro (m) arbitrator
archivio (m) (di un
computer)
computer file
archivio (m) *[docu-*
mentazione] records
area (f) *o* regione
(f) area *or* region
area (f) *[campo]* field
area (f) del dollaro
dollar area
area (f) di carico
loading bay

area (f) problemat-
ica problem area
area (f) uffici
office space
arenarsi (di tratta-
tive) break down
(v) *[of talks]*
argomento (m)
[questione] item on
agenda *or* matter to
be discussed
aria (f) air
armonizzazione (f)
harmonization
arredamento (m)
per ufficio office
furniture
arrestare check (v)
or stop
arresto (m) check
(n) *or* stop
arretrati (mpl)
arrears
arrivare arrive
arrivare a reach *or*
come to
arrivare ad una
decisione reach a
decision
arrivi (mpl)
arrivals

arrivo (m) arrival

**arrotondare aumen-
tando** round up

**arrotondare dimin-
uendo** round down

**articoli (mpl)
deperibili** perish-
able goods

**articoli (mpl) che
vendono rapidamente**
fast-selling items

**articoli (mpl) di
lusso** luxury goods

articoli (mpl) diversi
miscellaneous items

**articoli (mpl) non
ricorrenti** non-
recurring items

articoli (mpl) vari
sundries

**articolo (m) *[pro-
dotto]*** article *or* item

articolo (m) unico
one-off item

ascendere *[salire]*
climb

ascensore (m) lift (n)

**aspettativa (f)
*[congedo autoriz-
zato]*** leave of
absence

assalire *[attaccare]*
attack

assegnare award (v)

assegnatario (m)
assignee

**assegni (mpl) per-
sonalizzati** person-
alized cheques

assegno (m) cheque

**assegno (m) a cop-
ertura garantita**
certified cheque

**assegno (m) al
portatore** cheque
to bearer

**assegno (m) circo-
lare** banker's draft
or bank draft

**assegno (m) dello
stipendio** pay cheque
or salary cheque

**assegno (m) di
cassa** cashier's
check *[US]*

**assegno (m) in
bianco** blank cheque

**assegno (m) non
sbarrato** open
cheque

**assegno (m) sbar-
rato** crossed cheque

assemblea (f)
assembly *or* meeting
assemblea (f) del
personale staff
meeting
assemblea (f) gen-
erale general meeting
Assemblea (f)
Generale degli
Azionisti annual gen-
eral meeting (AGM)
assemblaggio (m)
[montaggio]
assembly *[putting*
together]
assente absent *or*
away from work
assenza (f) *[man-*
canza] absence
assicurabile insurable
assicurare insure
assicurare la vita di
qualcuno assure
someone's life
assicurarsi contro un
rischio cover a risk
assicuratore (m)
insurer
assicuratore (m)
marittimo marine
underwriter

assicurazione (f)
insurance *or* (life)
assurance
assicurazione (f)
[garanzia] in-
demnity
assicurazione (f)
auto motor insurance
assicurazione (f)
contro gli incendi
fire insurance
assicurazione (f)
globale compre-
hensive insurance
assicurazione (f)
malattie health
insurance
assicurazione (f)
marittima marine
insurance
assicurazione (f)
per danni verso
terzi third-party
insurance
assicurazione (f)
sulla casa house
insurance
assicurazione (f)
sulla vita life
assurance *or* life
insurance

assicurazione (f) temporanea term insurance

assistente (mf) [collaboratore] assistant

assistenza (f) [aiuto] assistance

assistenza (f) post-vendita alla clientela after-sales service

assistere assist

assistere a attend (meeting)

associato associate (adj)

associato (m) [socio] associate (n)

associato [affiliato] affiliated

associazione (f) [circolo] associa-tion or society

associazione (f) commerciale trade association

associazione (f) in compartecipazione copartnership

associazione (f) in partecipazione ['joint venture'] joint venture

assoluto outright

assumere [impiegare] employ

assumere del personale hire staff

assumersi la responsabilità di qualcosa accept liability for something

asta (f) auction (n)

attaccare attack

attaccare [unire] attach

attendere istruzioni await instructions

attendibile reliable

attendibilità (f) reliability

attenzione (f) attention

attenzione: all'attenzione di FAO (for the attention of)

atterrare land (v) [of plane]

atteso due [expected]

attestato (m) [referenze] reference [report on person]

attestazione (f) ufficiale affidavit

attirare appeal to (v) *or* attract

attività (f) activity

attività (fpl) e passività (fpl) assets and liabilities

attività (f) bancaria banking

attività (f) commerciale fiorente flourishing trade

attività (f) esterna di ricerca e di studio field work

attività (f) finanziaria [finanza] finance (n)

attività (f) illegale racketeering

attività (fpl) immateriali intangible assets

attività (fpl) liquide current assets

attività (fpl) occulte hidden asset

attività (f) previsionale forecasting

attività (f) promozionale merchandizing

attività (f) secondaria sideline

attività (f) trascurata neglected business

attivo working (adj)

attivo (m) mobiliare personal assets

attivo (m) esigibile [cespiti realizzabili] realizable assets

atto (m) deed

atto (m) costitutivo deed of partnership

atto (m) costitutivo di società articles of association

atto (m) di cessione deed of assignment

atto (m) di donazione deed of covenant

atto (m) di trasferimento deed of transfer

atto (m) di vendita
[fattura] bill of sale
attraccare [entrare
in porto dock (v)
[ship]
attrarre attract
attrezzare (una
fabbrica) tool up (a
factory)
attrezzatura (f) per
ufficio office
equipment
attribuire un diritto
a qualcuno assign
a right to someone
attuale present
(adj) [now]
attuale [moderno]
up to date [modern]
attuale: non
attuale out of date
attuare [realizzare]
implement (v)
attuario (m) actuary
attuazione (f)
implementation
aumentare gain or
increase or rise [get
bigger]
aumentare raise or
increase

aumentare di
prezzo increase in
price
aumentare di val-
ore appreciate or
increase in value
aumentare il
prezzo (di articoli)
mark up (an item)
aumentare pro-
porzionalmente
scale up
aumento (m)
increase or rise
[higher salary]
aumento (m)
increase or gain
[getting bigger]
aumento: in
aumento on the
increase or
mounting
aumento (m) del
costo della vita
cost-of-living increase
aumento (m) di
paga retroattivo
retroactive pay rise
aumento (m) di
prezzo mark-up
[action]

aumento (m) medio annuale mean annual increase

aumento (m) percentuale percentage increase

aumento (m) salariale pay rise

autenticare [legalizzare] authenticate

autenticare [certificare] certify

autentico [vero] genuine

autobus (m) bus

autobus (m) dell'aeroporto airport bus

autocopiante carbonless

autofinanziamento (m) self-financing (n)

autofinanziarsi: che può autofinanziarsi self-financing (adj)

automobile (f) car

automobile (f) di grande successo best-selling car

automobile (f) a noleggio hire car

autoregolatore self-regulatory

autoregolazione (f) self-regulation

autorità (f) authority

autorità (fpl) portuali port authority

autorizzare authorize or give permission or license

autorizzare (qualcuno a fare qualcosa) allow or permit (someone to do something)

autorizzare un pagamento authorize payment

autorizzato authorized

autorizzazione (f) authorization or permission

autorizzazione (f) warrant (n) [document]

avallante (m) guarantor

avallante (m) [sostenitore] backer

avallare stand security for

avallo (m) [sponsorizzazione] sponsorship

avanzare *[fare pro-gressi]* progress (v)

avaria (f) average (n) *[insurance]*

avaria (f) generale general average

aver bisogno di require *[need]*

avere (v) carry *[have in stock]*

avere (m) *[lato del-l'attivo]* credit side

avere come risultato result in

avere indietro get back *[something lost]*

avere lo scopo di aim (v)

avere luogo take place

avere successo *[riuscire]* succeed *[do well]*

avviamento (m) start-up

avviamento (m) commerciale goodwill

avvio (m) start (n)

avvisare *[infor-mare]* advise *[tell what happened]*

avviso (m) notice *or* piece of information

avviso (m) di ricevimento doganale customs receipt

avviso (m) di rinnovo renewal notice

avvocato (mf) lawyer; counsel

avvocato (mf) della parte querelante prosecution counsel

avvocato (mf) difensore defence counsel

azienda (f) *[impresa]* business *or* firm *or* company

azienda (f) autonoma independent company

azienda (f) commerciale business establishment

azienda (f) con forte indebitamento highly-geared company

aziende (f) in concorrenza competing firms

azione (f) share
(n) *[in a company]*
azione (f) action
[thing done]
azione (f) *[causa]*
action *or* lawsuit
azioni (fpl) ordi-
narie ordinary
shares *or* equities
azioni (fpl) privile-
giate preference
shares
azioni (fpl) privile-
giate cumulative
cumulative prefer-
ence shares
azioni (fpl) quotate
quoted shares
azioni (fpl) trascu-
rate neglected shares
azionista (m)
shareholder
azionista (m) di
maggioranza
majority shareholder
azionista (m) di
minoranza minority
shareholder
azionista (m)
principale major
shareholder

Bb

bacheca (f) showcase
bacino (m) dock (n)
bagagli (mpl) non
reclamati
unclaimed baggage
bagaglio (m) luggage
bagaglio (m) a
mano hand luggage
bagaglio (m) in
eccesso excess
baggage
banca (f) bank (n)
banca (f) centrale
central bank
banca (f) d'emis-
sione issuing bank
banca (f) di
compensazione
clearing bank
banca (f) di sconto
discount house *[bank]*
Banca (f) Europea
per gli Investimenti
(BEI) European
Investment Bank (EIB)
banca (f) mercan-
tile merchant bank

banchiere (m) banker
banco (m) counter
banco (m) dei paga-
menti pay desk
banco (m) di espo-
sizione display stand
banconota (f) ban-
knote; bill (n) [US]
barattare barter (v)
baratto (m) [scam-
bio] barter (n)
barriera (f) barrier
barriera (f) [pro-
tezione] hedge (n)
barriera (f)
doganale customs
barrier
barriere (fpl) tarif-
farie tariff barriers
base (f) base (n)
[place]
base: di base
basic (adj)
base (f) [fonda-
mento] basis
base (f) di dati
database
base (f) monetaria
monetary base
basilare [di base]
basic (adj) [simple]

basso [scadente]
low (adj)
basso: a basso
prezzo cheap
basso livello (m)
low (n)
battuta (f) d'ar-
resto setback
bene (m) [cespite]
asset
bene (m) [merce]
commodity
beneficiario (m)
beneficiary
beneficio (m) [util-
ità] benefit (n)
benestare (m)
approval
beni (mpl) di con-
sumo consumer goods
beni (mpl) di con-
sumo durevoli con-
sumer durables
beni (mpl) durevoli
durable goods
beni (mpl) invisi-
bili invisible assets
beni (mpl) reali
tangible assets
beni (mpl) strumen-
tali capital goods

benzina (f) a prezzo ridotto cut-price petrol

biasimare blame (v)

biasimo (m) [colpa] blame (n)

biglietto (m) business card; ticket

biglietto (m) aereo privo di prenotazione standby ticket

biglietto (m) aperto (senza data di ritorno) open ticket

biglietto (m) da visita business card

biglietto (m) di andata one-way fare

biglietto (m) di banca note (n)

biglietto (m) omaggio complimentary ticket

bilancia (f) balance (n)

bilancia (f) commerciale attiva favourable balance of trade

bilancia (f) commerciale in dollari dollar balance

bilancia (f) dei pagamenti balance of payments

bilancia (f) commerciale balance of trade

bilanciare balance (v)

bilancio (m) balance (n)

bilancio (m) d'apertura opening balance

bilancio (m) dello Stato budget (n) [government]

bilancio (m) di chiusura closing balance

bilancio (m) di verifica trial balance

bilancio (m) preventivo budget (n) [personal, company]

bilancio (m) d'esercizio balance sheet

bilaterale bilateral

bilione (m) billion (UK)

binario (m) platform *[in railway station]*
bloccare block (v)
bloccare i salari e i prezzi freeze *or* peg wages and prices
bloccare un assegno stop a cheque
bloccare un conto stop an account
bloccato *[congelato]* frozen
blocco (m) *[commerciale]* freeze (n)
blocco (m) degli affitti rent control
blocco (m) del credito credit freeze
blocco (m) del lavoro straordinario overtime ban
blocco (m) di fogli per lavagna flip chart
boicottaggio (m) boycott (n)
boicottare boycott (v)
bolla (f) di spedizione dispatch note *or* shipping note *or* delivery note

bolletta (f) bill *[list of charges]* **bolletta (f) d'avviso** advice note
bollettino (m) bulletin
bonifico (m) bank transfer
boom (m) boom (n)
bordo: a bordo on board
borsa (f) bag
borsa (f) *[cartella]* briefcase
borsa (f) di studio grant (n)
Borsa (f) Merci commodity exchange
Borsa (f) Valori stock exchange
bozza (f) rough draft
bozza (f) di un piano draft plan
bozza (f) di un progetto draft project
breve: a breve *o* a breve termine short-term (adj) *or* on a short-term basis

breve: nel più breve termine as soon as possible (asap)

brevettare un'invenzione patent an invention

brevettato patented

brevetto (m) patent

brevetto (m) richiesto *o* **in attesa di brevetto** patent applied for *or* patent pending

britannico [*inglese*] British

broker (m) broker

budget (m) [*bilancio preventivo*] budget (n) [*personal, company*]

budget (m) di gestione operational budget

budget (m) generale overhead budget

budget (m) operativo operating budget

budget (m) per le spese di promozione promotion budget

budget (m) provvisorio provisional budget

budget (m) pubblicitario publicity budget *or* advertising budget

budgetario [*relativo al budget*] budgetary

budgettare budget (v)

buon affare (m) good buy

buon guadagno (m) healthy profit

buona gestione (f) good management

buona qualità (f) good quality

buono good

buono (m) coupon *or* voucher

buono (m) premio gift coupon *or* gift voucher

busta (f) aperta unsealed envelope

busta (f) chiusa sealed envelope

bustarella (f) [*tangente*] bribe (n)

Cc

cadere fall (v) *or*
go lower
cadere *[calare]*
drop (v)
cadere *[crollare]*
collapse (v)
caduta (f) *[crollo]*
fall (n) *or* collapse
caduta (f) *[ribasso]*
drop (n)
calare *[cadere]*
drop (v)
calcolare calculate
calcolare 10% per il
trasporto allow
10% for carriage
calcolare una
media average (v)
calcolatore (m)
calculator
calcolatrice (f) tasca-
bile pocket calculator
calcolo (m)
calculation
calcolo (m)
approssimativo
rough calculation

calcolo (m)
sbagliato
miscalculation
calligrafia (f)
handwriting
calo (m) lowering
cambiale (f) bill of
exchange
cambiale (f) *[effetto]*
bill (n) *[written
promise to pay]*
cambiale (f) di
favore *[effetto di
comodo]* accommo-
dation bill
cambiali (fpl) da
incassare *[effetti
attivi]* bills receivable
cambiali (fpl) da
pagare *[effetti pas-
sivi]* bills payable
cambiamento (m)
change *or* difference
or shift
cambiamento (m)
[modifica]
alteration
cambiare change *or*
exchange *[money]*
cambiare switch *or*
change

cambiare *[modifi-care]* alter

cambiavalute (m) money changer

cambio (m) exchange (n) *[currency]*

cambio (m) incrociato cross rate

camera (f) room

Camera (f) di Commercio Chamber of Commerce

camion (m) lorry *or* truck

camion (m) articolato articulated lorry

camionista (m) lorry driver *or* trucker

campagna (f) campaign *or* drive

campagna (f) country *[not town]*

campagna (f) aggressiva hard selling

campagna (f) di vendite sales campaign

campagna (f) promozionale a mezzo posta mail shot

campagna (f) pubblicitaria publicity campaign *or* advertising campaign

campionamento (m) sampling

campionare sample (v) *or* test

campionatura (f) casuale random sampling

campionatura (f) per accettazione acceptance sampling

campione (m) sample (n)

campione (m) casuale random sample

campione (m) di prova trial sample

campione (m) gratuito free sample

campione (m) per dimostrazione demonstration model

campione (m) (statistico) di controllo check sample

campo (m) (area) area *or* field

canale (m) channel (n)

canali (mpl) di distribuzione distribution channels *or* channels of distribution

canalizzare channel (v)

cancellare cross out

cancellare *[annullare]* cancel

cancellazione (f) *[disdetta]* cancellation

cancelleria (f) d'uffi-cio office stationery

candidato (m) candidate

candidato (m) a un posto di lavoro applicant for a job

capace di capable of

capacità (f) capacity *[space]*

capacità (f) *[abilità]* capacity *[ability]*

capacità (f) di guadagno earning capacity

capacità (f) di produzione manufacturing capacity

capacità (f) in eccedenza overcapacity

capacità (f) industriale industrial capacity

capacità (f) produttiva capacity *[production]*

capacità (f) produttiva in eccesso excess capacity

capacità (f) produttiva inutilizzata spare capacity

caparra (f) rimborsabile refundable deposit

capi (mpl) d'intesa heads of agreement

capienza (f) di magazzino storage capacity

capire (rendersi conto di) realize *or* understand

capitale (m) o capitali (mpl) capital

capitale (m) d'apporto initial capital

capitale (m) d'esercizio working capital

capitale (m) di rischio risk capital

capitale (m) di rischio venture capital

capitale (m) disponibile available capital

capitale (m) effettivo equity capital

capitale (m) in fuga flight of capital

capitale (m) mutuato loan capital

capitale (m) nominale nominal capital

capitale (m) obbligazionario loan stock

capitale (m) sociale share capital

capitali (mpl) capital

capitalizzare capitalize

capitalizzazione (f) capitalization

capitalizzazione (f) di mercato market capitalization

capitalizzazione (f) delle riserve capitalization of reserves

capo (m) boss (informal)

capo (m) (direttore) principal (n) *[person]*

capo (m) del personale personnel manager

capo (m) reparto head of department; floor manager

capo (m) servizio departmental manager

capo (m) ufficio chief clerk

carenza (f) di manodopera manpower shortage

caricabile chargeable

caricare *[un camion o una nave]* load a lorry *or* a ship

caricare *[programma]* load (v) *[a computer program]*

carico (m) load (n) *or* cargo

carico (m) di camion lorry-load

carico (m) di coperta deck cargo

**carico (m) di
ritorno** homeward
freight
carico (m) lordo
deadweight cargo
carico (m) utile
payload
carnet (m) carnet
[document]
caro dear
carovita (m) *[costo
della vita]* cost of
living
**carrello (m) eleva-
tore (a forche)**
fork-lift truck
carro (m) merci
railway goods wagon
carta (f) assegni
cheque (guarantee)
card
carta (f) carbone
carbon paper
carta (f) d'imbarco
boarding card *or*
boarding pass
carta (f) d'imbarco
embarkation card
**carta (f) da imbal-
laggio** wrapping
paper

carta (f) da pacco
brown paper
carta (f) di credito
credit card; charge card
**carta (f) di credito
d'oro** gold card
**carta (f) di credito
telefonica** phone card
carta (f) di sbarco
landing card
carta (f) riciclata
recycled paper
cartella (f) *[borsa]*
briefcase
cartella (f) *[portfo-
lio]* portfolio
**cartellino (m) del
prezzo** price ticket *or*
price tag *or* price label
cartello (m) cartel
cartolina (f) postale
card *or* postcard
cartoncino (m)
card *[material]*
**cartoncino (m)
della società**
compliments slip
cartone (m)
cardboard
cartone (m) carton
[material]

cartone (m)
[imballo di cartone]
carton [box]
casa (f) house [for family]
casa: di casa in casa house-to-house
casella (f) postale P.O. box number
cassa (f) case or crate or box
cassa (f) checkout or till [in supermarket]
cassa (f) automatica prelievi cash dispenser
cassa (f) da imballaggio packing case
cassa (f) integrazione volontaria voluntary redundancy
cassa: in cassa integrazione redundant
cassaforte (f) safe (n)
cassiere (m),
cassiera (f) cashier
casuale (accidentale) random
catalogo (m) catalogue or list

catalogo (m) di vendita per corrispondenza mail-order catalogue
categoria (f) category or class
catena (f) chain [of stores]
catena (f) di montaggio assembly line or production line
cattiva amministrazione (f) mismanagement or maladministration
cattivo acquisto (m) bad buy
causa: a causa di owing to
causa (f) [azione] action [lawsuit]
causa (f) di forza maggiore act of God; force majeure
causa (f) legale court case
causa (f) per risarcimento action for damages
cavaliere (m) bianco white knight

cavarsela get along
cedente (m) *[parte*
venditrice] assignor
cedere *[accordare]*
allow *or* give
cedola (f) di divi-
dendo dividend
warrant
centrale central
centralino (m)
telefonico tele-
phone exchange *or*
switchboard
centralizzare
centralize
centralizzazione (f)
centralization
centro (m) centre
centro (m) (di
città) downtown (n)
centro: in centro
downtown (adv)
centro (m) assis-
tenza service
centre
centro (m) com-
merciale shopping
centre; shopping
mall *or* arcade
centro (m) d'affari
business centre

centro (m) di costi
cost centre
centro (m) di prof-
itto profit centre
centro (m) indus-
triale industrial
centre
certificare *[autenti-*
care] certify
certificato
certificated
certificato (m)
certificate
certificato (m)
azionario share
certificate
certificato (m)
d'iscrizione certifi-
cate of registration
certificato (m) d'o-
rigine certificate of
origin
certificato (m) di
accettazione cer-
tificate of approval
certificato (m) di
deposito certificate
of deposit
certificato (m) di
garanzia certificate
of guarantee

certificato (m) di sdoganamento clearance certificate
certificato (m) medico doctor's certificate
certificazione (f) [revisione contabile] auditing
cespite (m) (bene) asset
cespiti (mpl) congelati frozen assets
cespiti (mpl) realizzabili [attivo esigibile] realizable assets
cessare (finire) stop (v) [doing something]
cessare di lavorare stop work or knock off
cessazione (f) delle consegne suspension of deliveries
cessione (f) [trasferimento] cession or assignment
cessione (f) di una cambiale delivery [of bill of exchange]

check in (m) check-in counter
chiamare call (v) or telephone (v)
chiamata (f) telefonica phone call or telephone call
chiaro clear (adj) [easy to understand]
chiave key (adj) [important]
chiave (f) key [to door]
chiedere apply for [ask for]
chiedere (a qualcuno di fare qualcosa) ask [someone to do something]
chiedere [domandare] ask for [something]
chiedere informazioni enquire or inquire
chiedere ulteriori dettagli o particolari ask for further details or particulars

chiedere un rim-borso ask for a refund
chilo (m) *o* chilo-grammo (m) kilo *or* kilogram
chiudere shut (v)
chiudere *[finire]* close (v) *[after work]*
chiudere *[incollare]* seal (v) *[envelope]*
chiudere *[sospendere un'at-tività]* close down
chiudere a chiave lock (v)
chiudere a chiave un negozio *o* un ufficio lock up a shop *or* an office
chiudere un conto close an account
chiudere un conto bancario close a bank account
chiuso closed *or* shut
chiusura (f) clos-ing *or* close *or* end
chiusura (f) *[ter-mine]* closure
ciclico cyclical
ciclo (m) cycle
ciclo (m) econom-ico economic cycle *or* trade cycle
cifra (f) figure *or* digit
cifra (f) preventi-vata estimated figure
cifre (fpl) *[numeri]* figures
cifre (fpl) desta-gionalizzate season-ally adjusted figures
cifre (fpl) effettive historical figures
cifre (fpl) non verifi-cate unchecked figures
cima (f) *[vetta]* top (n) *[highest point]*
circolazione (f) cir-culation *[of money]*
circolo (m) *[associ-azione]* society or club
citare *[intentare causa]* sue
citazione (f) in giudizio summons
classe (f) class
classe (f) business business class

classe (f) turistica economy class *or* tourist class
classificare classify
classificazione (f) classification
clausola (f) clause; article
clausola (f) addizionale rider
clausola (f) condizionale proviso
clausola (f) di esclusione exclusion clause
clausola (f) di penalità penalty clause
clausola (f) di recessione waiver clause
clausola (f) di recupero dell'investimento payback clause
clausola (f) di rescissione cancellation clause *or* termination clause
clausola (f) di salvaguardia escape clause
cliente (mf) client *or* customer

cliente (mf) abituale regular customer
clientela (f) clientele
clienti (mpl) eventuali potential customers
coassicurazione (f) co-insurance
codice (m) code
codice (m) a barre bar code
codice (m) d'avviamento postale postcode *or* zip code *[US]*
codice (m) di etica professionale code of practice
codice (m) di magazzino stock code
codice (m) di zona area code
codice (m) fiscale tax code
codici (mpl) leggibili dal computer computer-readable codes
codifica (f) *o* **codificazione (f)** coding

coefficiente (m) di redditività profitability *[ratio of profit to cost]*
coefficiente (m) di carico load factor
cogliere *[raccogliere]* collect *or* fetch
coincidenza (f) connection
collaborare collaborate
collaboratore (m) *[assistente]* assistant
collaborazione (f) collaboration
collaterale collateral (adj)
collegamento (m) tie-up *or* link
collegare connect
collegare in rete network (v) *[computers]*
collettivo collective
collocazione (f) *[posizione]* situation *[place]*
colloquio (m) *[intervista]* interview (n)

colmare una lacuna (f) fill a gap
colonna (f) del dare debit column
colonna (f) dell'avere credit column
colpa (f) fault *or* blame
colpevole (mf) di appropriazione indebita embezzler
come consigliato as per advice
come da campione as per sample
come da fattura as per invoice
cominciare *[iniziare]* begin *or* start
comitato (m) commission *or* committee
commerciabile marketable
commerciale commercial (adj)
commercializzare *[vendere]* commercialize *or* market (v)
commercializzazione (f) commercialization

commerciante (m)
dealer *or* trader
commerciante (m)
all'ingrosso whole-
saler *or* wholesale
dealer
commerciante (m) in
proprio sole trader
commerciare han-
dle *or* deal in *or* sell
commerciare in o
trafficare in trade
in *[buy and sell]*
commercio (m)
commerce *or* trade
or business
commercio (m) a
senso unico one-
way trade
commercio (m)
bilaterale
reciprocal trade
commercio (m) d'e-
sportazione export
trade
commercio (m)
estero foreign trade
or overseas trade
commercio (m)
internazionale
international trade

commercio (m) in-
terno domestic trade
commercio (m) invis-
ibile invisible trade
commercio (m) legit-
timo lawful trade
commercio (m)
libero fair trading
commercio (m)
marittimo
maritime trade
commercio (m)
multilaterale mul-
tilateral trade
commesso (m) o
commessa (f) (di
negozio) salesman
or saleswoman *or*
shop assistant
commesso (m)
viaggiatore com-
mercial traveller
commettere
commit *[crime]*
commissione (f)
[percentuale] com-
mission *[money]*
commissione (f) di
mediazione broker-
age *or* broker's
commission

**commissione (f) di
studio** working
party
comodo convenient
**compagnia (f)
[società di capitali]**
company
**compagnia (f)
aerea** airline
**compagnia (f) di
assicurazione**
insurance company
compagno (m) o
**compagna (f)
[socio]** partner
comparabilità (f)
comparability
**compartecipazione
(f) agli utili** profit-
sharing
compensare com-
pensate; make up for
**compensare un
assegno** clear a
cheque
**compensazione (f)
di un assegno** clear-
ance of a cheque
**compenso (m)
[ricompensa]**
compensation

**compenso (m)
[emolumento]** fee
[for services]
**compenso (m) per
lavoro straordi-
nario** overtime pay
comperare buy or
purchase
**comperare a ter-
mine** buy forward
**comperare in con-
tanti** buy for cash
competenza (f)
remit (n)
**competere con qual-
cuno** o **con un'azienda**
compete with some-
one or with a company
competitività (f)
competitiveness
competitivo com-
petitive
**competizione (f) [con-
correnza]** competition
compilare make
out [invoice]
compilare un assegno
write out a cheque
**compito (m)
[impegno]** under-
taking or promise

complementare
complementary
complesso (m) produt-tivo production unit
completamento (m) completion
completare complete (v) *or* finalize
completo complete (adj)
comporre (for-mare) form (v)
comporre un numero dial a number
compratore (m) purchaser *or* buyer
compravendita (f) di azioni da parte degli stessi amministra-tori della Società insider dealing
comprensivo comprehensive
comprese tasse (fpl) inclusive of tax
compromesso (m) compromise (n)
comproprietà (f) co-ownership *or* joint ownership *or* part-ownership

comproprietario (m) co-owner *or* joint owner *or* part-owner
computer (m) computer
computerizzare computerize
comune common
comune: in comune jointly
comunicare communicate
comunicato (m) stampa press release
comunicazione (f) communication
comunicazione (f) orizzontale horizontal communication
comunicazione (f) verticale vertical communication
comunicazioni (fpl) communications
comunità (f) community
con cum
con coupon (m) cum coupon
con dividendo (m) cum dividend

concedente (m)
franchiser
concedere [accor-
dare] grant (v)
concedere il diritto
di esclusiva
franchise (v)
concessionario (m)
franchisee; licensee;
concessionaire
concessione (f)
concession *or* right;
franchise
concessione (f) di
licenze licensing
concessione (f) di
vendita distributor-
ship; franchising
concessione (f) fis-
cale tax concession
conciliazione (f)
conciliation
concludere con-
clude *[agreement]*
concludere
[finire] end (v)
concludere definiti-
vamente clinch
concordare [cor-
rispondere a] agree
with *or* be the same as

concordato [con-
venuto] agreed
concorrente (m)
competitor
concorrenza (f)
[competizione]
competition
concorrenza: in
concorrenza
competing (adj)
concorrenza (f)
accanita keen
competition
concorrenza (f) dura
stiff competition
concorrenza (f)
sleale unfair
competition
concorrenza (f)
spietata cut-throat
competition
condirettore (m)
joint managing
director
condirezione (f)
joint management
condizionato [con
riserve] qualified
[with reservations]
condizione (f) con-
dition *[terms]*

condizione: a condizione che on condition that
condizione (f) [stato] condition [state]
condizione (f) sociale status
condizioni (fpl) terms
condizioni: a condizioni vantaggiose on favourable terms
condizioni (fpl) di assunzione conditions of employment
condizioni (fpl) di impiego terms of employment
condizioni (fpl) di lavoro working conditions
condizioni (fpl) di pagamento terms of payment
condizioni (fpl) di vendita terms of sale
condizioni (fpl) moderate easy terms
condizioni (fpl) per pagamento in contanti cash terms; cash price

conducente (m) driver
condurre (guidare) drive (v) [a car]
condurre una trattativa conduct negotiations
conferenza (f) [congresso] conference
conferenza (f) stampa press conference
conferire il diritto entitle
conferma (f) confirmation or acknowledgement
confermare confirm
confermare l'assunzione di una persona confirm someone in a job
confermare una prenotazione confirm a booking
confermato: non confermato unconfirmed
confezionatore (m) wrapper

confezione (f) a bolla di plastica trasparente bubble pack

confezione (f) finta dummy pack

confezione (f) per esposizione display pack

conflitto (m) di interessi conflict of interest

conformarsi a (osservare) comply with

confrontare (paragonare) compare

confronto (m) comparison

congedo (m) leave (n)

congedo (m) autorizzato [aspettativa] leave of absence

congedo (m) per maternità maternity leave

congegno (m) device

congelamento (m) salariale wage freeze

congelare freeze (v) [prices]

congelare un credito freeze credits

congelato [bloccato] frozen

congiunto (unito) joint

congiuntura (f) economic trends

conglomerato (m) conglomerate

congresso (m) [conferenza] conference

consegna (f) di merci delivery of goods

consegna (f) gratuita free delivery

consegnare deliver; consign

consegnare: non consegnato undelivered

consegnatario (m) consignee

conseguibile [ottenibile] obtainable

Conservatore (m) del Registro delle Società Registrar of Companies

conservazione (f) in ambiente frigorifero cold storage
considerare consider
consigliare [raccomandare] advise or recommend [what should be done]
Consiglio (m) di Amministrazione board of directors
consistere in consist of
consocio (m) copartner
consolidamento (m) consolidation
consolidare consolidate
consolidare spedizioni consolidate [shipments]
consolidato consolidated
consorzio (m) consortium
consueto [fisso] regular [always at same time]
consulente (m) consultant or adviser

consulente (m) di direzione aziendale management consultant
consulente (m) fiscale tax consultant
consulente (m) legale legal adviser
consulente (m) tecnico consulting engineer
consulenza (f) consultancy
consulenza (f) legale legal advice
consultarsi consult
consumatore (m) consumer
consumo (m) consumption
consumo (m) interno o nazionale home consumption
contabile (mf) [ragioniere] bookkeeper
contabilità (f) accounting; bookkeeping

**contabilità (f) a
costi correnti** current cost accounting
**contabilità (f)
basata sui conti**
cost accounting
**contabilità (f) di
bilancio** budget
account *[in bank]*
**contabilità (f) di
fine mese** month-end accounts
**contabilità (f) di
metà mese** mid-month accounts
**contabilità (f) non
sottoposta a revisione contabile**
unaudited accounts
**contabilità (f)
semestrale** half-yearly accounts
container (m) container *[for shipping]*
containerizzare
containerize *[put into containers]*
**containerizzazione
(f)** containerization
*[putting into
containers]*

contanti: in contanti in cash
contare count
(v) *[add]*
contare su depend on
contatto (m)
contact (n)
contenere contain
or hold
contenitore (m)
container; holder
**contenitore (m) di
contanti** cash till
contenuto (m)
contents
**contenzioso: in
contenzioso** sub
judice
conti (mpl) attivi
accounts receivable
conti (mpl) gestione management
accounts
conti (mpl) passivi
accounts payable
**contingente (m) di
importazione**
import quota
contingenza (f)
contingency;
cost-of-living bonus

continuamente
continually
continuare
continue
continuazione (f)
continuation
continuo continual
or continuous
conto (m) account;
bill *[in restuarant]*
conto: per conto di
on behalf of
conto (m) *[dell'al-*
bergo] hotel bill
conto (m) a garanzia
escrow account
conto (m) aperto
open account
conto (m) assegni
cheque account
conto (m) bancario
bank account
conto (m) bloccato
account on stop
conto (m) capitale
capital account
conto (m) chiuso
dead account
conto (m) conge-
lato frozen account
conto (m) con-
giunto joint account

conto (m) corrente
current account
conto (m) creditori
credit account
conto (m) delle
entrate revenue
accounts
conto (m) det-
tagliato itemized
account
conto (m) di cassa
cash account
conto (m) di con-
tropartita contra
account
conto (m) di depos-
ito deposit account
conto (m) di
prestanome nomi-
nee account
conto (m) di
risparmio savings
account
conto (m) in cred-
ito account in credit
conto (m) numerato
numbered account
conto (m) person-
ale charge account
conto (m) profitti e
perdite profit and
loss account

conto (m) scoperto
overdrawn account
conto (m) spese
expense account
contraffare coun-
terfeit (v)
contraffatto *[falso]*
counterfeit (adj)
contraffazione (f)
forgery *[action]*
contrapporre set
against
contrario contrary
contrarre
contract (v)
contrarre debiti
incur debts *or* run
into debt
contrassegno (m)
countersign
contrasto (m)
contrast (n)
contrattare *[tirare sul*
prezzo] bargain (v)
contrattazione (f)
bargaining
contratti (mpl) a
termine su
materie prime
commodity futures
contratto (m)
contract (n)

contratto (m) a
breve termine
short-term contract
contratto (m) a
prezzo fisso fixed-
price agreement
contratto (m) a ter-
mine forward contract
contratto (m)
salariale collettivo
collective wage
agreement
contratto (m) di
assicurazione
insurance contract
contratto (m) di
lavoro contract of
employment
contratto (m) di
locazione tenancy
[agreement]
contratto (m) glob-
ale package *[of*
services]
contrattuale
contractual
contrattualmente
contractually
contribuente (m)
taxpayer
contribuire
contribute

contributo (m) contribution

controfferta (f) counter-offer *or* counterbid

controllabile [trattabile] manageable

controllante controlling (adj)

controllare control (v)

controllare [esaminare] check (v) *or* examine

controlli (mpl) dei prezzi price controls

controlli (mpl) valutari exchange controls

controllo (m) examination *or* check

controllo: a controllo statale government-controlled *or* government-regulated

controllo (m) [verifica] control (n) *or* check

controllo (m) budgetario budgetary control

controllo (m) dei materiali materials control

controllo (m) dei prezzi price control

controllo (m) del credito credit control

controllo (m) delle scorte stock control

controllo (m) di magazzino inventory control

controllo (m) di qualità quality control

controllo (m) doganale customs examination

controllo (m) passeggeri check-in *[at airport]*

controllore (m) controller *[who checks]*

controllore (m) della qualità quality controller

controreazione (f) feedback

controrichiesta (f) counter-claim (n)

contumace: essere contumace default (v)

conveniente good value (for money)

convenire covenant (v)

convenuto *[concordato]* agreed

convenzione (f) covenant (n)

conversione (f) conversion

conversione (f) della valuta currency conversion

conversione (f) di fondi conversion of funds

conversione (f) di un prestito refunding of a loan

convertibilità (f) convertibility

convertire convert

convocare call (v) or convene *[meeting]*

cooperare cooperate

cooperativa (f) cooperative (n)

cooperativo *[cooperativa]* co-operative (adj)

cooperazione (m) *[collaborazione]* cooperation

cooptare qualcuno co-opt someone

copertura (f) cover (n) *[top]*

copertura (f) assicurativa insurance cover

copia (f) copy (n)

copia (f) *[esemplare]* copy (n) *[book, newspaper]*

copia (f) autentica certified copy or true copy

copia (f) carbone carbon copy

copia (f) di riserva backup copy

copia (f) in chiaro hard copy

copiare *[riprodurre]* copy (v)

copiatrice (f) copier or copying machine

coprire cover (v)
coprire i costi
cover costs
**corona (f) (danese,
norvegese)** krone
*[currency used in
Denmark and
Norway]*
**corona (f)
(svedese)** krona
*[currency used in
Sweden]*
corporazione (f)
corporation
**corporazione (f)
*[gilda]*** guild
correggere correct
(v) *or* amend *or*
 rectify
corrente current *or*
ruling
correre un rischio
run a risk *or* take
a risk
corretto correct
(adj) *or* right
correzione (f) cor-
rection
**correzione (f)
strutturale** struc-
tural adjustment

**corriere (m) *[mes-
saggero]*** courier
[messenger]
**corrispondente
(mf)** correspondent
[who writes letters]
corrispondenza (f)
correspondence
**corrispondenza:
essere in corrispon-
denza con qualcuno**
correspond with
someone
**corrispondere a *[con-
cordare]*** agree with
or be the same as
**corrompere (con
denaro *o* doni)**
bribe (v)
**corso (m) a indi-
rizzo commerciale**
commercial course
**corso (m) d'aggior-
namento** refresher
course
**corso (m) in
amministrazione**
management course
**corso (m) introdut-
tivo** induction course
or induction training

corso (m) per oper-
azioni a termine
forward rate
corte (f) di
Giustizia court
costante constant
costare cost (v)
costi (mpl) d'eser-
cizio operating costs
or operating expenses
costi (mpl) di dis-
tribuzione distribu-
tion costs
costi (mpl) di factor-
ing factoring charges
costi (mpl) di ges-
tione operational
costs or running costs
or running expenses
costi (mpl) di lan-
cio launching costs
costi (mpl) di pro-
duzione production
costs or manufac-
turing costs
costi (mpl) diretti
prime cost
costi (mpl) ecces-
sivi excessive costs
costi (mpl) fissi
fixed costs

costi (mpl) fondiari
landed costs
costi (mpl) indi-
retti del lavoro
indirect labour costs
costi (mpl) per la
spedizione marit-
tima shipping
charges or shipping
costs
costi (mpl) sociali
social costs
costi (mpl) vari-
abili variable costs
costituire incorpo-
rate [a company]
costituire una soci-
età (f) set up a
company
costituzione (f)
incorporation
costo (m) cost (n)
costo (m) della
manodopera labour
costs
costo (m) della
vita [carovita] cost
of living
costo (m) delle
vendite cost of
sales

costo (m) diretto
direct cost
costo (m) effettivo
historic(al) cost
**costo (m) mar-
ginale** marginal cost
or incremental cost
**costo (m) più una
percentuale**
cost plus
**costo (m) simbol-
ico** token charge
costo (m) totale
total cost
costo (m) unitario
unit cost
**costo (m), assicu-
razione (f) e nolo
(m)** cost, insurance
and freight (c.i.f.)
costoso costly *or*
expensive
**costruire *[svilup-
pare]*** develop
[build]
**costruire riserve
*[stoccare]*** stock
pile (v)
**costruttore (m)
chiavi in mano**
turnkey operator

**costruzione: in
costruzione** under
construction
**coupon (m) con
risposta pagata**
reply coupon
**crediti (mpl) conge-
lati** frozen credits
credito (m) credit
(n) *or* credit balance
credito: a credito
on credit
credito (m) a breve
short-term credit
**credito (m) a breve
termine** short
credit
**credito (m) a lungo
termine** long credit
**credito (m) al con-
sumatore** con-
sumer credit
credito (m) aperto
open credit
**credito (m) ban-
cario** bank credit
**credito (m) d'im-
posta** tax credit
**credito (m) di
appoggio** standby
credit

credito (m) esente da interessi interest-free credit

credito (m) esigibile debts due

credito (m) immediato instant credit

credito (m) inesigibile bad debt

credito (m) prorogato extended credit

credito (m) rinnovabile automaticamente revolving credit

creditore (m) creditor

creditore (m) differito deferred creditor

creditore (m) in solido co-creditor

creditore (m) ipotecario mortgagee

creditore (m) non garantito unsecured creditor

creditore (m) privilegiato preferential creditor or secured creditor

crescente increasing

crescita (f) growth

crescita (f) economica economic growth

crisi (f) del dollaro dollar crisis

crisi (f) di mancanza di liquidità liquidity crisis

crisi (f) economica [crollo] slump (n) or depression

crisi (f) finanziaria financial crisis

crollare [cadere] collapse (v) or crash or fail

crollo (m) [crisi economica] slump (n) [depression]

crollo (m) [caduta] fall (n) or collapse (n) or crash (n)

cronico chronic

cubico cubic

cucire con punti metallici [graffare] staple (v)

cucitrice (f) [graffatrice] stapler

culminare *[raggiungere un punto massimo]* peak (v)

cumulativo cumulative

curricolo (m) track record

curriculum (m) vitae curriculum vitae (CV)

curva (f) curve

curva (f) delle vendite sales curve

Dd

da non restituire *o* da gettare disposable

da primato record-breaking

da ricevere receivable

danneggiare damage (v)

danneggiato damaged

danni (mpl) *[rotture]* damage; breakages

danni (mpl) causati da un temporale storm damage

danno (m) alla proprietà damage to property

danno (m) causato da un incendio fire damage

dare give

dare corso ad un'ordinazione deal with an order

dare e avere debits and credits

dare in affitto *[affittare]* lease out (v)

dare in prestito *[prestare]* loan (v)

dare in subappalto subcontract (v)

dare istruzioni brief (v)

dare la caccia a chase *[an order]*

dare soldi come anticipo put money down

data (f) date (n)
data (f) d'inizio
starting date
data (f) del lancio
launching date
data (f) di chiusura
[termine ultimo]
closing date
data (f) di con-
segna delivery date
data (f) di entrata in
vigore effective date
data (f) di ricevi-
mento date of
receipt
data (f) di rimborso
redemption date
data (f) di sca-
denza sell-by date;
expiry date *or* matu-
rity date
data (f) di sca-
denza *[termine*
ultimo] deadline
data (f) di ulti-
mazione comple-
tion date
datare date (v)
datario (m) date
stamp
datato dated

datato: non datato
undated
dati (mpl) data
dati (mpl) di emis-
sione computer
output
datore (m) di
lavoro employer
daziere (m) Excise
officer
dazio (m) duty *[tax]*
dazio (m) d'esport-
azione export duty
dazio (m) doganale
customs duty *or*
import duty
dazio (m) preferen-
ziale preferential
duty *or* preferential
tariff
debiti (mpl) a
lungo termine
long-term debts
debiti (mpl) inso-
luti outstanding
debts
debiti (mpl) privile-
giati secured debts
debito (m) debt
debito: a debito
[dovuto] owing

debito (m) *[registrazione]* debit entry
debito (m) inesigibile irrecoverable debt
debitore (m) debtor
debitore: essere debitore owe
debitore (m) autorizzato al concordato preventivo certificated bankrupt
debitore (m) ipotecario mortgager *or* mortgagor
debitore (m) riconosciuto da tribunale judgment debtor
decentramento (m) decentralization
decentrare decentralize
decidere decide *or* resolve
decidere una linea di condotta decide on a course of action
decimale (m) decimal (n)
decisione (f) decision

decisione (f) *[verdetto]* judgement *or* judgment
decisivo deciding
declino (m) decline (n)
decollare take off
decrescente decreasing (adj)
decretare rule (v) *[give decision]*
decreto (m) ruling (n)
decurtare dock (v) *or* deduct money
dedurre *[fare uno sconto di]* take off *or* deduct
deficit (m) *[disavanzo]* deficit
deficit (m) della bilancia commerciale trade deficit *or* trade gap
definire una domanda d'indennizzo settle a claim
deflazione (f) deflation
deflazionistico deflationary

**degrado (m) [nor-
male usura]** fair
wear and tear
delega (f) delega-
tion [action]
delega (f) [procura]
proxy [deed]
delegare delegate (v)
delegato (m)
delegate (n)
**delegato (m) [sos-
tituto]** deputy
delegazione (f)
delegation
denaro (m) money
**denaro (m) a buon
mercato** cheap
money
denaro (m) contante
cash (n) [money]
**denaro (m) per le
piccole spese**
spending money
denaro (m) scarso
tight money
**denominazione (f)
della mansione** job
title
**denuncia (f) dei
redditi** tax return
or tax declaration

depennare cross off
deperibile perishable
deporto (m)
backwardation
depositante (m)
depositor
**depositare docu-
menti** file documents
depositare in banca
bank (v)
**depositare un mar-
chio di fabbrica**
register a trademark
**depositi (mpl) ban-
cari** bank deposits
**depositi (mpl) frut-
tiferi** interest-bear-
ing deposits
deposito (m)
deposit (n) [in bank]
**deposito (m) [mag-
azzino]** store (n)
[place where goods
are kept]
**deposito (m) [mag-
azzinaggio]** storage
(n) [in warehouse]
**deposito (m) a ter-
mine** time deposit
deposito (m) a vista
demand deposit

**deposito (m) in cas-
setta di sicurezza**
safe deposit
**deposito (m) in con-
tanti** cash deposit
deposito (m) merci
goods depot
**deposito (m) non
rimborsabile** non-
refundable deposit
**deposito (m) vinco-
lato** fixed deposit
depressione (f)
depression
**deregolamentazione
(f)** deregulation
derivare result from
descrivere describe
descrizione (f)
description
**descrizione (f)
commerciale** trade
description
**descrizione (f) dei
compiti** job
description
**design (m) [proget-
tazione]** design (n)
**desktop publishing
(m)** desk-top
publishing (DTP)

destinare appropri-
ate (v) *[funds]*
destinatario (m)
addressee
destinazione (f)
destination
destituzione (f)
removal *or* sacking
[of someone]
destro right (adj)
[not left]
**deterioramento
(m) naturale** wear
and tear
determinare
determine
**determinazione (f)
del prezzo** pricing
**determinazione (f)
del prezzo di con-
correnza** competi-
tive pricing
**determinazione (f)
marginale del prezzo**
marginal pricing
detraibile deductible
**detraibile dal red-
dito imponibile**
tax-deductible
detrazione (f)
deduction

**detrazioni (fpl)
d'imposta** tax
deductions *[from
salary to pay tax]*
**detrazioni (fpl)
personali** personal
allowances
dettagli (mpl)
particulars
dettagliante (m)
retailer *or* retail
dealer
dettagliare detail
(v) *or* break down
(v) *or* itemize
dettagliato detailed
dettaglio (m)
detail (n)
dettare dictate
dettatura (f) dic-
tation
di mezzo *[medio]*
medium (adj)
diagramma (m)
diagram
**diagramma (m) a
barre** bar chart
**diagramma (m) del
ciclo di lavorazione**
flow diagram
diario diary

dichiarare declare
or state
**dichiarare le merci
alla dogana** declare
goods to customs
**dichiarare qualcuno
fallito** declare
someone bankrupt
**dichiarare sciolta
una riunione** wind
up a meeting
**dichiarare una
perdita** report a loss
dichiarato declared
dichiarazione (f)
declaration
**dichiarazione (f)
doganale**
customs declaration
**dichiarazione dei
redditi** declaration
of income
**dichiarazione di fal-
limento** declaration
of bankruptcy
dichiarazione IVA
VAT declaration
dicitura (f) wording
difendere defend
difendere una causa
defend a lawsuit

difensore (m) civico ombudsman

difesa (f) defence *[legal]*

difetto (m) defect *or* mechanical fault

difettoso defective *[faulty]*

differenza (f) difference

differenza (f) a credito credit balance

differenze (fpl) di prezzo differences in price

differenziale differential (adj)

differire (rinviare) defer *or* postpone *or* shelve

differire un pagamento defer payment

differito deferred

diffusione (f) nei mass-media media coverage

digitare keyboard (v)

dilazione (f) *[rinvio]* postponement

diluizione (f) della partecipazione azionaria dilution of equity

dimensione (f) size

dimensioni: di medie dimensioni medium-sized

dimettersi resign

diminuire decrease (v) *or* fall off

diminuzione (f) decrease (n)

diminuzione (f) dei prezzi price reduction *or* reduction in price; mark-down

diminuzione (f) del valore decrease in value

dimissioni (fpl) resignation

dimostrare demonstrate

dimostratore (m) demonstrator

dimostrazione (f) demonstration

dinamismo (m)
[energia] human
energy
dipartimentale
departmental
dipartimento (m)
department
dipartimento (m)
design design
department
dipendente (m)
employee
dipendenti (m)
pagati a ore
hourly-paid workers
diramare istruzioni
issue instructions
direttamente
direct (adv)
direttiva (f) direc-
tive *or* guideline
direttivo *[gestion-*
ale] managerial
diretto direct (adj)
direttore (m), diret-
trice (f) manager;
senior executive
direttore (m) com-
merciale sales
manager

direttore (m) d'al-
bergo hotel manager
direttore (m) del
progetto project
manager
direttore (m)
del reparto
esportazioni
export manager
direttore (m) del
servizio marketing
sales executive
direttore (m) del-
l'ufficio acquisti
purchasing manager
direttore (m) della
pubblicità advertis-
ing manager *or* pub-
licity manager
direttore (m) delle
distribuzioni distri-
bution manager
direttore (m) delle
finanze finance
director
direttore (m) delle
vendite sales exec-
utive
direttore (m) di
banca bank manager

direttore (m) di filiale branch manager
direttore (m) di marketing marketing manager
direttore (m) di produzione production manager
direttore (m) di zona area manager
direttore (m) esecutivo executive director
direttore (m) esterno outside director
direttore (m) facente funzione acting manager
direttore (m) generale *[amministratore delegato]* managing director (MD); chief executive
direttore (m) generale general manager
direttore (m) senza poteri esecutivi non-executive director
direttore (m) vendite esterne field sales manager
direzione (f) management *[managers]*

direzione (f) *[istruzione]* directions *or* instructions
direzione (f) al vertice top management
direzione (f) centrale *[sede centrale]* main office
direzione (f) del personale personnel management
dirigente (m) executive (n)
dirigente (m) delle pubbliche relazioni public relations officer
dirigente (m) delle vendite sales executive
dirigente (m) di grado inferiore junior executive *or* junior manager
dirigente (m) in capo senior manager *or* senior executive
dirigere direct (v) *or* run (v) *or* manage
dirigere male mismanage

**diritti (mpl) di
porto** port charges
or port dues
**diritti (mpl) portu-
ali** harbour dues
**diritti (mpl) spe-
ciali di prelievo
(DSP)** special draw-
ing rights (SDRs)
diritto (m) right *or*
entitlement; legal
title
diritto (m) law
[study]
diritto (m) civile
civil law
**diritto (m)
commerciale**
commercial law
**diritto (m) contrat-
tuale** contract law
**diritto (m) della
navigazione**
 maritime law
**diritto (m) di con-
cessione** royalty
**diritto (m) di pos-
sesso** tenure *[right]*
**diritto (m) di prece-
denza** right of way
diritto (m) di veto
right of veto

**diritto (m) inter-
nazionale** interna-
tional law
**diritto (m) soci-
etario** company law
**disavanzo (m)
*[deficit]*** deficit
discendente *[giù]*
down *or* downward
**discesa (f) delle
vendite** slump in
sales
dischetto (m)
diskette
disco (m) disk
**discorso (m) di
ringraziamento**
speech of thanks
discrepanza (f)
discrepancy
discussione (f)
discussion
**discussione (f)
*[disputa]*** argument
**discussione (f) collet-
tiva** joint discussions
**discussione (f) pro-
duttiva** productive
discussions
discutere discuss
**disdetta (f) *[cancel-
lazione]*** cancellation

disdire un affare call off a deal

disegno (m) industriale industrial design

disfarsi di get rid of

disoccupato out of work *or* unemployed

disoccupazione (f) unemployment

disoccupazione (f) strutturale structural unemployment

disonestamente fraudulently

disonesto [fraudolento] fraudulent

dispari odd [*not even*]

disparità (f) dei prezzi price differential

dispersione (f) leakage

disponibile available

disponibile: non disponibile unavailable

disponibilità (f) availability

disponibilità: non disponibilità (f) unavailability

disponibilità (f) di capitali money supply

disponibilità (fpl) finanziarie financial assets

disporre [sistemare] arrange *or* set out

disposizione (m) [sistemazione] arrangement *or* system

disposizioni (fpl) [regolamenti] regulations

disputa (f) argument

dissentire differ

dissolvere [risolvere] dissolve

distinta (f) d'imballaggio packing list *or* packing slip

distinta (f) di versamento paying-in slip *or* deposit slip

distretto (m) commerciale commercial district

distribuire distribute
distributore (m)
distributor
distribuzione (f)
distribution
distruggere wreck
(v) *or* ruin
ditta (f) (impresa)
firm (n) *or* business
or company
**ditta (f) a con-
duzione familiare**
family company
**ditta (f) di consule-
nza** consultancy firm
**ditta (f) di vendita
a rate** hire-purchase
company
**ditta (f) di noleggio
impianti** plant-hire
firm
dittafono (m)
dictating machine
divario (m) gap
diversificare
diversify
diversificazione (f)
diversification
diverso different
dividendo (m)
dividend

**dividendo (m)
finale** final dividend
**dividendo (m) in
acconto** interim
dividend
**dividendo (m)
minimo** minimum
dividend
dividere share (v)
**divieto (m) di
importazione**
import ban
divisa (f) forte
strong currency
**divise (fpl) *[mon-
eta straniera]*** for-
eign currency
divisione (f) divi-
sion *[part of a group]*
divulgare *[rivelare]*
disclose
**divulgare un'infor-
mazione** disclose a
piece of information
**divulgazione (f) *[riv-
elazione]*** disclosure
**divulgazione (f) di
un'informazione
riservata** disclo-
sure of confidential
information

documentario (m)
documentary
documentarsi su
[fare ricerche]
research (v)
documentazione (f)
documentation;
records
documenti (mpl)
documents
documenti (mpl)
falsi faked
documents
documento (m)
document
documento (m)
provvisorio scrip
dogana (f) customs
doganiere (m)
customs officer
dollaro (m) dollar
domanda (f)
demand (n)
domanda: fare
domanda scritta
apply in writing
domanda (f)
[istanza] application
domanda (f)
d'impiego applica-
tion for a job

domanda
d'impiego: fare
domanda d'impiego
apply for a job
domanda (f) d'in-
dennizzo claim (n)
domanda (f) di
lavoro job
application
domanda (f)
effettiva effective
demand
domanda (f) finale
final demand
domandare
demand (v)
domandare
[chiedere] ask for
[something]
domandare
[richiedere]
request (v)
domestico domestic
domicilio (m)
domicile
domicilio: a domi-
cilio door-to-door
donna (f) d'affari
businesswoman
dono (m) [omag-
gio] free gift

doppia tassazione
(f) double taxation
doppio double (adj)
dorso (m) [retro]
back (n)
dossier (m) [prat-
ica] dossier
dover rispondere a
qualcuno report to
someone
dovere (m)
[impegno] obliga-
tion or duty
dovutamente [rego-
larmente] duly or
legally
dovuto [a debito]
due or owing
dovuto: essere
dovuto fall due or
be due
dozzina (f) dozen
DSP (diritti speciali
di prelievo) special
drawing rights (SDRs)
duplicare
duplicate (v)
duplicato (m)
duplicate (n)
duplicato: fare il
duplicato di una

fattura duplicate
an invoice
duplicazione (f)
duplication
durata (f) [periodo]
term [of validity]
durata (f) in carica
tenure [time]
duty free shop
[negozio esente da
tasse] duty-free shop

Ee

eccellente excellent
eccessivo excessive
eccesso excess
eccetto [tranne]
except
eccezionale [straor-
dinario] exceptional
economia (f)
economy
economia (f) [scie-
nze economiche]
economics

economia (f) con-trollata controlled economy

economia (f) dell'offerta supply side economics

economia (f) di massa economies of scale

economia (f) di mercato libero free market economy

economia (f) di tipo misto mixed economy

economia (f) matura mature economy

economia (f) nera black economy

economia (f) solida stable economy

economico [*a basso prezzo*] economical *or* cheap

economico [*finanziario*] economic *or* financial

economista (mf) economist

economista (mf) di mercato market economist

economizzare economize *or* save

ecu (m) (Unità di Conto Europea) ecu *or* ECU (= European currency unit)

edificio (m) facility *[building]*

edificio (m) principale main building

effetti (mpl) a breve termine short-dated bills

effetti (mpl) all'incasso bills for collection

effetti (mpl) attivi receivables *or* bills receivable

effetti (mpl) bancabili [*strumenti scontabili*] bankable paper

effetti (mpl) passivi [*cambiali da pagare*] bills payable

effettivo effective

effettivo (reale) actual

effetto (m) effect (n)

effetto (m) *[cambiale]* bill (n) *or* promise to pay

effetto (m) a catena knock-on effect

effetto (m) a lunga scadenza long-dated bill

effetto (m) accettato irrevocabilmente irrevocable acceptance

effetto (m) bancario bank bill *[GB]*

effetto (m) di comodo *[cambiale di favore]* accommodation bill

effettuare effect (v)

efficacia (f) effectiveness

efficiente efficient

efficienza (f) efficiency

elaborare cifre process figures

elaborato a mezzo computer computerized

elaboratore (m) ad uso personale *[personal computer]* personal computer (PC)

elaborazione (f) delle ordinazioni order processing

elaborazione (f) dei dati data processing

elaborazione (f) delle informazioni processing of information

elaborazione (f) di massa batch processing

elasticità (f) elasticity

eleggere elect

elementi (m) ciclici cyclical factors

elemento (m) decisivo deciding factor

elencare list (v) *or* index (v)

elencazione (f) scheduling

elenco (m) classificato classified directory

**elenco (m) delle
cause** docket
**elenco (m) di indi-
rizzi** mailing list
**elenco (m) telefon-
ico** telephone book *or*
telephone directory
elezione (f) election
eliminare delete
**eliminare gradual-
mente** phase out
**eliminare le scorte
in eccesso** dispose
of excess stock
embargo (m)
embargo (n)
**emendamento
(m) [rettifica]**
amendment
emergenza (f)
emergency
emettere issue (v)
[shares]
**emettere allo scop-
erto** overdraw
**emettere un
assegno** draw [a
cheque]
**emettere una fat-
tura** raise an
invoice

**emissione (f)
azionaria** share issue
**emissione (f) di
certificati azionari
provvisori** scrip
issue
**emissione (f) di
diritti** rights issue
**emissione (f) gra-
tuita di azioni**
bonus issue
**emolumento (m)
[compenso]** fee
[for services]
energia (f) elettrica
energy [electricity]
**energia (f) [dina-
mismo]** human
energy
ente (m) locale
local government
entrare enter *or*
go in
entrare: far entrare
admit *or* let in
**entrare in porto
[attraccare]** dock
(v) [ship]
**entrare in possesso
di una società**
acquire a company

entrare in vigore
run (v) *or* be in force
entrata (f) entry
[going in]
entrate (fpl) receipts
equalizzazione (f)
equalization
equipaggiare equip
**equivalere a qual-
cosa** correspond
with something
equo (giusto)
fair (adj)
erodere erode
errore (m) error *or*
mistake
errore (m) casuale
random error
**errore (m) di com-
puter** computer error
**errore (m) di trasc-
rizione** clerical error
esame (f)
examination
esame: in esame
on approval
esaminare examine
or inspect
**esaminare [control-
lare]** check (v) *or*
examine

esatto exact (adj)
esattamente exactly
**esattore (m) dei
crediti** debt collector
**esattore (m) delle
imposte** tax collector
**esattore (m) di
affitti** rent collector
**esaurire [vendere
tutto]** sell out *[all
stock]*
esaurire run out of
esaurito out of
stock
esborso (m) outlay
or disbursement
escludere exclude
esclusione (f)
exclusion
esclusività (f)
exclusivity
escluso excluding;
exclusive of
esecutivo
executive (adj)
esecuzione (f)
execution
eseguire execute
**esemplare (m)
[copia]** copy (n) *[of
book, newspaper]*

esentare exempt (v)
esentasse tax-exempt
esente exempt (adj)
esente da canone d'affitto rent-free
esente da dazio duty-free
esente da pedaggio toll free *[US]*
esente da tassa exempt from tax
esente da tasse tax-free *or* free of tax
esenzione (f) exemption
esenzione (f) fiscale tax exemption *or* exemption from tax
esercitare exercise (v)
esercitare il commercio di un prodotto merchandize a product
esercitare un'opzione exercise an option *or* take up an option
esercizio (m) exercise (n)
esercizio (m) di un'opzione exercise of an option
esercizio (m) finanziario financial year
esibire exhibit (v)
esigenza (f) di manodopera manpower requirements
esigere exact (v)
espansione (f) industriale industrial expansion
esperto experienced
esperto (m) *[professionista]* expert (n) *or* professional (n)
esperto (m) di statistica statistician
esplorare explore
esporre display (v)
esportare export (v)
esportatore exporting (adj)
esportatore (m) exporter
esportazione (f) export (n)
esportazioni (fpl) exports

espositore (m)
[standista]
exhibitor
esposizione (f)
[mostra] exhibition
or display
esposizione (f) in
vetrina window
display
espresso ex
press (adj)
esprimere express
(v) [state]
espropriazione (f)
per pubblica utilità
compulsory purchase
essere in ritardo
(nel fare una cosa)
fall behind or be late
essere valido run
(v) or be in force
estendersi [variare]
range (v)
esteriore outside
esterno external
[outside a company]
estero [straniero]
external or foreign
estero (m) [i paesi
stranieri] over
seas (n)

estero: all'estero
abroad or overseas
estinguere [un deb-
ito] redeem or pay
off or clear [a debt]
estratto (m) conto
statement of account
estratto (m) conto
bancario bank
statement
età (f) della pen-
sione retirement age
etichetta (f)
label (n)
etichetta (f) di
posta aerea airmail
sticker
etichetta (f) indi-
rizzata address
label
etichettare label (v)
etichettatura (f)
labelling
ettaro (m) hectare
euro (m) euro
euroassegno (m)
Eurocheque
eurodollaro (m)
Eurodollar
euromercato (m)
Euromarket

euromoneta (f)
Eurocurrency
evadere evade
evadere un'ordi-
nazione fulfil an
order
evasione (f) d'im-
posta evasion
evasione (f) di
un'ordinazione
order fulfilment
evasione (f) fiscale
tax avoidance or tax
evasion
evidenziatore (m)
marker pen
ex cedola (f) ex
coupon
ex dividendo (m)
ex dividend
expertise (f) [per-
izia] expertise
extra extra

Ff

fabbrica (f) factory
or plant
fabbricante (m)
[produttore]
manufacturer
fabbricare [pro-
durre] manufacture
(v) or produce or
make
fabbricazione (f)
[lavorazione]
manufacture (n)
faccenda (f) [prob-
lema] matter (n) or
problem
facente funzione di
[sostituto] acting
facile easy
facile da usare
[accessibile] user-
friendly
facilitazioni (fpl) di
scoperto overdraft
facility
facoltativo optional
factoring (m)
factoring

factoring: fare del
factoring factor (v)
fallimento (m)
bankruptcy
fallire fail
fallire: fare fallire
ruin (v) *or* bank
rupt (v)
fallire *[non arrivare
a compimento]* fall
through
fallito bankrupt (adj)
fallito (m) bank-
rupt (n)
fallito (m) non
riabilitato undis-
charged bankrupt
falsificare falsify
or fake (v) *or*
forge
falsificazione (f)
falsification
falso (m) forgery
[copy]
falso *[contraf-
fatto]* false *or*
counterfeit (adj)
falso *[fittizio]*
dummy
far entrare admit
[let in]

far pagare charge
(v) *[money]*
far pagare meno
undercharge
far pagare troppo
overcharge (v)
fare pratica train
(v) *[learn]*
fare progressi *[av-
anzare]* progress (v)
fare riferimento a
refer *[to item]*
fare soldi make
money
fare un'ordinazione
place an order
farsi ritirare l'usato
trade in *[give in old
item for new]*
fascia (f) tax bracket
fascicolo (m) file
(n) *[documents]*
fascicolo (m) dello
schedario card-
index file
fascicolo (m) sup-
plementare (in una
rivista) magazine
insert
fattibilità (f)
feasibility

**fatto apposita-
mente** custom-built
or custom-made
fattore (m) factor
(n) *[influence]*
fattore (m) costo
cost factor
**fattore (m) nega-
tivo** minus factor *or*
downside factor
**fattore (m) posi-
tivo** plus factor
**fattori (mpl) di
produzione** factors
of production
fattorino (m)
deliveryman *or*
messenger
fattura (f) invoice
(n) *or* bill
fattura (f) *[atto di
vendita]* bill of sale
fattura (f) con IVA
VAT invoice
**fattura (f) dettagli-
ata** itemized invoice
**fattura (f) pro-
forma** pro forma
(invoice)
fatturare invoice
(v) *or* bill (v)

fatturato (m) *[ven-
dite]* sales (revenue)
fatturazione (f)
invoicing *or* billing
**fatture (fpl) inso-
lute** unpaid invoices
favorevole
favourable
fax (m) fax (n)
**fedeltà (f) alla
marca** brand loyalty
fede: in buona fede
bona fide; in good
faith
**fedeltà (f) dei cli-
enti** customer loyalty
fermare
countermand
fermarsi stay (v)
fermo (stabile)
stable
fermoposta (m)
poste restante
ferrovia (f) railway
or rail *or*
railroad *[US]*
festa (f) nazionale
public holiday; bank
holiday
fiasco: fare fiasco
fail (v) *or* flop (v)

fiducia (f) confidence

fiera (f) campi- onaria trade fair

file (m) *[archivio]* computer file

filiale (f) branch office; subsidiary

finale final

finanza (f) *[attiv- ità finanziaria]* finance (n)

finanza (f) pub- blica public finance

finanze (fpl) finances

finanziamento (m) financing

finanziamento (m) del disavanzo (m) deficit financing

finanziare finance (v) *or* fund (v) *or* pay costs

finanziare un'oper- azione finance an operation

finanziariamente financially

finanziario *[eco- nomico]* financial

finanziatore (m) moneylender

fine fine (adv) *[very small]*

fine (f) *[scadenza]* expiry

fine (f) *[termine]* end (n)

fine (f) del mese month end

fine (f) esercizio year end

finestra (f) window

finire *[concludere]* end (v)

finire *[portare a termine]* complete (v)

finire *[cessare]* stop (v) *[doing something]*

finito finished

fino a *[conforme a]* up to

fiorente booming *or* flourishing

firma (f) signature

firmare sign (v)

firmare come testi- mone witness (v) *[a document]*

firmare il registro
check in *or* register
[at hotel]
firmare un accordo
come testimone wit-
ness an agreement
firmare un assegno
sign a cheque
firmare un contratto
sign a contract
firmatario (m)
signatory
firmatario (m)
congiunto joint
signatory
fiscale fiscal
fissaggio (m) fixing
fissare fix *or* arrange
fissare obiettivi
set targets
fissare una riu-
nione per le 3 del
pomeriggio fix a
meeting for 3 p.m.
fissato fixed
fissato (m) bollato
contract note
fisso fixed *or* flat
fisso (consueto)
regular *[always at*
same time]

fittizio (falso)
dummy
flessibile flexible
flessibilità (f)
flexibility
fluire flow (v)
flusso (m) flow (n)
flusso (m) di cassa
cash flow
flusso (m) di cassa
positivo positive
cash flow
fluttuante
fluctuating
fluttuante *[galleg-*
giante] floating
fluttuare *[oscillare]*
fluctuate
fluttuare: far
fluttuare float (v)
[a currency]
fluttuazione (f)
fluctuation
foglietto (m) slip
(n) *[piece of paper]*
foglio (m) di cal-
colo elettronico
spreadsheet
[computer]
foglio (m) di carta
sheet of paper

fondamentale [di base] basic or most important
fondamento (m) [base] basis
fondi (mpl) insufficienti insufficient funds [US]
fondi (mpl) pubblici public funds
fondo (m) fund or reserve (n)
fondo (m) comune di investimento unit trust
fondo (m) di cassa cash float; cash in hand
fondo (m) di previdenza contingency fund
fondo (m) pensioni pension fund
Fondo Monetario Internazionale (FMI) International Monetary Fund (IMF)
fonte (f) di reddito source of income

formale formal
formalità (f) formality
formalità (fpl) doganali customs formalities
formare (comporre) form (v)
formare un numero telefonico dial (v) a number
formato (m) normale regular size
formazione (f) training
formulazione (f) form of words
fornire (approvvigionare) supply (v)
fornire di personale staff (v)
fornitore (m) supplier
fornitore (m) allo stato o statale government contractor
fornitura (f) supply (n) [action]
forte strong
forte richiesta (f) keen demand

forti costi (mpl)
heavy costs
forza (f) lavoro
labour force *or*
workforce
forza (f) vendita
[personale addetto
alle vendite] sales
force
forzato forced
forze (fpl) di mer-
cato market forces
fotocopia (f)
photocopy (n)
fotocopiare
photocopy (v)
fotocopiatrice (f)
photocopier
fotocopiatura (f)
photocopying
fragile fragile
franco *[senza*
spese] franco
franco a bordo free
on board (f.o.b.)
franco di porto
carriage free
franco di spese *[gra-*
tuito] free of charge
franco dogana free
of duty

franco posta
post free
franco su rotaia
free on rail
francobollo (m)
postage stamp
fraudolento
fraudulent
frequente frequent
frode (f) fraud
fronte: far fronte a
una spesa meet an
expense
frontiera (f) border
fruttare *[rendere]*
earn *or* bear *or* pro-
duce (v) *[interest]*
fuga (f) *[di denaro]*
flight *[of money]*
fungere da inter-
faccia interface (v)
funzionamento (m)
[marcia] running
(n) *[of machine]*
funzionare *[operare]*
act *or* operate *or* work
funzionare: far fun-
zionare operate (v)
or run a machine
funzionario (m)
official (n)

funzionario (m) addetto all'addestramento training officer

funzionario (m) di banca banker

fuoco (m) [incendio] fire (n)

fuori controllo out of control

fuori orario d'ufficio outside office hours

fuori stagione off-season

furgone (m) van

furgone (m) per le consegne delivery van

furto (m) theft

furto (m) di scarsa entità pilferage or pilfering

fusione (f) merger

futura consegna (f) future delivery

Gg

galleria (f) [con negozi] shopping mall or shopping arcade

gamma (f) range (n) or series of items

gamma (f) dei prezzi price range

gamma (f) di prodotti product mix

garante (m) surety; sponsor (n)

garantire guarantee (v)

garantire [sponsorizzare] sponsor (v)

garantire per qualcuno stand surety for someone

garantire un debito guarantee a debt

garanzia (f) guarantee (n) or security

garanzia (f) collaterale collateral (n)

generale general

generi (mpl) di consumo consumables

gestionale [direttivo] managerial

gestione (f) [amministrazione] administration *or* management

gestione (f) del portafoglio portfolio management

gestire [amministrare] manage

gettare throw away

gettare: da gettare disposable

giacenze (fpl) finali alla chiusura dell'esercizio closing stock

gilda (f) [corporazione] guild

giornale (m) newspaper

giornale (m) di categoria trade journal

giorno (m) day

giorno (m) festivo legale statutory holiday

giorno (m) per giorno day-to-day

giovane [junior] junior (adj)

girante (m) endorser

girare un assegno endorse a cheque

girata (f) endorsement [action]

giratario (m) endorsee

giroconto (m) giro system

giù [discendente] down

giudicare judge (v)

giudice (m) adjudicator

giudice (m) [magistrato] judge (n)

giudizio (m) [aggiudicazione] adjudication

giudizio (m) arbitrale award (n)

giungere ad un accordo reach an agreement

giungere al punto di pareggio break even (v)

giuridico legal *[referring to law]*

giurisdizione (f) jurisdiction

giustificare justify *or* warrant (v)

giusto rightful

giusto *[equo]* fair (adj)

globale *[totale]* all-in *or* total (adj)

governativo *[del governo]* government (adj)

governo (m) government (n)

grado (m) di solvibilità credit rating

graduale gradual

graduato graduated

graffare *[cucire con punti metallici]* staple (v)

graffare insieme fogli staple papers together

graffatrice (f) *[cucitrice]* stapler

graffetta (f) paperclip

grafico (m) a settori pie chart

grafico (m) delle vendite sales chart

grammo (m) gram *or* gramme

grande magazzino (m) department store

grande quantità (f) *[massa]* mass *[of things]*

grande quantità (f) *[volume]* bulk

grande supermercato (m) superstore

gratifica (f) (premio) bonus

gratifica (f) di bilancio incentive bonus

gratifica (f) natalizia *[tredicesima]* Christmas bonus

gratis gratis *or* free

gratuitamente free (adv) *[no payment]*

gratuito *[franco di spese]* free of charge

**gravare d'imposta
*[tassare]*** tax (v)
grave heavy
[important]
**griglia (f)
*[reticolo]*** grid
grinta (f) drive (n)
[energy]
**grossa (f) *[dodici
dozzine]*** gross
(n) (= 144)
gru (f) crane
**gruppi (mpl) socioe-
conomici** socio-
economic groups
gruppo (m) batch
(n) *[of orders]*;
group *[of people]*
**gruppo (m) di col-
locamento** under-
writing syndicate
**gruppo (m) indus-
triale** group *[of
businesses]*
**gruppo (m) sele-
zionato di consuma-
tori** consumer panel

guadagnare earn
[money]
guadagni (mpl)
earnings *[salary]*
guadagno (m) gain
(n) *[increase in
value]*
**guadagno (m)
*[profitto]*** return
(n) *[profit]*
guadagno (m) lordo
gross earnings
guardia (f) giurata
security guard
guasto (m) break-
down (n) *[machine]*
**guerra (f) dei
prezzi** price war
**guerra (f) della dim-
inuzione dei prezzi**
price-cutting war
guida (f) (turistica)
courier *[guide]*
guida (f) stradale
street directory
guidare *[condurre]*
drive (v) *[a car]*

Hh Ii

hard disk (m) hard disk

holding (f) *[società controllante]* holding company

hotel (m) *[albergo]* hotel

illecito illicit

illegale illegal

illegalità (f) illegality

illegalmente illegally

imballaggio (m) packing *or* packaging; wrapping

imballaggio (m) ermetico airtight packaging

imballaggio (m) termocontrattile shrink-wrapping

imballare *[impacchettare]* pack (v)

imballare (merce) in casse crate (v) *or* pack goods into cartons

imballato con metodo termocontrattile shrink-wrapped

imballo (m) a perdere non-returnable packing

imballo (m) di cartone carton *or* box

imbarcare o imbarcarsi embark *or* board

imbarcarsi in embark on

imbarco (m) embarkation

imbonimento (m) sales pitch

imbrogliare fiddle (v)

imbroglio (m) *[truffa]* fiddle (n)

imitazione (f) imitation *or* fake (n)

immagazzinare store *or* stock up *or* keep in warehouse

immagine (f) aziendale corporate image

immagine (f) del prodotto brand image

immagine (f) pubblica public image

immediatamente immediately

immediato [istantaneo] immediate or instant

immetere [informazioni nel computer] input information [on computer]

immissione (f) mediante tastiera keyboarding

immobile (m) con chiusura di sicurezza lock-up premises

immobilizzazioni (fpl) capital assets

immobilizzi (mpl) fixed assets

immobilizzi (mpl) tecnici capital equipment

immutato unchanged

impaccare wrap up [goods]

impacchettare [imballare] pack (v) or parcel (v)

impacchettatore (m) packer

impadronirsi capture

impegni (mpl) commitments

impegno (m) [compito] undertaking or promise

impegno (m) [dovere] obligation or duty

imperfetto imperfect

imperfezione (f) imperfection

impianti (mpl) plant (n) or machinery

impianti (mpl) di magazzinaggio storage facilities

impianti (mpl) portuali harbour facilities

impianto (m) di magazzinaggio storage unit

impiegare [assumere] employ

impiegatizio [d'uffi-cio] clerical

impiegato employed

impiegato (m) clerk

impiegato (m) addetto al parti-tario delle vendite sales ledger clerk

impiegato (m) addetto alle infor-mazioni informa-tion officer

impiegato (m) alla biglietteria book-ing clerk

impiegato (m) di spedizioniere shipping clerk

impieghi (mpl) disponibili appoint-ments vacant

impiego (m) [lavoro] job or employment

impiego (m) [posto] position or post or job

impiego (m) a tempo pieno full-time employment

imporre impose

imporre [una tassa] levy (v) [a duty]

importante important

importanza (f) importance

importanza: avere importanza be im-portant or matter (v)

importanza: di scarsa importanza petty or minor

importare [merci] import (v)

importatore (m) importer

importatore, -trice importing (adj)

importazione (f) importation

importazioni (fpl) imports

importazioni (fpl) visibili visible imports

importazioni-esportazioni import-export (adj)

importo (m) [ammontare] amount [of money]

importo (m) aggiuntivo
premium *[on lease]*
importo (m) dovuto amount owing
importo (m) fisso flat rate
importo (m) forfettario lump sum
importo (m) maturato accrual
importo (m) pagato amount paid
importo (m) totale total amount
imposizione (f) enforcement
imposta (f) *[tassa]* tax (n) *or* duty
imposta (f) arretrata back tax
imposta (f) di bollo stamp duty
imposta (f) diretta direct tax
imposta (f) generale sugli acquisti purchase tax
imposta (f) indiretta excise duty

imposta (f) pagata tax paid
imposta (f) progressiva graded tax
imposta (f) progressiva sul reddito graduated income tax
imposta (f) sul reddito income tax
imposta (f) sul valore aggiunto (IVA) value added tax (VAT)
imposta (f) sul volume di affari sales tax *or* turnover tax
imposta (f) sulla società corporation tax
imposta (f) sulle plusvalenze capital gains tax
imposta (f) trattenuta alla fonte tax deducted at source
imposte (f) indirette indirect tax
imposte (f) progressive progressive taxation

imprenditore (m)
contractor; entre-
preneur
imprenditoriale
entrepreneurial
impresa (f) busi-
ness *or* company
impresa (f) di
trasporti [trasporta-
tore] carrier *or*
haulage contractor
impronta (f)
mark (n)
impulso (m) impulse
in acconto on
account
in aumento on the
increase *or* mounting
in buona fede
bona fide
in comune jointly
in concorrenza
competing (adj)
in contanti
cash (adv)
in media on an
average
in orario [puntuale]
on time
in ritardo [tardi]
late (adv)

in scala naturale
full-scale (adj)
in scala ridotta
small-scale (adj)
in vendita for sale
inabile [privo di
validità] invalid
inabilità (f) [inva-
lidità] invalidity
inadempiente (m)
defaulter
inadempienza (f)
default (n)
inadempienza (f)
nel pagamento
default on payments
inadempimento
(m) del contratto
breach of contract
incapace in
competent
incarico (m)
assignment [work]
incartamenti (mpl)
papers
incassabile cashable
incassare cash (v)
or encash
incassare un
assegno cash a
cheque

incassi (mpl)
takings *or* returns
incassi (mpl) netti
net receipts
incasso (m) take
(n) *[money received]*
incendio (m)
[fuoco] fire (n)
incentivo (m)
incentive
incidente (m) acci-
dent *or* crash (n)
**incidente (m) pro-
fessionale** occupa-
tional accident
includere count (v)
or include
incluso inclusive
incollare *[chiud-
ere]* seal (v) *[an
envelope]*
incondizionato
unconditional
incontrare meet
[someone]
incorporare merge
incorporato *[inser-
ito]* built-in
incorrere (in) incur
incrementativo
incremental

incremento (m)
increment
indagare inquire
indagine (f) *[anal-
isi]* investigation *or*
examination
indebitamento (m)
indebtedness
**indebitamento (m)
a breve** short-term
debts
indebitarsi get
into debt
indebitato indebted
indennità (f)
[indennizzo]
indemnification
**indennità (f) di
contingenza** cost-
of-living allowance
indennizzare *[risar-
cire]* indemnify;
make good *[a defect
or loss]*
indennizzo (m)
[indennità]
indemnification
indicare un prezzo
[quotare] quote
(v) *or* estimate
costs

indicare un profitto
show a profit
indicatore (m)
indicator
**indicatori (mpl)
economici** eco-
nomic indicators
indice (m) index (n)
**indice (m) dei
prezzi al consumo**
consumer price index
**Indice (m) dei
prezzi al dettaglio**
retail price index
**indice (m) dei
prezzi all'ingrosso**
wholesale price
index
**indice (m) del
costo della vita**
cost-of-living index
**indice (m) di cre-
scita** growth index
**indice (m) di rendi-
mento** rate of return
**indice (m) econom-
ico** index number
**indice (m) ponder-
ato** weighted index
indicizzato index-
linked

indicizzazione (f)
indexation *or*
index-linking
indipendente
independent
indiretto indirect
**indirizzare una let-
tera *o* un pacco**
address a letter *or* a
parcel
**indirizzo (m) *[re-
capito]*** address (n)
**indirizzo (m) cablo-
grafico** cable address
**indirizzo (m)
d'inoltro** forwarding
address
**indirizzo (m) d'uffi-
cio** business address
**indirizzo (m) del
mittente** return
address
**indirizzo (m) di
comodo** accommo-
dation address
**indirizzo (m)
personale** home
address
**indiscriminato *[uni-
forme]*** across-the-
board

indispensabile
essential
indossatrice (f)
model (n) *[person]*
industria (f) industry
industria (f) a
forte assorbimento
di capitali capital-
intensive industry
industria (f) che si
è sviluppata ra-
pidamente boom
industry
industria (f) chiave
key industry
industria (f) di base
staple industry
industria (f) pesante
heavy industry
industria (f) pri-
maria primary
industry
industria (f) secon-
daria secondary
industry
industria (f) statal-
izzata nationalized
industry
industria (f)
terziaria tertiary
industry

industriale industrial
industriale (m)
industrialist
industrializzare
industrialize
industrializzazione
(f) industrialization
inefficiente in
efficient
inefficienza (f)
inefficiency
inferiore *[più
basso]* lower (adj)
inferiore *[meno di]*
under *or* less than
inflazione (f)
inflation
inflazione (f) da
costi cost-push
inflation
inflazionistico
inflationary
influenza (f)
influence (n)
influenzare
influence (v)
informare *[avvisare]*
inform *or* advise
informazione (f)
riservata tip (n)
[advice]

informazioni (fpl) commerciali status inquiry

informazioni (fpl) di volo flight information

infortunio (m) sul lavoro industrial accident

infrangere infringe

infrangere un accordo break an agreement

infrastruttura (f) infrastructure

infrazione (f) fiscale tax offence

ingegnere (m) edile site engineer

ingiusto unfair

inglese *[britannico]* English or British

ingranaggio (m) gear

ingrosso: all'ingrosso wholesale (adv)

ininterrotto *[senza scalo]* non-stop

iniziale initial (adj) or starting or opening

iniziare *[cominciare]* begin or start (v) or initiate

iniziare un dibattito (m) initiate discussions

iniziativa (f) initiative

iniziativa (f) commerciale commercial undertaking

iniziativa (f) privata private enterprise

iniziativa (f) su scala ridotta small-scale enterprise

inizio (m) beginning

innovare innovate

innovativo innovative

innovatore (m) innovator

innovazione (f) innovation

inoltrare file (v) *[a request]*

inoltrare una domanda di brevetto file a patent application

inoltro (m)
forwarding
inondare flood (v)
inondazione (f)
flood (n)
inquilino (m) tenant
insegna (f) sign (n)
inseguire chase *or*
follow up
inserimento (m) in
un nuovo lavoro
induction
inserire insert *or*
put in
inserire in una lista
di proscrizione
blacklist (v)
inserito *[incorpo-*
rato] built-in
inserzione (m)
advertisement
inserzione: pubblicare
un'inserzione per un
impiego disponibile
advertise a vacancy
inserzioni (fpl)
[annunci economici
su giornale]
classified ads
inserzionista (m)
advertiser

insolvente insol-
vent
insolvenza (f)
insolvency
inspiegato unac-
counted for
insuccesso (m)
failure *or* flop
insuccesso (m)
commerciale com-
mercial failure
intangibile
intangible
integrazione (f)
orizzontale hori-
zontal integration
integrazione (f)
verticale vertical
integration
intendere propose
to *[do something]*
intensificare
escalate
intentare azione
legale take legal
action
intentare causa
[citare] sue
intentare causa
civile bring a civil
action

interdire *[vietare]*
ban (v)
interdizione (f)
ban (n)
interessare
interest (v)
interessarsi di con-
cern (v) *or* deal with
interesse (m)
interest (n)
interesse (m) alto
high interest
**interesse (m) com-
posto** cumulative
interest
**interesse (m) com-
posto** compound
interest
interesse (m) fisso
fixed interest
**interesse (m)
maturato** accrued
interest
**interesse (m)
semplice** simple
interest
**interessi (mpl)
costituiti** vested
interest
interfaccia (f)
interface (n)

intermediario (m)
intermediary *or*
intermediary
internazionale
international
interno internal *or*
in-house
interno (m) tele-
phone extension
**interno (del terri-
torio nazionale)**
inland
intero (pieno) full
interpretare
interpret
interprete (mf)
interpreter
interrompere
discontinue
**intervallo (m) *[fra
ordinazione e con-
segna]*** lead time
**intervista (f) *[col-
loquio]*** inter
view (n)
intervistare
interview (v)
intervistato (m)
interviewee
intervistatore (m)
interviewer

intesa (f)
understanding
intesa (f) *[accordo]*
arrangement *or*
understanding *or*
compromise
intraprendente go-
ahead (adj)
intraprendere
undertake
introdurre introduce
introdurre gradual-
mente phase in
introduzione (m)
introduction *or*
bringing into use
invalidare *[annullare]*
invalidate *or* void (v)
invalidità (f)
[inabilità] invalidity
invecchiamento
(m) obsolescence
invenduto unsold
inventariare *[fare*
l'inventario] take
stock *or* inventory (v)
inventario (m)
stocklist; inventory
inventario (m)
[stock] stock *or*
[US] inventory

inventario (m)
stocktaking
inventario: fare
l'inventario inven-
tory (v) *or* take
stock
inversione (f)
reversal
inversione (f) di
tendenza turn-
round *[making*
profitable]
inverso reverse
(adj)
invertire
reverse (v)
investigare
investigate
investimenti (mpl)
ad interessi fissi
fixed-interest
investments
investimenti (mpl)
esteri foreign
investments
investimenti (mpl)
in titoli di prim'or-
dine blue-chip
investments
investimento (m)
investment

**investimento (m)
garantito** secure
investment
**investimento (m)
privo di rischio**
risk-free investment
**investimento (m)
sicuro** safe
investment
investire invest
investire capitali
invest in *or* lock up
capital
investito invested *or*
employed *[money]*
investitore (m)
investor
**investitori (mpl)
istituzionali** insti-
tutional investors
inviare send
inviare per fax
fax (v)
**inviare rimessa a
mezzo assegno**
remit by cheque
inviato (m) corre-
spondent *[journalist]*
invio (m) consign-
ment *[things sent,
received]*

**invio (m) *[per
posta]*** mailing
**invio (m) di riviste
per posta** magazine
mailing
invitare invite *or*
call *[on someone to
do something]*
invito (m) invitation
**involucro (m)
*[imballaggio]***
wrapping
ipermercato (m)
hypermarket
ipoteca (f)
mortgage (n)
ipotecare
mortgage (v)
irregolare irregular
irregolarità (fpl)
irregularities
irrevocabile
irrevocable
**iscrivere una
società** register a
company
iscriversi register
(v) *[in official list]*
iscrizione (f) mem-
bership *[being a
member]*

ispettivo [di super-visione] supervisory
ispettore (m) aziendale factory inspector
ispettore (m) delle tasse tax inspector
ispettore (m) IVA VAT inspector
ispezionare [esam-inare] survey (v) or inspect
ispezione (f) inspection
istantaneo [imme-diato] instant (adj) or immediate
istanza (f) [do-manda] application
istituire institute (v) or establish
istituto (m) institute (n)
istituto (m) di credito credit bank
istituto (m) di credito fondiario building society
istituto (m) finanziario financial institution

istituzionale institutional
istituzione (f) institution
istruire train (v) or teach
istruzione (f) instruction
istruzioni (fpl) per l'uso directions for use
istruzioni (fpl) per la spedizione shipping instructions or forwarding instructions
itinerario (m) itinerary
IVA (imposta sul valore aggiunto) VAT (= value added tax)

Jj Ll

joint venture (f)
*[associazione in
partecipazione]*
joint venture
junior *[giovane]*
junior (adj)
lanciare launch (v)
or bring out
**lanciare una soci-
età** float a company
lancio (m) launch
(n) *or* launching
**lancio (m) di una
società** flotation *or*
floating of a company
lasciar vuoto vacate
lasciare *[abban-
donare]* leave (v)
[resign]
lasciare *[partire]*
leave (v) *or* go away
**lasciare libera la
camera dell'albergo**
check out of hotel
lato (m) side
lato (m) dell'attivo
[avere] credit side

**laureato (m) che fa
tirocinio come diri-
gente** graduate
trainee
lavorare work (v)
lavorare al nero
moonlight (v)
**lavorare: che lavora
in proprio**
selfemployed
lavorare *[trattare]*
process (v) *[raw
materials]*
**lavoratore (m), lavo-
ratrice (f)** worker
**lavoratore (m) a
domicilio**
homeworker
**lavoratore (m) al
nero** moonlighter
**lavoratore (m) a
orario ridotto**
part-timer
**lavoratore (m) saltu-
ario** casual worker
**lavoratore che fa
parte del consiglio di
amministrazione e
che agisce come por-
tavoce del personale**
worker director

lavoratori (mpl) parzialmente quali-ficati semi-skilled workers

lavorazione (f) [fabbricazione] manufacture (n)

lavoro (m) labour; job *or* piece of work

lavoro (m) [impiego] position *or* job

lavoro (m) a contratto contract work

lavoro (m) a cont-ratto a termine temporary employment

lavoro (m) a cot-timo piecework

lavoro (m) a orario ridotto part-time work *or* part-time employment

lavoro (m) arretrato backlog

lavoro (m) ben pagato well-paid job

lavoro (m) con turni shift work

lavoro (m) d'ufficio clerical work

lavoro (m) di rou-tine routine work

lavoro (m) in corso work in progress

lavoro (m) man-uale manual work

lavoro (m) nero moonlighting

lavoro (m) saltu-ario casual work

lavoro (m) stabile secure job

lavoro (m) straor-dinario overtime

lavoro (m) urgente rush job

leasing (m) leasing

leasing (m) immo-biliare lease-back

legale legal *or* according to the law

legalizzare [auten-ticare] authenticate

legge (f) law *[rule]*

legge (f) del rendi-mento decrescente law of diminishing returns

legge (f) dell'offerta e della domanda law of supply and demand

leggibile dal computer computer-readable
legislazione (f) legislation
legittimazione (f) standing
legittimo lawful
lento slow
lento [stagnante] slack
lettera (f) letter
lettera: fare una lettera raccomandata register (v) [letter]
lettera (f) aerea air letter
lettera (f) circolare circular letter
lettera (f) circolare circular (n)
lettera (f) d'affari business letter
lettera (f) di accompagnamento covering letter
lettera (f) di assunzione letter of appointment
lettera (f) di credito letter of credit (L/C)

lettera (f) di credito circolare circular letter of credit
lettera (f) di credito irrevocabile irrevocable letter of credit
lettera (f) di intenti letter of intent
lettera (f) di presentazione letter of introduction
lettera (f) di reclamo letter of complaint
lettera (f) di referenze letter of reference
lettera (f) di sollecito follow-up letter
lettera (f) di vettura consignment note; waybill
lettera (f) espresso express letter
lettera (f) standard standard letter
leva (f) finanziaria leverage
levata (f) postal collection

libbra (f) [peso]
pound [weight:
0.45kg]
liberare free (v) or
release
liberarsi di qual-
cosa get rid of
something
libero free (adj)
libero profession-
ista (m) freelancer
libero scambio (m)
free trade
libretto (m) assegni
cheque book
libretto (m) di ver-
samento bank book
libro (m) book (n)
libro (m) cassa
cash book
libro (m) contabile
[registro] register
(n) or journal
libro (m) giornale
journal or
accounts book
libro (m) mastro
ledger
libro (m) mastro
degli acquisti
purchase ledger

libro (m) vendite
sales book
licenza (f) licence
licenza (f) d'es-
portazione export
licence or export
permit
licenza (f) di
importazione
import licence or
import permit
licenziamento (m)
dismissal
licenziamento (m)
ingiustificato
wrongful dismissal
licenziamento (m)
ingiusto unfair
dismissal
licenziare
discharge orsack or
dismiss [employees]
licenziare: essere
licenziato get
the sack
licitazione (f)
tendering
licitazione (f)
[offerta d'appalto]
tender (n) [offer
to work]

limitare limit (v) *or* restrict
limitare il credito restrict credit
limitato limited
limitazione (f) agli scambi commerciali restraint of trade
limite (m) limit (n)
limite (m) del pre-stito lending limit
limite (m) di cred-ito credit limit
limite (m) di peso weight limit
limite (m) massimo ceiling
linea (f) line (n)
linea: in linea on line *or* online
linea (f) aerea *[compagnia aerea]* airline
linea (f) di carico load line
linea (f) di naviga-zione shipping line
linea (f) di prodotti product line
linea (f) esterna outside line

linea (f) gerarchica line management
linea (f) telefonica telephone line
linguaggio (m) burocratico officialese
linguaggio (m) di computer computer language
linguaggio (m) di programmazione programming language
liquidare clear (v) *[stock]*
liquidare (pagare) una fattura settle *[an invoice]*
liquidare le ordi-nazioni inevase release dues
liquidatore (m) liquidator *or* official receiver
liquidazione (f) liquidation *or* winding up
liquidazione (f) coatta compulsory liquidation

liquidazione (f) volontaria voluntary liquidation

liquidità (f) liquid assets *or* liquidity

lira (f) lira *[currency used in Turkey]*

lira (f) sterlina pound sterling

lista (f) list (n)

lista (f) di indirizzi address list

lista (f) di selezione picking list

lista (f) nera black list (n)

lista (f) ristretta (di candidati) shortlist (n)

listino (m) *[catalogo]* list (n) *or* catalogue

listino (m) prezzi price list

litro (m) litre

livelli (mpl) salariali wage levels

livello (m) level (n)

livello: di livello inferiore low-level

livello (m) delle scorte stock level

livello (m) di organico manning levels

livello (m) di riordinazione reorder level

livello (m) massimo di produzione peak output

locale *[del luogo]* local

locali (mpl) premises

locali (mpl) d'azienda *o* locali commerciali business premises

locatore (m) landlord

locazione (f) tenancy *[period]*

logogramma (m) logo

lordo gross (adj)

lungaggine (f) burocratica red tape

lungo *[per molto tempo]* long

lungo: a lungo termine long-term

luogo (m) site *or* place

luogo: avere luogo
take place
**luogo (m) d'incon-
tro** meeting place
**luogo (m) di
ritrovo** venue

Mm

macchina (f)
machine; car
**macchina (f)
affrancatrice**
franking machine
**macchina (f) che ca-
mbia denaro in spic-
cioli** change machine
**macchinario (m)
pesante** heavy
machinery
macroeconomia (f)
macro-economics
**magazzinaggio (m)
[deposito]** ware-
housing or storage
(n) [in warehouse]

magazziniere (m)
warehouseman
magazzino (m)
warehouse (n);
stockroom or
storeroom; store
**magazzino (m) a
prezzi scontati**
discount store
**magazzino (m)
doganale** bonded
warehouse
**magazzino (m) frig-
orifero** cold store
maggioranza (f)
majority
maggiorazione (f)
premium or extra
charge
maggiore major
**magistrato (m)
[giudice]** magis-
trate or judge (n)
malinteso (m)
misunderstanding
malpagato
underpaid
**mancanza (f)
[assenza]** absence
**mancanza (f) di
fondi** lack of funds

mancare miss
mancare il bersaglio miss a target
mancata consegna (f) non-delivery
mancia (f) tip (n) [money]
mandare indietro [respingere] return (v) or send back
mandare un carico per mare send a shipment by sea
mandatario (m) proxy [person]
mandato (m) mandate; writ
mandato (m) di pagamento [vaglia] money order
maneggevole [pratico] handy
maneggio (m) [gestione] handling
manifatturiero manufacturing
manifesto (m) manifest
manodopera (f) manpower

manodopera (f) qualificata skilled labour
manodopera (m) a basso prezzo cheap labour
manodopera (m) locale local labour
manovale (m) manual worker
mantenere maintain [keep at same level]
mantenere una promessa keep a promise
mantenimento (m) maintenance
mantenimento (m) delle provvigioni maintenance of supplies
mantenimento (m) di contatti maintenance of contacts
manuale manual (adj)
manuale (m) manual (n)
manuale (m) di manutenzione service manual

manuale (m) operativo operating manual

manufatti (mpl) manufactured goods

manutenzione (f) [revisione] maintenance *or* service (n) *[of machine]*

marca (f) [nome del prodotto] brand name

marca (f) [marchio] brand

marchio (m) trademark *or* trade name *or* brand

marchio (m) di fabbrica depositato registered trademark

marchio (m) di qualità quality label

marcia (f) [funzionamento] running (n) *[of machine]*

marginale marginal

margine (m) margin *[profit]*

margine (m) di errore margin of error

margine (m) di utile profit margin

margine (m) lordo gross margin

margine (m) netto net margin

marina (f) mercantile merchant navy

marittimo marine *or* maritime

marketing (m) marketing

marketing (m) di massa mass marketing

mass-media (m) [mezzi di comunicazione di massa] mass media

massa (f) mass

massimale (m) di credito credit ceiling

massimizzare maximize

massimizzazione (f) maximization

massimo maximum (adj)

massimo (m) maximum (n)

master (m) in gestione d'impresa Master's degree in Business Administration (MBA)

mastro (m) dei conti dei creditori bought ledger

mastro (m) nominale nominal ledger

materiale (m) d'imballaggio packaging material

materiale (m) da esposizione display material

materiale (m) di recupero salvage (n) or things saved

materiale (m) illustrativo delle vendite sales literature

materiale (m) per punto di vendita point of sale material (POS material)

materiale (m) pubblicitario con buono coupon ad

materie (fpl) prime raw materials

matrice (f) counterfoil

matrice (f) dell'assegno cheque stub

maturare [accumularsi] accrue

maturazione (f) degli interessi accrual of interest

media (f) average (n) or mean (n)

media: in media on an average

media (f) ponderata weighted average

mediare mediate

mediatore (m) mediator or troubleshooter

mediatore (m) assicurativo insurance broker

mediazione (f) mediation

mediazione (f) di cambio stockbroking

medio average (adj) or medium

medio: a medio termine medium-term

meglio: il meglio
best (n)
memorandum (m)
memorandum or
memo
**memoria (f) del
computer** computer
memory
meno [negativo]
minus
meno di [inferiore]
under or less than
meno: a meno di
short of
mensile
monthly (adj)
mensilmente
monthly (adv)
mercanteggiare
haggle
mercante (m)
merchant
**mercati (mpl)
esteri** overseas
markets
**mercati (mpl) mon-
etari** money markets
mercato (m)
market (n)
**mercato (m) a ter-
mine** forward market

**mercato (m) al
rialzo** bull market
**mercato (m) al rib-
asso** buyer's market
**mercato (m) azio-
nario** stock market
mercato (m) chiuso
closed market
**mercato (m) con-
trollato da un solo
fornitore** captive
market
**mercato (m) dei
cambi** foreign
exchange market
**mercato (m) delle
materie prime**
commodity market
**mercato (m)
favorevole ai vendi-
tori** seller's market
mercato (m) fiacco
weak market
mercato (m) interno
domestic market
mercato (m) libero
open market
**mercato (m) limi-
tato** limited market
**mercato (m) mon-
diale** world market

mercato (m) nazionale home market
mercato (m) nero black market
mercato (m) potenziale potential market
mercato (m) prescelto target market
Mercat (m) Europeo Unico Single European Market
merce (f) merchandise (n) *or* goods
merce (f) a prezzo ridotto cut-price goods
merce (f) con dazio pagato duty-paid goods
merce (f) danneggiata da incendio fire-damaged goods
merce (f) in transito goods in transit
merce (f) non venduta returns *or* unsold goods
merce (f) per la vendita al dettaglio retail goods

merchant bank (f) *[banca mercantile]* merchant bank
merci (fpl) deperibili perishable goods
merci (fpl) vendute sottocosto distress merchandise
merito (n) merit
mese (m) month
mese (m) solare calendar month
messaggero (m) *[corriere]* courier *or* messenger
messaggio (m) message
metà (f) half (n)
metà settimana (f) mid-week
metodo (m) LIFO (ultimo a entrare, primo a uscire) LIFO (= last in first out)
metodo (m) per tentativi trial and error
mettere put (v) *or* place
mettere *[posare]* place (v)

mettere a verbale
[verbalizzare]
minute (v)
mettere al corrente
[aggiornare]
update (v)
mettere da parte
denaro save up
mettere francobolli
[affrancare] stamp
(v) *[a letter]*
mettere in liquida-
zione scorte di
magazzino liqui-
date stock
mettere in liq-
uidazione una soci-
età liquidate *or*
wind up *[a company]*
mettere in ordine
put in a certain order
mettere in serbo
store (v) *[keep for
future]*
mettere in vendita
release (v) *or* put on
the market
mettere insieme
batch (v)
mettere insieme le
risorse pool resources

mettere l'embargo
su embargo (v)
mettere per iscritto
put in writing
mettersi in affari
go into business *or*
set up in business
mettersi in contatto
con contact (v)
mezza dozzina (f)
half a dozen *or* a
half-dozen
mezzi (mpl) means
[money]
mezzi (mpl) *[stru-
menti]* means *[ways]*
mezzi (mpl) di
comunicazione di
massa mass media
mezzo half (adj)
mezzo (m)
medium (n)
microeconomia (f)
micro-economics
microelaboratore
(m) microcomputer
miglior offerente
(m) successful
bidder
miglioramento (m)
upturn

migliore best (adj)
migliore *[piu alto]*
top (adj)
migliore offerente
(m) highest bidder
miliardario (m)
millionaire
miliardo
billion *[US]*
milione (m) million
millantato credito
(m) false
pretences
minimo minimum
(adj)
minimo (m)
minimum (n)
ministero (m) min-
istry *or* government
department
Ministero del
Tesoro Treasury
ministro (m) gov-
ernment minister *or*
secretary
minoranza (f)
minority
minuto (m) minute
(n) *[time]*
miscellaneo *[vario]*
miscellaneous

missione (f) com-
merciale trade
mission
misto mixed
misura (f) della red-
ditività measure-
ment of profitability
misura (f) standard
stock size
misure (fpl) meas-
urements
misure (fpl) cubiche
cubic measure
misure (fpl) di
sicurezza safety
measures *or* safety
precautions
mittente (m)
sender *or* consignor
mobilità (f) mobility
mobilizzare mobilize
mobilizzare capitali
mobilize capital
modalità (fpl) di
pagamento mode
of payment
modello (m)
model (n)
modello (m) eco-
nomico economic
model

modello (m) in scala scale model *or* mock-up
modem (m) modem
moderare moderate (v)
moderato moderate (adj)
moderno [attuale] modern *or* up to date
modifica (f) [cambiamento] alteration
modificare [cambiare] alter
modo (m) mode
moduli (mpl) a striscia continua continuous stationery
modulo (m) form (n)
modulo (m) d'iscrizione registration form
modulo (m) delle tasse tax form
modulo (m) di dichiarazione doganale customs declaration form
modulo (m) per domanda di assunzione application form

molo (m) quay *or* wharf
moltiplicare multiply
moltiplicazione (f) multiplication
molto bene fine (adv) *or* very good
mondiale world-wide (adj)
mondo (m) world
mondo: in tutto il mondo world wide (adv)
moneta (f) (metallica) coin
moneta (f) a corso legale legal tender
moneta (f) inflazionata inflated currency
moneta (f) legale legal currency
moneta (f) spicciola small change
moneta (f) stabile stable currency
moneta (f) straniera foreign currency
monetario monetary

monitor (m) monitor (n) *or* screen
monopolio (m) monopoly
monopolio perfetto (m) absolute monopoly
monopolizzare monopolize
monopolizzazione (f) monopolization
montacarichi (m) goods elevator
montaggio (m) [assemblaggio] assembly *[putting together]*
montatura (f) giornalistica hype (n)
moratoria (f) moratorium
morto dead (adj) *[person]*
mostra (f) [esposizione] exhibition *or* display
mostrare show (v)
motivato motivated
motivazione (f) motivation

movimentazione (f) dei materiali materials handling
movimenti (m) di capitali movements of capital
movimento (m) movement *or* turnover *[of stock]*
multa (f) (penale) fine *or* penalty
multare fine (v)
multilaterale multilateral
multinazionale (f) multinational (n)
multiplo multiple (adj)
mutuare borrow; lend
mutuatario (m) borrower
mutuo (m) borrowing
mutuo (m) [prestito] loan (n)
mutuo (m) a breve scadenza short-term loan
mutuo (m) a lunga scadenza long-term loan

mutuo (m) garan-
tito secured loan
mutuo (reciproco)
mutual (adj) or
reciprocal

Nn

nastro (m) mag-
netico magnetic
tape or mag tape
navale (marittimo)
maritime
nave (f) ship (n)
nave (f) da carico
cargo ship or
freighter
nave (f) di sal-
vataggio salvage
vessel
nave (f) gemella
sister ship
nave (f) mercantile
merchant ship
or merchant
vessel

nave (f) per tras-
porto di container
container ship
nazionale national
nazionale: di
dimensioni nazion-
ali nationwide
nazionalizzazione
(f) nationalization
nazione (f) [paese]
country [state]
nazione (f) più
favorita most-
favoured nation
necessario necessary
negativo (meno)
minus
negligente
negligent
negligenza (f)
negligence
negoziabile
negotiable
negoziante (m)
shopkeeper
negoziare negotiate
negoziare [commer-
ciare] deal in (v)
negoziato (m)
[negoziazione]
negotiation

**negoziato (m)
salariale** wage
negotiations
negoziatore (m)
negotiator
**negoziazione (f)
[negoziato]**
negotiation
negozio (m) shop
or store
**negozio (m) appar-
tenente a una cat-
ena** multiple store
**negozio (m) che fa
parte di una catena**
chain store
**negozio (m) con
merce a prezzi
ridotti** cut-price
store
**negozio (m) d'an-
golo** corner shop
**negozio (m) di ven-
dita a prezzi ridotti**
discount store
**negozio (m) esente
da tasse** duty-free
shop
**negozio (m) per
articoli da regalo**
gift shop

netto net (adj)
nicchia (f) niche
**nodo (m) della
questione** bottom
line
noleggiare
charter (v)
**noleggiare un
aeroplano** charter
an aircraft
**noleggiare un'auto-
mobile** hire a car
**noleggiatore (m)
(di navi, aerei)**
charterer
noleggio (m) char-
tering *or* charter (n)
**noleggio (m) in
blocco** block
booking
nome (m) name
nome: a nome di
on behalf of
**nome (m) del
prodotto [marca]**
brand name
nomina (f) appoint-
ment *[to a job]*
**nomina (f) del
personale** staff
appointment

nomina (f) di amministratratore giudiziario letters of administration
nominare appoint
non datato undated
non disponibile unavailable
non disponibilità (f) unavailability
non pagato outstanding *or* unpaid
non specializzato unskilled
non ufficiale [ufficioso] unofficial
non verificato unaudited
norma (f) standard (n) *or* rule (n) *or* norm
normale [regolare] regular *or* ordinary
normale usura e degrado fair wear and tear
norme (fpl) antincendio fire regulations
norme (fpl) di sicurezza safety regulations
nota (f) note (n)

nota (f) di accredito credit note
nota (f) di addebito debit note
notaio (m) notary public
notare note (v) *or* mark (v) *[details]*
notificare notify
notificazione (f) notification
notte (f) night
nulla (m) [zero] nil
nullo null *or* void *or* not valid
numerare number (v)
numeri (mpl) [cifre] figures
numeri (m) dispari odd numbers
numerico numeric *or* numerical
numero (m) number (n) *or* figure
numero (m) dell'assegno cheque number
numero (m) di conto corrente di corrispondenza giro account number

numero (m) di fattura invoice number
numero (m) di matricola registration number
numero (m) di partita batch number
numero (m) di riferimento reference number
numero (m) di serie serial number
numero (m) di telefono phone number
numero (m) minimo legale quorum
numero (m) telefonico telephone number *or* phone number
nuova domanda (f) reapplication
nuova ordinazione (f) reorder (n)
nuovo accertamento (m) reassessment
nuovo di zecca brand new
nuovo orientamento (m) departure *[new venture]*

Oo

obbligatorio compulsory
obbligazione (f) bond *[borrowing by government]*
obbligazione (f) *[di società private]* debenture
obbligazione (f) al portatore bearer bond
obbligazione (f) irredimibile irredeemable bond
obbligazione (f) redimibile callable bond
obbligazioni (fpl) 'cartastraccia' junk bonds
obbligazioni (fpl) convertibii convertible loan stock
obbligazionista (m) debenture holder
obbligo (m) liability

obiettivi (mpl) di produzione production targets

obiettivo (m) objective (n) *or* target (n)

obiettivo (m) di rilevamento takeover target

obiettivo (m) di vendita sales target

obiettivo [oggettivo] objective (adj)

obsolescente obsolescent

occasione (f) [affare] bargain (n) *[cheaper than usual]*

occultamento (m) di beni concealment of assets

occupante (m) occupant

occupare occupy

occupare: chi occupa occupant

occuparsi di attend to *or* handle (v) *or* deal with

occupato busy; engaged *[telephone]*

occupazionale [professionale] occupational

occupazione (f) occupancy

offerente (m) tenderer; bidder

offerta (f) offer (n); bid

offerta (f) d'apertura opening bid

offerta (f) d'appalto tender (n) *[offer to work]*

offerta (f) d'occasione bargain offer

offerta (f) di propaganda introductory offer

offerta (f) di vendita offer for sale

offerta (f) e domanda supply and demand

offerta (f) in busta chiusa sealed tenders

offerta (f) per contanti cash offer

offerta (f) premio premium offer

offerta (f) pubblica d'acquisto takeover bid

offerta (f) reale cash offer

offerta (f) speciale special offer

offerte (fpl) d'impiego situations vacant

officina (f) workshop

offrire [proporre] offer (v) [to buy]

offrire [presentare] present (v) or give

offshore [all'estero] offshore

olio (m) edible oil or cooking oil

omaggio (m) [dono] free gift

omaggio: in omaggio complimentary

omesso pagamento (m) di un debito non-payment [of a debt]

omettere [trascurare] omit

omissione (f) omission

onorare honour (v)

non onorare dishonour

non onorare un effetto dishonour a bill

onorare una cambiale honour a bill

onorare una firma honour a signature

onorario (m) honorarium

operativo operational or operative (adj)

operatore (m) operator or operative (n)

operatore (m) in cambi foreign exchange dealer

operatore (m) su tastiera keyboarder

operazione (f) operation

operazione (f) [affare] deal (n)

operazione (f) a denominazione valutaria multipla multi-currency operation

operazione (f) chiavi in mano
turnkey operation
operazione (f) disonesta fraudulent transaction
operazioni (fpl)
[transazioni] dealing
opinione (f) pubblica public opinion
opportunità (f)
opportunity
opuscoli (mpl) pubblicitari junk mail
opzione (f) d'acquisto call (n)
[stock exchange]
opzione (f) per l'acquisto option to purchase
ora (f) hour
ora (f) di accettazione
check-in time
ora (f) di chiusura
closing time
ora (f) di punta
rush hour
ora (f) lavorativa
man-hour
orario hourly

orario (m)
timetable (n)
[trains, etc.]
orario: in orario
[puntuale] on time
orario (m) d'apertura opening hours
orario (m) d'ufficio
office hours
orario (m) di banca
banking hours
orario (m) pieno
full-time
orario (m) ridotto
part-time
ordinare order (v)
[goods]
ordinaria amministrazione (f)
routine (n)
ordinario ordinary
ordinato on order
ordinazione (f)
order (n) *[for goods]*
ordinazioni (fpl) inevase back orders *or* dues *or* unfulfilled orders
ordinazione (f) rinnovata repeat order

**ordinazione (f)
urgente** rush order
**ordinazioni (fpl) da
evadere** outstand-
ing orders
**ordinazioni (fpl)
per corrispondenza**
mail-order
ordine (m) order (n)
**ordine (m) alfa-
betico** alphabetical
order
ordine (m) bancario
banker's order
**ordine (m) crono-
logico** chronologi-
cal order
**ordine (m) d'ac-
quisto** purchase
order
**ordine (m) del
giorno** agenda
**ordine (m) di con-
segna** delivery order
**ordine (m) di paga-
mento di valuta
estera** foreign
money order
**ordine (m) perma-
nente** standing
order

ore (fpl) d'ufficio
business hours
organico (m)
manning
organigramma (m)
organization chart
organizzare organ-
ize *or* arrange *or* plan
organizzativo orga-
nizational
organizzazione (f)
organization
**Organizzazione (f)
dei paesi** esporta-
tori di petrolio
Organization of
Petroleum Exporting
Countries (OPEC)
**organizzazione (f) e
metodo (m)** organi-
zation and methods
**organizzazione (f)
gerarchica** line
organization
**Organizzazione (f)
Internazionale del
Lavoro (OIL)**
International Labour
Organization (ILO)
originale (m)
original (n)

originario
original (adj)
origine (f) origin
ormeggiare
berth (v)
ormeggio (m)
berth (n)
oro (m) in verghe
gold bullion
oscillare *[fluttuare]*
fluctuate
osservare *[confor-marsi]* comply with
ottenere obtain *or*
gain *or* get
ottenere la liber-azione (su cau-zione) di qualcuno
bail someone out
ottenibile *[con-seguibile]*
obtainable
ottenibile: non
ottenibile
unobtainable
output (m) *[dati di emissione]*
computer output

Pp

pacchetto (m)
packet
pacchetto (m)
[azionistico] block
(n) *[of shares]*
pacchetto (m) di
buste pack of
envelopes
pacchetto (m) di
sigarette packet of
cigarettes
pacchetto (m)
rivendicativo
package deal
pacco (m) package
or pack *or* parcel
paese (m) *[nazione]*
country *[state]*
paese (m) d'origine
country of origin
paese (m) in via di
sviluppo deve-loping country
paesi (mpl)
esportatori di
petrolio oil-exporting countries

**paesi (mpl) indus-
trializzati** industri-
alized societies
**paesi (mpl) produt-
tori di petrolio** oil-
producing countries
**paesi (mpl) sot-
tosviluppati** under-
developed countries
**paesi (mpl)
stranieri** *[l'estero]*
overseas (n)
paga (f) *[salario]*
pay (n) *[salary]*
pagabile payable
**pagabile a sessanta
giorni** payable at
sixty days
**pagabile alla con-
segna** payable on
delivery
**pagabile antici-
patamente** payable
in advance
pagabile su richiesta
payable on demand
**pagamenti (mpl)
ipotecari** mortgage
payments
**pagamenti (mpl)
mensili** monthly
payments

**pagamenti (mpl)
scaglionati** staged
payments
pagamento (m)
payment *or*
settlement
pagamento (m)
[esborso] dis
bursement
**pagamento (m) a
carico del desti-
natario** charges
forward
**pagamento (m) a
saldo *o* totale** full
payment
**pagamento (m)
alla consegna** cash
on delivery (c.o.d.)
**pagamento (m)
annuale** yearly
payment
**pagamento (m)
anticipato** advance
payment *or*
prepayment
**pagamento (m)
degli arretrati** back
payment
**pagamento (m) di
un debito** discharge
(n) *[of debt]*

pagamento (m) dif-ferito deferred payment

pagamento (m) in acconto payment on account

pagamento (m) in base al lavoro effettuato payment by results

pagamento (m) in contanti payment in cash *or* cash payment; prompt payment

pagamento (m) in natura payment in kind

pagamento (m) in più overpayment

pagamento (m) minimo minimum payment

pagamento (m) parziale partial payment

pagamento (m) progressivo progress payments

pagamento (m) provvisiorio interim payment

pagamento (m) semestrale half-yearly payment

pagamento (m) simbolico token payment

pagamento (m) tramite assegno payment by cheque

pagare [remunerare] pay (v) [worker]

pagare [saldare] pay (v) [bill]

pagare: far pagare charge someone

pagare: far pagare meno under charge (v)

pagare: far pagare troppo overcharge (v)

pagare a rate pay in instalments

pagare anticipata-mente pay in advance

pagare con carta di credito pay by credit card

pagare con un assegno pay by cheque

pagare gli interessi
pay interest
pagare in anticipo
prepay
pagare in contanti
pay cash
pagare un conto
pay a bill
pagare un debito
service a debt
pagare un dividendo
pay a dividend
pagare una fattura
pay or settle an
invoice
pagato paid [invoice]
pagato *[remuner-*
ato] paid [for work]
pagato: non pagato
outstanding or
unpaid
pagato in anticipo
prepaid
pagatore (m) tar-
divo slow payer
pagherò (m) prom-
issory note or IOU
pagherò (m) cam-
biario note of hand
Pagine Gialle (fpl)
yellow pages

palazzo (m) block
(n) or large building
paletta (f) pallet
palettizzare
[trasportare a mezzo
di palette] palletize
pannello (m) panel
paragonabile com-
parable
paragonabile:
essere paragonabile
compare with
paragonare *[con-*
frontare] compare
pareggiare un
budget balance (v)
[a budget]
pari par
parità (f) parity
parte (f) part (n)
parte (f) *[leg]*
party
parte (f) contraente
contracting party
parte (f) quere-
lante prosecution
[party in legal
action]
parte (f) superiore
top (n) or upper
surface

parte (f) venditrice [cedente] assignor

partecipazione (f) investment or interest (n)

partecipazione (f) azionaria share-holding

partenza (f) departure or going away

partenze (fpl) departures

partire (lasciare) leave (v) or go away

partita (f) (di merci) batch or lot [of items]

partitario (m) delle vendite sales ledger

partite (fpl) varie sundry items

partite (fpl) visibili visible trade

partner (m) commerciale trading partner

parziale one-sided

passare a switch over to

passare il tempo a spend [time]

passibile di liable to

passività (fpl) liabilities

passività (fpl) a lungo termine long-term liabilities

passività (fpl) correnti current liabilities

passivo (m) patrimoniale equity

patto: a patto che provided that or providing

pausa (f) break (n)

pavimento (m) floor [surface]

pedaggio (m) toll

penale (f) penalty

penalità (f) [multa] forfeit (n)

penalizzare penalize

pendente pending

pendolare (m) commuter

pendolare: fare il pendolare commute [travel]

penetrazione (f) di mercato market penetration

pensionamento (m)
retirement
pensione (f) pension
per affari on
business
per cento per cent
per conto di on
behalf of
per persona per head
percentuale (f)
percentage
percentuale (f)
d'errore error rate
percentuale (f) di
crescita growth rate
percentuale (f) di
occupazione
occupancy rate
percentuale (f) per
il servizio service
charge
percorso (m) run
(n) *or* regular route
perdere miss
[train, plane]
perdere *[un diritto]*
forfeit (v) *[a right]*
perdere denaro
lose money
perdere un depos-
ito forfeit a deposit

perdere un'ordina-
zione lose an
order
perdita (f) loss
perdita (f) *[di un*
diritto] forfeiture
[of a right]
perdita (f) d'eser-
cizio trading loss
perdita (f) di capi-
tale capital loss
perdita (f) di clien-
tela loss of
customers
perdita (f) di un'or-
dinazione loss of
an order
perdita (f) netta
net loss
perdita (f) parziale
partial loss
perdita (f) secca
dead loss
perdita (f) sulla
carta paper loss
perdite (fpl) record
record losses
perenzione (f)
time limitation
perfetta sintonia
(f) fine tuning

periferiche (fpl) peripherals

periodico periodic *or* periodical (adj)

periodico (m) *[rivista]* journal *or* magazine

periodico *[stagionale]* seasonal

periodo (m) period *or* term

periodo (m) *[stagione]* season *[time for something]*

periodo (m) di avviamento make-ready time

periodo (m) di massima attività peak period

periodo (m) di preavviso period of notice

periodo (m) di prova trial period

periodo (m) di recupero payback period

periodo (m) di validità period of validity

periodo (m) medio di permanenza di un prodotto shelf life of a product

perito (m) surveyor

perizia (f) d'avaria damage survey

permanenza (f) stay (n) *[time]*

permesso (m) permit (n)

permesso (m) di lavoro work permit

permesso (m) di soggiorno residence permit

permettere allow *or* permit

permuta (f) come pagamento parziale part exchange; trade-in

perseguire *[legalmente]* prosecute

persona (f) addetta al controllo delle scorte stock controller

persona (f) che prende decisioni decision maker

**persona (f) che
risolve problemi**
problem solver
**personal computer
(m) [elaboratore]**
personal com
puter (PC)
personale personal
personale (m) staff
(n) *or* personnel
**personale (m)
addetto alle vendite
[forza vendita]** sales
force *or* sales team
**personale (m) al
banco** counter staff
**personale (m)
alberghiero**
hotel staff
**personale (m)
avventizio**
temporary staff
**personale (m) d'uf-
ficio** office staff
**personale (m) di
ruolo** regular staff
**personale (m) diri-
gente** managerial
staff
**personale (m) impie-
gatizio** clerical staff

personale-chiave
key personnel *or* key
staff
personalizzato
personalized
pesa a ponte (f)
weighbridge
pesante heavy
[weight]
pesare weigh
peso (m) weight
peso (m) lordo
gross weight
peso (m) morto
deadweight
peso (m) netto net
weight
petroliera (f) tanker
petrolio (m) oil *or*
petroleum
**pezza (f) giusti-
ficativa di cassa**
cash voucher
pezzo (m) piece
**pezzo (m) di ricam-
bio** spare part
**pianificare
investimenti** plan
investments
pianificatore (m)
planner

pianificazione (f)
planning
**pianificazione (f) a
lunga scadenza**
long-term planning
**pianificazione (f)
strategica** strategic
planning
**piano (m) [di
edificio]** floor
**piano (m) [prog-
etto]** plan (n) or
project
piano (m) continuo
rolling plan
**piano (m) di
contingenza**
contingency plan
piano (m) globale
overall plan
piano (m) pensioni
pension scheme
piano [livello] level
pianta (f) plan (n)
or drawing
piatto flat or dull
**piazza (f) del mer-
cato** marketplace
[in town]
piccola cassa (f)
petty cash

**piccole imprese
(fpl)** small
businesses
piccole spese (fpl)
petty expenses
**piccoli annunci
(mpl)** small ads
piccolo small
**piccolo affarista
ouomo d'affari**
small businessman
pieno [intero] full
**pieno scarico (m)
di un debito** full
discharge of a debt
**PIL (prodotto
interno lordo)**
gross domestic
product (GDP)
pilota pilot (adj)
pilota (m) pilot (n)
[person]
pioniere (m) pio-
neer (n)
**pioniere: fare da
pioniere in**
pioneer (v)
più alto [migliore]
top (adj)
**più basso [inferi-
ore]** lower (adj)

planimetria (f)
floor plan
plusvalenza (f)
capital gains
PNL (prodotto
nazionale lordo)
gross national
product (GNP)
politica (f) policy
[way of working]
politica (f) credi-
tizia credit policy
politica (f) dei pre-
zzi flessibile flexible pricing policy
politica (f) della
determinazione dei
prezzi pricing policy
politica (f) di
budget budgetary
policy
polizza (f) policy
[insurance]
polizza (f) contro
tutti i rischi
all-risks policy
polizza (f) di assi-
curazione
insurance policy
polizza (f) di carico
bill of lading

polizza (f) provvi-
soria covering note
ponderazione (f)
weighting
popolare popular
porta (f) door
porta (f) di com-
puter computer port
portafoglio (m)
portfolio *or* share-
holding
portare bring *or*
bear *or* carry
portare [trasportare]
carry *or* transport
portare qualcuno in
tribunale take
someone to court
portata (f) lorda
deadweight tonnage
portatile portable
portatore (m), por-
tatrice (f) bearer
portfolio (m)
[cartella] portfolio
portiere (m)
reception clerk
portineria (f)
reception (desk)
porto (m) port *or*
harbour

**porto (m) asseg-
nato** carriage for-
ward *or* freight
forward
**porto (m) d'arma-
mento** port of
registry
**porto (m) d'im-
barco** port of
embarkation
porto (m) di scalo
port of call
**porto (m) di tran-
sito** entrepot port
porto (m) franco
free port
porto (m) pagato
carriage paid *or*
postage paid
posare (mettere)
place (v) *or* put
positivo positive
**posizione (f) [collo-
cazione]** situation
or place
**posizione (f) [situ-
azione]** position
[state of affairs]
**posizione (f)
finanziaria** finan-
cial position

posporre hold over
possedere possess
or own (v)
**possibile
acquirente (m)**
prospective buyer
possibilità (f)
possibility
**possibilità (fpl) di
mercato** market
opportunities
possibile possible
**possibile: se non è
possibile**
failing that
posta (f) post (n)
or mail (n)
posta (f) aerea
airmail (n)
**posta (f) elettron-
ica** electronic
mail *or* e-mail
posta (f) in arrivo
incoming mail
**posta (f) in part-
enza** outgoing mail
posta (f) ordinaria
surface mail
postale postal
postdatare
postdate

posticipare put back *[till later]*

posto (m) *[impiego]* place (n) *or* position *or* job

posto (m) *[luogo]* spot *or* place

posto (m) chiave key post

posto (m) di lavoro place of work; computer workstation

posto (m) vacante job vacancy

potenziale potential (adj)

potenziale (m) potential (n)

potere (m) *[controllo]* power *or* control (n)

potere (m) contrattuale bargaining power

potere (m) d'acquisto purchasing power; spending power

potere (m) per ricorrere al prestito borrowing power

pranzo (m) d'affari business lunch

pratica (f) *[dossier]* dossier

pratica (f) spregiudicata sharp practice

pratiche (fpl) restrittive restrictive practices

pratica: fare pratica train (v) *[learn]*

pratico *[maneggevole]* practical *or* handy

preavviso (m) notice *[time allowed]*

precedente previous *or* prior

precisare *[dichiarare]* state (v)

preciso *[accurato]* precise *or* accurate

preconfezionare prepack *or* prepackage

predere parte in enter into *[discussion]*

preferenza (f) preference

preferenziale preferential
preferire prefer
prefinanziamento (m) pre-financing
prefisso (m) telefonico dialling code
prelevare withdraw *[money]*
prelievo (m) sulle importazioni import levy
premio (m) *[gratifica]* bonus
premio (m) addizionale additional premium
premio (m) agli assicurati che non hanno denunciato sinistri no-claims bonus
premio (m) d'operosità incentive payments
premio (m) di assicurazione insurance premium
premio (m) di merito merit award *or* merit bonus

premio (m) di produttività productivity bonus
premio (m) di rinnovo renewal premium
premio (m) di rischio risk premium
premio (m) finale terminal bonus
prendere a prestito *[mutuare]* borrow
prendere in affitto rent (v) *[pay money for]*
prendere in consegna un carico di merce accept delivery of a shipment
prendere l'iniziativa take the initiative
prendere nota take note
prendere un carico (m) a bordo take on freight
prendere una telefonata take a call
prendersi giorni di ferie take time off work

prenotare book (v)
**prenotare una cam-
era oun tavolo oun
posto** reserve a room
or a table or a seat
**prenotazione (f)
[registrazione]** book-
ing or reservation
**prenotazione antic-
ipata (f)** advance
booking
**prenotazioni (fpl)
di camera** room
reservations
preoccupazione (f)
concern (n) or worry
**preparare lo schema
di un contratto**
draft a contract
**preparazione (f) del
budget** budgeting
prescrizione (f)
statute of limitations
presentare pres-
ent (v) [show a
document]
**presentare [un
modello]** model (v)
[clothes]
**presentare [intro-
durre]** introduce

presentare [offrire]
present (v) or give
[a gift]
**presentare (pro-
durre)** produce (v)
or bring out
presentare un conto
render an account
**presentare un
effetto (m) per il
pagamento** present
a bill for payment
**presentare un eff-
etto (m) per l'ac-
cettazione** present
a bill for acceptance
**presentare una
controrichiesta**
counter-claim (v)
presentarsi report
(v) [go to a place]
**presentarsi al
check in** check in
[at airport]
**presentarsi per
un colloquio di
lavoro** report for an
interview
presentazione (f)
production or
presentation

presentazione (f) in cofanetto boxed set
presente present (adj) *[being there]*
presidente (m) chairman
presidente e amministratore delegato chairman and managing director
presso care of (c/o)
prestanome (m) nominee
prestare lend *or* advance *[money]*
prestatore (m) lender
prestazione (f) performance
prestigio (m) prestige
prestiti (mpl) bancari bank borrowings
prestito (m) [mutuo] loan (n)
prestito (m) a termine term loan
prestito (m) agevolato soft loan
prestito (m) bancario bank loan

presto: al più presto possibile as soon as possible (asap)
pretendente (m) di diritto rightful claimant
prevedere forecast (v)
prevenire prevent
preventivo preventive
preventivo (m) estimate (n) *or* quote (n)
prevenzione (f) prevention
previdenza (f) sociale social security
previsione (f) forecast (n)
previsione (f) a lungo termine long-term forecast
previsione (f) della necessità di manodopera manpower forecasting
previsione (f) provvisoria delle vendite provisional forecast of sales

previsione (f) di vendita sales budget

previsione (f) di vendita sales forecast

previsioni (fpl) del flusso di cassa cash flow forecast

previsioni (fpl) di mercato market forecast

prezzi (mpl) concorrenziali keen prices

prezzi (mpl) correnti common pricing

prezzi (mpl) effettivi di vendita actuals

prezzi (mpl) equi fair price

prezzi (mpl) flessibili flexible prices

prezzi (mpl) franco banchina price ex quay

prezzi (mpl) franco magazzino price ex warehouse

prezzi (mpl) franco stabilimento price ex works

prezzi (mpl) inflazionati inflated prices

prezzi (mpl) popolari popular prices

prezzi (mpl) stabili stable prices

prezzo (m) price (n)

prezzo: ad alto prezzo highly-priced

prezzo (m) al dettaglio retail price

prezzo (m) al rivenditore trade price

prezzo (m) allineato competitive price

prezzo (m) concordato agreed price

prezzo (m) consigliato di fabbrica manufacturer's recommended price

prezzo (m) corrente current price

prezzo (m) d'acquisto purchase price

prezzo (m) d'apertura opening price

prezzo (m) d'entrata threshold price

prezzo (m) d'intervento intervention price

prezzo (m) d'occasione bargain price

prezzo (m) d'offerta supply price

prezzo (m) del coperto cover charge

prezzo (m) del petrolio oil price

prezzo (m) del trasporto haulage costs *or* haulage rates

prezzo (m) di catalogo catalogue price

prezzo (m) di chiusura closing price

prezzo (m) di fabbrica factory price

prezzo (m) di fattura invoice value

prezzo (m) di listino list price

prezzo (m) di mercato market price *or* market rate

prezzo (m) di permuta trade-in price

prezzo (m) di rivendita resale price

prezzo (m) di sostegno support price

prezzo (m) di vendita selling price

prezzo (m) eccessivo overcharge (n)

prezzo (m) franco delivered price

prezzo (m) intero full price

prezzo (m) massimo maximum price *or* ceiling price

prezzo (m) medio average price

prezzo (m) minimo reserve price

prezzo (m) netto net price

prezzo (m) per contanti cash price

prezzo (m) per merce pronta spot price

prezzo (m) ridottissimo rock-bottom prices

prezzo (m) ridotto cut price (n)

prezzo ridotto: a prezzo ridotto cut-price (adj)

prezzo (m) scontato discount price

prezzo (m) sotto costo cost price

prezzo (m) stabile firm price

prezzo (m) stabilito set price

prezzo (m) tutto compreso all-in price

prezzo (m) unitario unit price

prima classe first class

prima: di prima classe first-class (adj) *or* A1

prima: di prima qualità prime *or* top grade

prima opzione (f) first option

primario primary

primato (m) record (n) *[better than before]*

primo first

primo *[di prima qualità]* prime

primo ad entrare primo ad uscire first in first out (FIFO)

primo giorno (m) del trimestre quarter day

primo trimestre (m) first quarter

principale principal (adj) *or* main *or* chief

principio (m) principle

privatizzare privatize

privatizzazione (f) privatization

privato private

privilegio (m) lien

privo di validità (inabile) invalid

privo di valore worthless

pro-capite per capita

probabile prospective

probatorio probationary

problema (m) problem

procacciare canvass
procedere proceed
procedimenti (mpl) legali judicial processes
procedimento (m) giudiziario prosecution *[legal action]*
procedura (f) procedure
procedura (f) di selezione selection procedure
processi (mpl) industriali industrial processes
processo (m) process (n)
processo (m) trial *[court case]*
processo (m) decisionale decision making
procura (f) power of attorney; proxy
procurarsi get
procurarsi fondi secure funds
procuratore (m) attorney

procuratore (m) legale solicitor
prodotti (mpl) agricoli agricultural produce
prodotti (mpl) che si fanno concorrenza competing products
prodotti (mpl) competitivi competitive products
prodotti (mpl) con etichetta propria own label goods
prodotti (mpl) con marchio proprio own brand goods
prodotti (mpl) di alta qualità high-quality goods
prodotti (mpl) di seconda qualità seconds
prodotti (mpl) essenziali staple product
prodotti (mpl) finiti finished goods
prodotti (mpl) semilavorati semi-finished products

prodotto (m) product or article

prodotto (m) derivato by-product

prodotto (m) di prestigio prestige product

prodotto (m) finito end product

prodotto (m) nazionale lordo (PNL) gross national product (GNP)

prodotto (m) per il mercato di massa mass market product

prodotto (m) sensibile ai cambiamenti di prezzo price-sensitive product

prodotto (m) interno lordo (PIL) gross domestic product (GDP)

prodotto-guida (m) del mercato market leader

produrre [fabbricare] produce (v) or manufacture or make

produrre [presentare] produce or show or bring out

produrre in eccesso overproduce

produrre in serie mass-produce

produrre automobili in serie mass-produce cars

produttività (f) productivity

produttivo productive

produttore (m) [fabbricante] producer or manufacturer

produzione (f) production or making or output

produzione (f) in eccesso overproduction

produzione (f) in serie mass production

produzione (f) totale total output

produzione (f) nazionale domestic production

professionale pro-
fessional *or* occupa-
tional
professionista (m)
[esperto] profes-
sional (n) *or* expert
proficuo profitable
profitto (m) (utile)
profit *or* earnings
**proforma: fattura
(f) proforma** pro
forma (invoice)
progettare
design (v)
progettare *[orga-
nizzare]* plan (v)
progettato projected
progettazione (f)
[design] design (n)
**progettazione (f)
del prodotto**
product design
progetto (m) *[pia-
no]* project *or* plan
**progetto (m) di
legge** bill (n) *[in
Parliament]*
**progetto (m)
edilizio di
ricostruzione**
redevelopment

progetto (m) pilota
pilot scheme
**progetto (m)
redditizio** money-
making plan
programma (m) pro-
gramme *or* timetable
**programma (m)
aziendale** cor
porate plan
**programma (m) di
computer** computer
program
**programma (m) di
ricerca** research
programme
programmare
timetable (v)
**programmare un
computer** program
a computer
**programmatore (m)
di computer** com-
puter programmer
**programmazione
(f) aziendale** cor-
porate planning
**programmazione
(f) delle assunzioni
di manodopera**
manpower planning

programmazione (f) di computer computer programming
programmazione (f) economica economic planning
progresso (m) [sviluppo] progress or development
progresso: fare progressi progress (v) or make progress
proibire forbid
proibitivo prohibitive
prolungamento (m) extension [making longer]
prolungare extend [make longer]
promessa (f) promise (n)
promettere promise (v)
promozionale promotional
promozione (f) promotion [better job, publicity]
promozione (f) delle vendite sales promotion

promozione (f) di un prodotto promotion of a product
promuovere promote [give better job, advertise]
promuovere un'immagine aziendale promote a corporate image
pronosticare tip (v) [say what might happen]
pronta cassa (f) ready cash
pronto ready
pronunciarsi in una vertenza adjudicate in a dispute
propaganda (f) canvassing
propagandista (m) canvasser
proporre propose or move [a motion]
proporre [offrire] offer (v) [to buy]
proporzionale proportional or pro rata
proporzione (f) proportion

proposito (m)
[scopo] aim (n)
proposta (f) pro-
posal *or* suggestion
proposta (f) *[di
assicurazione]*
insurance proposal
**proposta (f) unica
di vendita** unique
selling point *or*
proposition (USP)
proprietà (f)
ownership
**proprietà (f) collet-
tiva** collective
ownership
**proprietà (f)
comune** common
ownership
**proprietà (f) immo-
biliare** real estate
**proprietà (f) multi-
pla** multiple owner-
ship
proprietà (f) privata
private property; pri-
vate ownership
proprietaria (f)
proprietress
proprietario (m)
proprietor *or* owner

**proprietario (m)
legittimo** rightful
owner
prorata *[pro-
porzionale]* pro rata
prosperare flourish
or prosper
prospettive (fpl)
prospects
prospetto (m)
prospectus
prossimo early
protesta (f)
[reclamo] protest
or complaint
**protesta (f) con
occupazione**
sit-down protest
protestare *[recla-
mare]* complain
(about)
**protestare contro
qualcosa** protest
(v) *[against
something]*
**protestare una cam-
biale** protest a bill
protesto (m) *[per
mancato paga-
mento]* protest (n)
[official document]

protettivo protective
protezione (f) protection
protezione (f) [barriera] hedge (n)
protezione (f) del consumatore consumer protection
prova (f) test (n); protection; proof; trial
prova: in prova on approval
prova (f) documentata documentary proof
prova (f) gratuita free trial
provare test (v)
proventi (mpl) da partite invisibili invisible earnings
provvedere provide
provvedere a provide for; make provision for
provvedere di generi alimentari cater for
provvedimenti (mpl) fiscali fiscal measures

provvisorio provisional
provvista (f) supply (n) or stock of goods
prudente [sicuro] safe (adj)
pubblicazione (f) periodica periodical (n)
pubbliche relazioni (fpl) public relations (PR)
pubblicità (f) (reclame) publicity or advertising
pubblicità: fare pubblicità [reclamizzare] advertise
pubblicità (f) (spot) TV commercial
pubblicità (f) [annuncio pubblicitario] advertisement
pubblicità (f) a mezzo posta direct-mail advertising
pubblicità (f) di un prodotto product advertising

pubblicità (f) su tutto il territorio nazionale national advertising

pubblicizzare publicize

pubblicizzare un nuovo prodotto promote a new product

pubblico public (adj)

punto (m) point

punto (m) di pareggio fra costi e ricavi breakeven point

punto (m) di partenza starting point

punto (m) di riferimento benchmark

punto (m) di vendita point of sale (p.o.s. *or* POS)

punto (m) di vendita al dettaglio retail outlets

punto (m) di vendita diretta della fabbrica factory outlet

punto (m) di vendita elettronico electronic point of sale (EPOS)

punto (m) metallico staple (n)

punto (m) morto deadlock (n)

punto: essere a un punto morto be deadlocked

punto (m) per la dichiarazine doganale d'entrata customs entry point

punto (m) percentuale percentage point

puntuale on time

Qq

quadri (mpl) direttivi management team

quadri (mpl) intermedi middle management

quadro (m) generale survey (n) *or* general report

qualificarsi
qualify as
qualificato [abile]
qualified *or* skilled
qualifiche (fpl) pro-
fessionali profes-
sional qualifications
qualità (f) quality
qualità (f) extra
premium quality
qualità: di qualità
inferiore low-grade
or low-quality
qualità (f) sca-
dente poor quality
qualità (f) superi-
ore top quality
qualità superiore di
qualità superiore
high-quality
quantità (f)
quantity
quartiere (m) [zona]
area *or* quarter *or*
district [of town]
quarto (m) quarter
[25%]
quarto trimestre
(m) fourth quarter

querelante (m)
plaintiff
questione (f)
[argomento] item
[on agenda] or mat-
ter (n) *[to be*
discussed]
quietanza (f) finale
final discharge
quota (f) quota
quota (f) (tariffa)
rate (n) *or* price
quota (f) d'ammor-
tamento
depreciation rate
quota (f) d'iscri-
zione admission fee
quota (f) di mer-
cato market share
quotare quote (v)
[a reference number]
quotare [indicare un
prezzo] quote (v)
[estimate costs]
quotazione (f)
quotation *or* quote
[estimate of cost]
quotidiano daily

Rr

raccogliere
[cogliere] collect
(v) *or* fetch
raccogliere fondi
raise (v) *or* obtain
money
raccoglitore (m)
collector
raccomandare *[con-
sigliare]* recommend
or advise *[what
should be done]*
raccomandata (f)
registered letter
raccomandazione
(f) recommendation
raddoppiare
double (v)
raduno (m) dei
venditori sales
conference
rafforzarsi rally (v)
raggiungere reach
or arrive at
raggiungere un
obiettivo meet a
target

raggruppare
bracket together
ragione (f) sociale
corporate name
ragioniere (m) *o*
ragioniera (f) *[con-
tabile]* accountant
ragioniere (m)
iscritto all'albo
*[revisore ufficiale
dei conti]* certified
accountant
rallentamento (m)
slowdown
rallentare slow down
rammentare remind
rampa (f) di carico
loading ramp
rapidamente *[velo-
cemente]* fast (adv)
rapporto (m)
report (n); ratio
rapporto (m) cor-
so/utili price/earn-
ings ratio (P/E ratio)
rapporto (m) di
indebitamento
gearing
rapporto (m) fra
utile e dividendo
dividend cover

rapporto (m) riser-vato confidential report

rappresentante (m) sales representative

rappresentante (m) *[agente]* agent *or* representative

rappresentante (m) **commissionario** commission rep

rappresentante (m) **(di commercio)** salesman *or* representative

rappresentante (m) **esclusivo** sole agent

rappresentanza (f) **esclusiva** sole agency

rappresentare represent

rappresentare qual-cuno deputize for someone

rappresentativo representative (adj)

rata (f) instalment

ratifica (f) ratification

ratificare ratify

razionalizzare rationalize

razionalizzazione (f) rationalization

reale real

realizzabile viable

realizzare realize *or* sell for money

realizzare (attuare) implement (v) *or* put into practice

realizzare beni realize property

realizzare la pene-trazione di un mer-cato penetrate a market

realizzare un piano oun progetto realize a plan

realizzazione (f) di cespiti realization of assets

reato (m) di omis-sione nonfeasance

reazione (f) response

recapito (m) *[indi-rizzo]* address (n)

recentissimo latest

recessione (f) recession

reciproco [mutuo]
reciprocal or mutual
reclamare
[protestare]
complain (about)
reclame (f) [pub-
blicità] advertising
reclamizzare un
nuovo prodotto
advertise a new
product
reclamo (m)
[domanda d'inden-
nizzo] claim (n)
reclamo (m)
[protesta] complaint
recuperabile
recoverable
recuperare collect
(v) [money]
recuperare
repossess
recuperare [sal-
vare] salvage (v)
recuperare un deb-
ito collect a debt
recupero (m) col-
lection [of money];
salvage [of goods]
recupero (m) dell'in-
vestimento payback

recupero (m) di
crediti debt
collection
redditività (f)
profitability
redditività (f) dei
costi cost-
effectiveness
redditizio paying
(adj); money-making
or cost-effective
reddito (m) rev-
enue or income
reddito (m) comp-
lessivo total revenue
reddito (m) da affit-
tanze rental income
reddito (m) da divi-
dendi dividend yield
reddito (m) da
investimenti
investment income
reddito (m) effet-
tivo real income or
real wages
reddito (m) fisso
fixed income or
regular income
reddito (m)
imponibile taxable
income

reddito (m) lordo
gross income
reddito (m) netto
net income *or* net
salary
reddito (m) non
imponibile non-
taxable income
reddito (m) per-
sonale personal
income
reddito (m) soci-
etario negativo
negative cash flow
reddito (m) sugli
investimenti return
on investment (ROI)
reddito (m) totale
total income
reddito (m) uffi-
ciale official return
redigere *[abbozzare]*
draw up *or* draft (v)
redimibile
redeemable
referenze (fpl)
[attestato] refer-
ence *[on person]*
regalare give
(away) *[as gift]* or
present (v)

regalo (m) gift *or*
present (n)
regionale regional
regione (f) *[area]*
region *or* area
registrare record
(v) *or* write in
registrare chiamate
log calls
registrare una voce
[contabile] post an
entry
registrato
registered (adj)
registratore (f) di
cassa cash register
registrazione (f)
registration; registry
registrazione (f)
[prenotazione]
booking
registrazione (f) a
credito credit entry
registrazione (f) a
debito debit entry
registrazione (f) di
storno contra
entry
registrazione (f)
sul computer
computer listing

registro (m) regis-
ter (n) *or* official list
registro (m) *[libro
contabile]*
register (n)
registro (m) degli
amministratori
register of directors
registro (m) degli
azionisti o registro
(m) delle azioni reg-
ister of shareholders
registro (m) delle
ordinazioni
order book
registro (m) delle
ricevute
receipt book
Registro (m) delle
SPA companies'
register
regolamenti (mpl)
[disposizioni] regu-
lations
regolamento (m)
regulation
regolamento (m)
finanziario finan-
cial settlement
regolare (v)
regulate *or* adjust

regolare *[normale]*
regular *or* normal *or*
ordinary
regolarizzare regu-
late *[by law]*
regolarmente
[dovutamente] duly
[legally]
regresso (m)
downturn
reimportare
reimport (v)
reimportazione (f)
reimportation;
reimport (n)
reinvestimento (m)
reinvestment
reinvestire reinvest
relativo relevant
relativo a relating to
relazione (f)
annuale al bilancio
annual report
relazione (f)
provvisoria interim
report
relazione (f) sull'a-
vanzamento
progress report
relazioni (fpl)
relations

relazioni (fpl) industriali indus-trial relations

remunerare (pagare) pay (v) [worker]

remunerativo [redditizio] profitable

remunerato [pagato] paid [for work]

rendere [apportare] bring in or yield

rendere [fruttare] produce (v) [interest]

rendere conto account for

rendere effettivo un accordo imple-ment an agreement

rendere saturo il mercato saturate the market

rendersi conto di [capire] realize [understand]

rendiconti (mpl) annuali annual accounts

rendiconto (m) statement

rendiconto (m) del flusso di cassa cash flow statement

rendiconto (m) delle spese state-ment of expenses

rendimento (m) effettivo effective yield

rendimento (m) immediato current yield

rendimento (m) lordo gross yield

rendimento (m) netto net yield

rendita (f) yield (n) [on investment]

rendita (f) vitalizia [usufrutto] life interest

reparto (m) depart-ment [in shop]; divi-sion [of company]

reparto (m) esportazioni export department

reparto (m) marketing marketing division

reparto (m) contabilità accounts department

reperimento (m) retrieval

reperire retrieve

replica (f) repeat

rescindere rescind

rescindere [invalidare] void or invalidate

rescindere un accordo terminate an agreement

residente resident (adj)

residente (m) [abitante] resident (n) or inhabitant

residenza (f) residence

resoconto (m) dettagliato detailed account

resoconto (m) mensile monthly statement

resoconto (m) semestrale half-yearly statement

respingere [mandare indietro] return (v) or send back

respingere [rifiutare] reject (v)

responsabile (m) dei reclami claims manager

responsabile (m) del mastro dei conti dei creditori bought ledger clerk

responsabile (m) di un prodotto product engineer

responsabile (m) di un ufficio acquisti buyer [for a store]

responsabile di o per responsible or liable (for)

responsabilità (f) responsibility or responsibilties

responsabilità (f) [obbligo] liability

responsabilità (f) contrattuale contractual liability

responsabilità (f) illimitata unlimited liability

responsabilità (f) limitata limited liability

restare remain

resti in linea per favore hold the line please *or* please hold

restituibile returnable

restituire [consegnare] hand in *or* deliver *or* consign

restringere tighten up on

restringimento (m) shrinkage

restrittivo restrictive

restrizione (f) restraint *or* restriction *or* limitation

restrizione (f) endorsement [on insurance]

restrizioni (fpl) alle importazioni import restrictions

rete (f) network (n)

rete (f) di distribuzione distribution network

reticolo (m) grid

retribuire remunerate

retribuzione (f) remuneration

retribuzione (f) [stipendio] pay (n) *or* salary

retribuzione (f) a cottimo piece rate

retribuzione (f) a ore hourly rate

retribuzione (f) ferie holiday pay

retro (m) (dorso) back (n)

retroattivo retroactive

retrodatare antedate

rettifica (f) [emendamento] rectification *or* amendment

revisionare service (v) *[a machine]*

revisione (f) *[manutenzione]* service (n) *[of machine]*

revisione (f) contabile audit (n)

revisione (f) contabile periodica general audit

revisione (f) dello stipendio salary review

revisione (f) esterna external audit

revisione (f) interna internal audit

revisore (m) esterno external auditor

revisore (m) interno internal auditor

revisore (m) ufficiale dei conti auditor

revoca (f) di una nomina cancellation of an appointment

revocare revoke

riacquistare buy back

riadattare readjust

riaddestramento (m) retraining

riaddestrare retrain

riassestamento (m) readjustment

riassicurare reinsure

riassicuratore (m) reinsurer

riassicurazione (f) reinsurance

riassumere *[una persona]* re-employ *[someone]*

riassunzione (f) re-employment

ribassista (m) bear (n) *[on Stock Exchange]*

ribasso (m) *[caduta]* reduction *or* drop (n)

ribasso: in ribasso falling

ribasso (m) delle vendite drop in sales

ricambio (m)
turnover *[of staff]*
ricavare al netto
net (v)
ricavi (mpl) netti
net sales
ricavo (m) dalla
pubblicità revenue
from advertising
ricavo (m) nullo
nil return
ricerca (f)
research (n)
ricerca: fare ricerche
do research *or*
research (v)
ricerca (f) auto-
matica dell'infor-
mazione data
retrieval
ricerca (f) di
mercato market
research
ricerca (f) e
sviluppo (RS)
research and devel-
opment (R & D)
ricercatore (m),
ricercatrice (f)
research worker *or*
researcher

ricettività (f)
alberghi hotel
accommodation
ricevente receiving
ricevere receive
ricevimento (m)
receipt *[receiving]*
ricevuta (f) receipt
[piece of paper]
ricevuta (f) (di
vendita) sales
receipt
ricevuta (f) in
duplicato duplicate
receipt *or* duplicate
of a receipt
richiamo (m)
appeal (n) *or*
attraction
richiamo (m) per i
clienti customer
appeal
richiedere [doman-
dare] demand *or*
request (v)
richiedere [volere]
take (v) *or* need
richiesta (f)
request (n); inquiry
richiesta: su richi-
esta on request

richiesta (f)
[domanda] demand
(n) *[for payment]*
**richiesta (f) di
indennizzo assicu-
rativo** insurance
claim
**richiesta (f) di
informazioni**
enquiry
**richiesta (f) di
iscrizione** letter of
application
**richiesta (f) di
pagamento** call (n)
[for money]
**richiesta (f) sta-
gionale** seasonal
demand
richieste (fpl)
requirements
riciclare recycle;
launder *[money]*
ricollocamento (m)
reappointment
ricollocare reappoint
ricompensa (f)
[compenso] com-
pensation
riconciliare
reconcile

riconciliazione (f)
reconciliation
**riconciliazione (f)
dei conti** reconcilia-
tion of accounts
**riconoscere un sin-
dacato** recognize a
union
riconoscimento (m)
recognition
**riconoscimento (m)
scritto di un debito**
[pagherò] IOU (= I
owe you)
**riconoscimento (m)
sindacale** union
recognition
ricorrente recurrent
**ricorrere a con-
sulenza legale** take
legal advice
ricorrere in appello
[appellare] appeal
(v) *[against a
decision]*
**ricorso (m) *[appe-
llo]*** appeal (n)
[against a decision]
ricuperare
recover *or* get some-
thing back

**ricuperare medi-
ante tassazione**
clawback
ricupero (m)
recovery *[getting
something back]*
ridistribuire
redistribute
ridurre *[abbassare]*
reduce *or* knock
down (v) *[price]*
ridurre il valore
write down *[assets]*
ridurre le spese
reduce expenditure
ridurre un prezzo
reduce a price
riduzione (f)
[sconto] rebate *or*
price reduction
**riduzione (f) d'im-
posta** tax allowance
**riduzione (f) dei
costi** cost-cutting
**riduzione (f) delle
spese** retrenchment
**riduzione (f) di posti
lavorativi** job cuts
**riduzione (f) di
prezzi** knockdown
prices

**riduzioni (fpl)
d'imposta** tax
reductions
rieleggere re-elect
rielezione (f)
re-election
riesaminare revise
riesportare
re-export (v)
riesportazione (f)
re-export (n)
rifarsi delle perdite
recoup one's losses
riferimento (m)
reference *[dealing
with]*
**riferimento: fare
riferimento a** refer
[to item]
riferire report (v)
**riferirsi (fare riferi-
mento a)** refer (to)
**rifinanziamento (m)
di un prestito** refi-
nancing *or* restruc-
turing of a loan
rifiutare fall *or*
decline (v)
rifiutare *[respingere]*
refuse *or* reject (v) *or*
turn down

rifiutare un accordo repudiate an agreement

rifiuto (m) refusal *or* rejection

rifornimento (m) restocking

rifornire restock

rifugio (m) fiscale tax haven

riguardante regarding

riguardare apply to *or* affect

rilasciare release (v) *[make public]*

rilascio (m) release (n) *or* issue *[of shares]*

rilevamento (m) takeover

rimandare [aggiornare] adjourn

rimandare una lettera al mittente return a letter to sender

rimanenze (fpl) iniziali opening stock

rimanere indietro fall behind *[be in a worse position]*

rimborsabile refundable

rimborsabile repayable *or* repayable

rimborsare pay back

rimborsare un'obbligazione redeem a bond

rimborso (m) reimbursement *or* refund *or* repayment

rimborso (m) delle spese reimbursement of expenses

rimborso (m) totale full refund

rimessa (f) remittance

rimetterci out of pocket

rimettere remit (v)

rimuovere remove

ringraziamento (m) vote of thanks

rinnovare renew

rinnovare un abbonamento renew a subscription

rinnovare un contratto d'affitto renew a lease

rinnovare una cambiale renew a bill of exchange

rinnovo (m) renewal

rinnovo (m) di un contratto d'affitto renewal of a lease

rinnovo (m) di un abbonamento renewal of a subscription

rinnovo (m) di una cambiale renewal of a bill

rinuncia (f) renunciation; waiver [of right]

rinunciare waive

rinunciare ad un pagamento waive a payment

rinunciare ad un'azione (f) abandon an action

rinviare [differire] postpone

rinvio (m) return (n); deferment or postponement

rinvio (m) di pagamento deferment of payment

riordinare reorder (v)

riorganizzare reorganize

riorganizzazione (f) reorganization

riorganizzazione (f) di una società restructuring of the company

ripagare repay

riparare [aggiustare] repair (v) or fix or mend

riparazione (m) repair (n)

riparo (m) shelter

ripartire un rischio spread a risk

ripartizione (f) breakdown (n) [of items]

ripetere un'ordinazione repeat an order

riportare a nuovo carry forward

riportare un pareggio carry over a balance

riprendere resume

riprendere le trattative resume negotiations

riprendersi recover *or* get better *or* stage a recovery

ripresa (f) recovery *or* getting better; rally

riprodurre *[copiare]* copy (v)

ripudiare repudiate

risarcimento (m) di danni damages *or* compensation for damage

risarcire *[indennizzare]* indemnify

risarcire qualcuno per una perdita indemnify someone for a loss

riscattare surrender (v) *[an insurance]*

riscattare un pegno redeem a pledge

riscattare una polizza surrender a policy

riscatto (m) surrender (n) *[of an insurance policy]*

riscatto (m) *[di un prestito]* redemption *[of a loan]*

rischiare risk (v) *[money]*

rischio (m) risk (n)

rischio (m) d'incendio fire risk

rischio (m) finanziario financial risk *or* exposure

rischioso risky

riscossione (f) delle imposte tax collection

riserva (f) store *[of items kept]* *or* reserve *[of supplies]*

riserva (f) *[accantonamento]* reserve *or* provision *[money put aside]*

riserva: di riserva backup (adj) *[copy]*

riserva (f) di cassa
cash reserves
riserva (f) di materia prima stock of
raw materials
riservare reserve (v)
riservatezza (f)
confidentiality
riservato
confidential
riserve (fpl)
reserves
**riserve: con riserve
[condizionato]** with
reservations
**riserve (fpl)
d'emergenza**
emergency reserves
**riserve (fpl)
occulte** hidden
reserves
**riserve (fpl)
valutarie** currency
reserves
risoluzione (f)
resolution
**risoluzione (f) di
problemi** problem
solving
risolvere un problema solve a problem

risorse (fpl)
resources
**risorse (fpl)
finanziarie** financial resources
risorse (fpl) naturali natural resources
risparmi (mpl)
savings
risparmiare [economizzare] save (v)
**risparmiare: che
risparmia energia**
energy-saving (adj)
rispettare
respect (v)
rispettare una scadenza (f) meet a
deadline
rispondere answer
(v) *or* reply (v)
**rispondere: dover
rispondere a qualcuno** report to
someone
**rispondere: che
deve rispondere a
qualcuno** responsible to someone
rispondere a una lettera answer a letter

rispondere al telefono answer the telephone

risposta (f) answer (n) *or* reply (n)

ristagno (m) stagnation

ristrutturare restructure

ristrutturazione (f) restructuring

risultati (mpl) results *[company's profit or loss]*

risultato (m) result *[in general]*

risultato: avere come risultato result in

ritaglio (m) (di campioni) swatch

ritardare delay (v)

ritardo (m) delay (n) *or* hold-up (n)

ritardo: in ritardo late (adv)

ritardo: essere in ritardo *[nel fare una cosa]* fall behind *or* be late *[in doing something]*

ritelefonare phone back

ritenuta (f) d'acconto withholding tax

ritirare withdraw *[an offer]*

ritirare la propria candidatura stand down

ritiro (m) collection *[of goods]*; withdrawal *[of money]*

ritorno (m) return (n) *or* going back

ritrattare un'offerta di rilevamento withdraw a takeover bid

riunione (f) meeting; conference

riunione (f) del consiglio di amministrazione board meeting

riuscire *[avere successo]* succeed *or* do well

riuscire a manage to

riuscire: non riuscire fail *[not to do something]*

rivalutare
revalue (v)
rivalutazione (f)
revaluation; appreciation *[in value]*
rivelare (divulgare)
reveal *or* disclose
rivelazione (f)
[divulgazione] revelation *or* disclosure
rivendicare claim
(v) *[insurance]*
rivendicazione (f)
salariale wage
claim
rivendita (f) resale
rivenditore (m)
stockist
rivista (f) (periodico) magazine *or*
journal
rivista (f)
aziendale house
magazine
rivista (f) di
categoria trade
magazine
rivolgere la parola
a qualcuno address
(v) *or* speak to
someone

rivolto a una fascia
alta del mercato
up-market
roll on/roll off
[traghetto per
automezzi] roll
on/roll off ferry
rompere break (v)
[a contract]
rompersi break
down (v) *[of*
machine]
rotazione (f)
turnround *[goods*
sold]
rotazione (f) delle
scorte stock
turnover
rottura (f) breakdown (n) *[of talks]*
rotture (fpl)
[danni] breakages
routine (f) *[ordi-*
naria amministra-
zione] routine (n)
rovinare (viziare)
spoil
RS (ricerca e
sviluppo) R&D (=
research and
development)

Ss

sacchetto (m) di carta paper bag

saggio (m) [campione] sample (n)

sala (f) di esposizione showroom

sala (f) di vendita all'asta auction rooms

sala (f) esposizioni exhibition hall

sala (f) per VIP VIP lounge

sala (f) riunioni boardroom; conference room

sala (f) transiti transit lounge

salario (m) wage

salario (m) minimo minimum wage

salario (m) minimo garantito guaranteed minimum wage

salario (m) orario hourly wage

saldare [pagare] pay (v) or settle [bill]

saldare un conto settle an account

saldezza (f) steadiness

saldi (mpl) per inventario stocktaking sale

saldo (m) sale (n) [at a low price]

saldo (m) a metà prezzo half-price sale

saldo (m) da riportare balance brought down or brought forward

saldo (m) debitore debit balance

saldo (m) di cassa cash balance

saldo (m) di un debito clearing or paying [of a debt]

saldo (m) dovuto balance due to us

saldo (m) in banca bank balance

saldo (m) riportato
balance carried down
or carrried forward
salire *[ascendere]*
climb
salire alle stelle soar
**salone (m) delle
partenze** departure
lounge
salvaguardia (f)
safeguard
salvare *[su disco]*
save (v) *[on
computer]*
**salvare *[recuper-
are]*** salvage (v)
**salvo errori e omis-
sioni (S.E. & O)**
errors and omissions
excepted (e. & o.e.)
**salvo vista e veri-
fica** on approval
saturare saturate
or glut (v)
saturare di prodotti
overstock (v)
saturazione (f)
saturation *or* glut
sbagliato wrong
sbarcare land (v)
[passengers, cargo]

sbarrare un assegno
cross a cheque
sbocco (m) outlet
sborsare pay out
scadente *[basso]*
low (adj)
scadenza (f) *[fine]*
expiry
scadere *[terminare]*
expire *or* mature *or*
lapse
scaduto overdue
scaffalatura (f)
shelving *or* shelves
scaffale (m) shelf
scaglionare stagger
scala (f) scale
[system]
**scala: in scala nat-
urale** full-scale
(adj) *or* full-size
**scala: in scala
ridotta** small-scale
**scala (f) *[vari-
azioni]*** range (n) *or*
variation
**scala (f) incremen-
tale** incremental
scale
**scala (f) retribu-
tiva** wage scale

scala (f) temporale
time scale
scalo (m) merci
freight depot
**scalo (m) per con-
tainer** container port
scambiabile
exchangeable
scambiare swap (v)
or exchange
scambiare con
exchange (v) *[one
thing for another]*
scambio (m) swap
(n) *or* exchange
scambio (m)
[baratto] barter (n)
**scambio (m) di
merci e prodotti**
bartering
**scappatoia (f) fis-
cale** tax shelter
scaricare unload
[goods]
**scaricare merce in
un porto** land
goods at a port
**scaricatore (m) (di
porto)** *[stivatore]*
stevedore
scarsità (f) shortage

scarto (m) reject (n)
**scatola (f) di car-
tone** cardboard box
**scatola (f) per la
piccola cassa** petty
cash box
scegliere choose
**scegliere la strada
più facile** take the
soft option
scelta (f) choice (n)
**scelta (f) del
momento oppor-
tuno** timing
scendere
[diminuire] fall off
scheda (f) filing
card *or* index card
schedare
card-index (v)
schedario (m)
card index; filing
cabinet
schedatura (f)
filing *[action]*; card-
indexing
**schema (m) del
ciclo** flow chart
**scienze (fpl) eco-
nomiche** *[economia]*
economics *[study]*

sciogliere una società di persone dissolve a partnership

scioglimento (m) *[liquidazione]* winding up

sciolto loose

scioperante (m) striker

scioperare strike (v)

sciopero (m) strike (n)

sciopero (m) bianco go-slow *or* work-to-rule

sciopero (m) con occupazione sit-down strike

sciopero (m) di protesta protest strike

sciopero (m) di solidarietà sympathy strike

sciopero (m) generale general strike

sciopero (m) selvaggio wildcat strike

scontabile discountable

sconti (mpl) al rivenditore trade terms

scontista (m) discounter

sconto (m) *[riduzione]* discount *or* rebate *or* price reduction

sconto: con sconto di off *[reduced by]*

sconto: fare uno sconto di take off *or* deduct

sconto (m) ai rivenditori trade discount

sconto (m) all'ingrosso wholesale discount

sconto (m) cassa cash discount

sconto (m) del valore attuale discounted cash flow (DCF)

sconto (m) di base basic discount

sconto (m) percentuale percentage discount

sconto (m) per pagamento in contanti cash discount

sconto (m) sul quantitativo quantity discount *or* volume discount

scontrarsi con crash (v) into

scoperto (di c/c) overdraft

scopo (m) [*proposito*] aim (n)

scopo: avere lo scopo di aim (v)

scorrettamente incorrectly

scorretto incorrect

scorta (f) [*di materie prime*] stockpile (n)

scorte (fpl) stock (n) *or* goods *or* inventory (n)

scritto a mano handwritten

scrittura (f) writing

scrittura (f) contabile entry [*writing*]

scrivania (f) desk

scrivere write

scuola (f) per segretarie d'azienda secretarial college

scuola (m) superiore di commercio commercial college

scusa (f) apology

scusarsi apologize

S. E. & O. (salvo errori e omissioni) e. & o.e. (errors and omissions excepted)

seconda categoria oseconda classe second-class

seconda mano: di seconda mano secondhand

secondo second (adj)

secondo: a secondo di according to *or* under

secondo i termini convenuti according to the terms agreed; on agreed terms

secondo trimestre (m) second quarter

sede (f) head office

sede (f) legale
registered office
sede (f) centrale
headquarters
(HQ); main office
segnale (m) di linea
libera dialling tone
segnale (m) di
linea occupata
engaged tone
segno (m) place
(n) *[in a text]*
segretaria (f),
segretario (m)
secretary
segretaria (f) per-
sonale personal
assistant (PA)
segretaria (f) tem-
poranea temp (n)
segretario (m) del
consiglio
d'amministrazione
company secretary
segreteria (f) tele-
fonica answering
machine
segreto secret (adj)
segreto (m)
secret (n)
seguire follow

seguito: fare
seguito follow
seguito: in seguito
a further to
selezionare candid-
ati screen candidates
selezione (f)
selection
sembrare appear
semestre (m)
half-year
senza scalo *[inin-*
terrotto] non-stop
senza scopo di lucro
non profit-making
senza sovvenzioni
unsubsidized
senza spese
[franco] franco
senza tener conto
di regardless of
separare
separate (v)
separato
separate (adj)
sequela (f) *[serie]*
run (n) *[work*
routine]
sequestrare
sequester *or*
sequestrate *or* seize

sequestratario (m) sequestrator
sequestro (m) sequestration *or* seizure
serie (f) set (n); run (n)
serratura (f) lock (n)
servire serve
servire un cliente serve a customer
servizi (mpl) facilities
servizi (mpl) di elaborazione elettronica computer services
servizi (mpl) di trasporto transport facilities
servizio (m) service (n)
servizio (m) di marketing marketing department
servizio (m) in camera room service
servizio (m) pacchi postali parcel post
servizio (m) postale postal service

servizio (m) scadente poor service
servizio (m) segreteria telefonica answering service
servizio (m) sollecito prompt service
servizio (m) spedizioni dispatch department
servizio (m) stralci giornalistici clipping service
servizio (m) telefonico gratuito toll free number *or* 0800 number
settimana (f) week
settimanale weekly
settore (m) sector *or* branch
settore (m) privato private sector
settore (m) pubblico public sector
settore (m) terziario tertiary sector
sezione (f) *[reparto]* department *[in office]*

sfavorevole
unfavourable
sforzo (m) effort
sfruttare exploit
sgravio (m) per
doppia tassazione
double taxation
agreement
sicurezza (f)
security *or* safety
sicurezza (f) del
posto di lavoro
job security
sicurezza (f) del-
l'impiego security
of employment
sicurezza (f) di
possesso security
of tenure
sicuro (prudente)
safe (adj)
sigillare seal (v)
[attach a seal]
sigillo (m) seal (n)
sigillo (m)
doganale
customs seal
siglare initial (v)
silo (m) grain
elevator

simbolo (m) token
simbolo (m) di suc-
cesso status symbol
sindacalista (m)
trade unionist
sindacato (m)
(trade) union
sindacato (m)
degli inquilini rent
tribunal
sindrome (f)
della fenice
phoenix syndrome
sinergia (f) synergy
singolo single
sinistro left *[not*
right]
sistema (m) system
sistema (m) *[rete]*
network (n)
sistema (m) di
acquisti a rate hire
purchase (HP)
sistema (m) di
controllo control
systems
sistema (m) di
recupero delle
informazioni
retrieval system

sistema (m) di sorveglianza dell'ufficio office security

sistema (m) elettronico di elaborazione computer system

sistema (m) in tempo reale real-time system

Sistema (m) Monetario Europeo (SME) European Monetary System (EMS)

sistema (m) operativo operating system

sistema (m) tributario tax system

sistemare settle *or* arrange things

sistemare (disporre) arrange *or* set out

sistemazione (f) *[disposizione]* system *or* arrangement

situato situated

situazione (f) *[posizione]* situation *or* position *or* state of affairs

situazione (f) contrattuale bargaining position

SME (Sistema Monetario Europeo) EMS (= European Monetary System)

smentita (f) disclaimer

sociale social

società (f) society *[in general]*

società (f) a responsabilità limitata (Srl) private limited company

società (f) collegata (f) associate company

società (f) commerciale trading company

società (f) controllante parent company; holding company

società (f) cooperativa cooperative society
società (f) (di capitali) company
società (f) di capitali a responsabilità limitata limited (liability) company (Ltd)
società (f) di capitali a sottoscrizione pubblica (SpA) Public Limited Company (Plc)
società (f) di factoring factor (n) [company]
società (f) di medie dimensioni middle-sized company
società (f) di navigazione shipping company
società (f) di persone partnership
società (f) di servizi service (n) (business)
società (f) di vendita per corrispondenza mail-order business or mail-order firm

società (f) esistente solo di nome shell company
società (f) fiduciaria trust company
società (f) finanziaria finance company
società (f) in accomandita semplice limited partnership
società (f) mutua (di assicurazioni) mutual (insurance) company
società (f) orientata al profitto profit-oriented company
società (f) quotata in Borsa quoted company
società (f) rivale rival company
società (f) sorella sister company
socio (m) member [of a group]
socio (m) [compagno] partner
socio (m) [associato] associate (n)

socio (m) accomandante sleeping partner

socio (m) anziano senior partner

soddisfacente [accettabile] satisfactory or acceptable

soddisfare satisfy [customer]; meet [a need]

soddisfare una richiesta satisfy a demand

soddisfazione (f) satisfaction

soddisfazione (f) dei clienti customer satisfaction

soddisfazione (f) sul lavoro job satisfaction

software (m) software

soggetto a subject to

soggetto a condizioni conditional

soglia (f) threshold

soldi (mpl) in anticipo money up front

solido [stabile] solid or firm (adj)

solito [abituale] usual or normal

sollecitare ordinazioni solicit orders

sollecito prompt

sollecito (m) reminder or follow-up

sollevare raise (v) [a question]

solo [unico] sole

soluzione (f) solution

solvente solvent (adj)

solvibile credit-worthy

solvibilità (f) solvency

somma (f) sum [of money]

somma (f) [addizione] sum or addition [calculation]

sommare [aggiungere] add

sommare una colonna di cifre add up a column of figures

sondaggio (m)
random check
**sondaggio: fare un
sondaggio** sample
(v) *or* ask questions
**sondaggio (m)
d'opinione**
opinion poll
**soprattassa (f) di
importazione**
import surcharge
sopravvalutare
overvalue *or*
overestimate (v)
**sorpassare *[super-
are]*** exceed *or* go
higher than
sorvegliare
supervise
sospendere suspend
**sospendere i paga-
menti** stop payments
**sospendere le trat-
tative** break off
negotiations
**sospendere un'at-
tività *[chiudere]***
close down
sospensione (f)
suspension *or*
stoppage

**sospensione (f) dei
pagamenti** suspen-
sion of payments
sospensiva (f) stay
of execution
**sostegno (m)
*[contenitore]***
holder *[thing]*
sostegno (copia)
backup copy
sostenere bear (v)
or pay for
**sostenere le spese
di qualcuno** defray
someone's
expenses
sostenere spese
incur *[costs]*
**sostenitore (m)
[avallante backer
sostituire replace
*sostituto (m) [dele-
gato]*** replacement
or deputy
**sostituto *[facente
funzione di]*** acting
sostituzione (f)
replacement *[of an
item]*
**sotterfugio (m) fis-
cale** tax loophole

sotto contratto
under contract
sotto controllo
under control
**sotto nuova ges-
tione** under new
management
sottoporre refer *or*
pass to someone
sottoprodotto (m)
spinoff
sottoscritto
undersigned
sottoscrittore (m)
contributor
**sottoscrivere una
polizza** take out a
policy
**sottrarsi al paga-
mento delle tasse**
evade tax
**sovraccarico (m) di
scorte** overstocks
**sovrappiù (m)
[surplus]** surplus
sovrapprezzo (m)
surcharge
sovrapprofitti (mpl)
excess profits
sovvenzionare
subsidize

**sovvenzione (f)
[sussidio]** subven-
tion *or* subsidy
spaiato odd *[not
a pair]*
spartire [dividere]
share (v) *or* divide
among
spartire un ufficio
share an office
spazio (m) space
or room
spazio (m) [vuoto]
blank (n)
**spazio (m) pubblic-
itario** advertising
space
speciale special
specialista (m)
specialist
specializzato skilled
**specializzato:
essere specializ-
zato** specialize in
**specializzato: non
specializzato**
unskilled
specializzazione (f)
specialization
specifica (f)
specification

specificare specify

specificare *[det-tagliare]* itemize

specificazione (f) delle mansioni job specification

speculatore al rialzo bull *[on stock exchange]*

spedire dispatch (v) *or* send *or* forward *or* ship (v)

spedire merce in container ship in containers

spedire per espresso express (v) *or* send fast

spedire per posta post (v) *or* mail (v)

spedire per posta aerea airmail (v)

spedire un pacco per posta ordinaria send a package by surface mail

spedire un pacco per via aerea send a package by airmail

spedire una fattura (per posta) send an invoice by post

spedizione (f) dispatch (n) *or* sending

spedizione (f) consolidata consolidated shipment

spedizione (f) in massa bulk shipments

spedizione (f) marittima shipping

spedizione (f) per espresso express delivery

spedizioniere (m) (per via terra) forwarding agent

spedizioniere (m) marittimo shipper *or* shipping agent

spendere spend *[money]*

spendere meno underspend

spendere oltre il proprio budget overspend one's budget

spendere oltre le proprie possibilità overspend

spesa (f) shopping

spesa (f) (conto) expense

spesa (f) compresa inclusive charge

spesa (f) non autorizzata unauthorized expenditure

spesa (f) postale postage

spesa (f) totale total expenditure

spese (fpl) expenditure *or* expenses *or* outgoings

spese (fpl) bancarie bank charges

spese (fpl) conto capitali capital expenditure

spese (fpl) d'ammissione ospese (fpl) d'entrata admission charge *or* entrance charge

spese (fpl) d'esercizio running costs *or* running expenses *or* operating costs *or* operating expenses

spese (fpl) d'imballo packing charges

spese (fpl) d'incasso collection charges *or* collection rates

spese (fpl) di amministrazione administrative expenses

spese (fpl) di avviamento start-up costs

spese (fpl) di confezione o spedizione handling charges

spese (fpl) di consumo consumer spending

spese (fpl) di immagazzinamento storage cost

spese (fpl) di scarico (da nave) landing charges

spese (fpl) di trasporto freight costs

spese (fpl) extra extra charges

spese (fpl) generali overhead costs *or* overheads

**spese (fpl) gener-
ali di produzione**
manufacturing
overheads
**spese (fpl) impre-
viste** incidental
expenses
spese (fpl) legali
legal costs *or* legal
charges *or* legal
expenses
spese (fpl) postali
postal charges *or*
postal rates
**spese (fpl) postali
e imballo** postage
and packing (p & p)
**spese (fpl) pub-
blicitarie** publicity
expenditure
**spese (fpl) straor-
dinarie** below-the-
line expenditure
**spese (fpl) supple-
mentari** additional
charges *or* extras
**spese (fpl)
trasporto merci via
aerea** air freight
charges *or* rates

spiccioli (mpl)
change (n) *or* cash
spiegare explain
spiegazione (f)
explanation
spina (f) elettrica
electric plug
spinta (f) boost (n)
**spionaggio (m)
industriale** indus-
trial espionage
**sponsor (m)
[garante]**
sponsor (n)
**sponsorizzare
[patrocinare]**
sponsor (v)
**sponsorizzato dal
governo** government-
sponsored
**sponsorizzazione
(f) [avallo]**
sponsorship
sportellista (m)
teller
**sportello (m) di
cassa** cash desk
**spot (m)
[pubblicità]** TV
commercial (n)

sprecare waste (v)
(use too much)
spreco (m) waste
(n) *or* wastage
stabile *[solido]*
firm (adj) *or* stable
stabilimento (m)
[fabbrica] plant
(n) *or* factory
stabilire *[istituire]*
establish
stabilire *[organiz-*
zare] arrange
[meeting]
stabilire come obi-
ettivo target (v)
stabilire il prezzo
price (v) *or* fix a
price
stabilire il valore
[accertare] assess
stabilità (f) stability
stabilità (f) dei
prezzi price stability
stabilizzare stabilize
stabilizzarsi level
off *or* level out
stabilizzazione (f)
stabilization
stadio (m) stage (n)

stagionale *[period-*
ico] seasonal
stagione (f) season
stagnante stagnant
stampa (f) press
stampante (f)
printer *[machine]*
stampante (f) a
matrice d'aghi
dot-matrix printer
stampante (f) con
testina a
margherita daisy-
wheel printer
stampante (f) laser
laser printer
stampante (f) lin-
eare line printer *or*
computer printer
stampare print out
stampato (m)
printout
stand (m) stand
(n) *[at exhibition]*
standard standard
(adj) *or* stock (adj)
or normal
standard (mpl) di
produzione produc-
tion standards

standardizzare
standardize
standardizzazione
(f) standardization
standista (m) [esp-
ositore] exhibitor
stanziamento (m)
promozionale pro-
motional budget
stanziare allocate
star del credere
del credere
stare al passo
con la richiesta
keep up with the
demand
statistica (f)
statistics
statistico statistical
stato (m)
[nazione] state (n)
or country
stato (m) [con-
dizione] state (n)
or condition
stato (m) giuridico
legal status
stato (m) ordinato:
essere stato ordi-
nato on order
statutario statutory

statuto (m) soci-
etario articles of
association
stazione (f) fer-
roviaria railway
station
sterlina (f) pound
sterling
stima: fare una
nuova stima
reassess
stimare [valutare]
estimate (v) or
value (v)
stimatore (m) valuer
stimolare l'econo-
mia stimulate the
economy
stimolo (m) stimulus
stipendiato salaried
stipendio (m) salary
stipendio (m)
iniziale starting
salary
stipendio (m)
interessante
attractive salary
stipendio (m) lordo
gross salary
stipula (f)
stipulation

stipulare stipulate
stipulare un contratto
draw up a contract
stiva (f) hold (n)
[of ship]
stivatore (m) *[scar-*
icatore di porto]
stevedore
stoccare *[costruire*
riserve] stockpile (v)
stock (m) *[scorte]*
stock (n) *[goods]*
stop (m) *[fine]*
stop (n)
stornare una regis-
trazione contra an
entry
strada (f) road
straniero *[estero]*
foreign *or* external
straordinario
extraordinary; out-
standing *or* unusual
strategia (f) strategy
strategia (f) com-
merciale business
strategy
strategia (f) di
marketing market-
ing strategy
strategico strategic

strozzatura (f) *[nel*
processo aziendale]
bottleneck
strumenti (mpl)
[mezzi] ways *or*
means
strumenti (mpl)
scontabili *[effetti*
bancabili] bankable
paper
strumento (m)
instrument *or*
implement (n)
strumento (m)
[documento] instru-
ment *[document]*
strumento (m)
negoziabile nego-
tiable instrument
strumento (m) non
negoziabile non-
negotiable instrument
struttura (f) struc-
ture (n)
struttura a rete
grid structure
strutturale structural
strutturare struc-
ture (v) *or* arrange
studiare study (v)
studio (m) study (n)

studio (m) dei tempi e dei movimenti time and motion study
studio (m) della fattibilità feasibility report
su richiesta on request
subaffittante (m) sublessor
subaffittare sublease (v) or sublet
subaffitto (m) sublease (n)
subaffittuario (m) sublessee
subappaltatore (m) subcontractor
subappalto (m) subcontract (n)
subire un danno suffer damage
subire una forte flessione slump (v)
succedere succeed or take over [from someone else]
successo (m) success
successo: avere successo [riuscire] succeed [do well]

successo: che non ha successo unsuccessful
successo: di successo successful
sufficiente sufficient; adequate
superare (sorpassare) exceed or go higher than
superficie (f) area [surface]
superficie (f) di pavimento floor space
superiore superior (adj) [better quality]
superiore (m) superior (n) [person]
supermercato (m) supermarket
supermercato (m) all'ingrosso cash and carry
supervisione (f) [vigilanza] supervision
supervisione: di supervisione supervisory
supervisore (m) supervisor
supplementare supplementary; additional

surplus (m)
[sovrappiù] surplus
sussidiario
subsidiary (adj)
sussidio (m) *[sovv-
enzione]* subsidy
**sussidio (m) di
disoccupazione**
unemployment pay
svalutare devalue
or depreciate *or*
lose value
svalutazione (f)
devaluation *or*
depreciation *or* loss
of value
svendere sell off
**svendere merci sul
mercato** dump
goods on a market
**svendita (f) per
chiusura d'esercizio**
closing-down sale
**svendite (fpl) di
fine stagione** end
of season sales
sviluppare develop
or plan
sviluppare *[costru-
ire]* develop *or* build
sviluppo (m) *[pro-
gresso]* development

**sviluppo (m) del
prodotto** product
development
**sviluppo (m) eco-
nomico** economic
development
**svincolo (m)
doganale** customs
clearance
**svolgere esercizio
d'impresa** carry on
a business

Tt

**tabella (f) fissa dei
prezzi** fixed
scale of charges
tabellone (m)
hoarding *[for posters]*
tabulare tabulate
tabulato (m)
computer printout
tabulatore (m)
tabulator
tabulazione (f)
tabulation

taccheggiare
shoplifting
taccheggiatore (m)
shoplifter
tachigrafo (m)
tachograph
tacito consenso
(m) tacit approval
taglia (f) size
taglia (f) standard
stock size
taglia: di taglia
forte outsize (OS)
tagliare cut (v)
tagliare i prezzi *o*
le condizioni di
credito slash prices
or credit terms
taglio (m) cut (n)
tangente (f) *[bus-*
***tarella]* bribe (n)
tangibile tangible
tappare plug (v)
or block
tara (f) tare
tardi *[in ritardo]*
late (adv)
tariffa (f) tariff; fare;
scale of charges *or* rate
tariffa (f) a tempo
time rate

tariffa (f) doganale
customs tariff
tariffa (f) in vigore
going rate
tariffa (f) notturna
night rate
tariffa (f) pro-
tezionistica
protective tariff
tariffa (f) ridotta
cheap rate
tariffe (fpl) delle
inserzioni pubblici-
tarie advertising rates
tariffe (fpl) di assi-
curazione insur-
ance rates
tariffe (fpl) di nolo
freight rates
tariffe (fpl) dif-
ferenziali differen-
tial tariffs
tariffe (fpl) pub-
blicitarie differen-
ziali graded
advertising rates
tasca (f) pocket (n)
tassa (f) (im
posta) tax (n)
tassa (f) ad valorem
ad valorem tax

tassa (f) di base
basic tax
**tassa (f) di circo-
lazione** road tax
**tassa (f) di registra-
zione** registration fee
tassa (f) esclusa
exclusive of tax
tassabile taxable
tassare *[gravare
d'imposta]* tax (v)
tassazione (f)
taxation
tassazione (f) alta
high taxation
**tassazione (f) dire-
tta** direct taxation
**tassazione (f) indi-
retta** indirect taxation
**tasse (fpl) aero-
portuali** airport tax
**tassi (mpl) mone-
tari** money rates
tasso (m) rate (n)
or amount
**tasso (m) d'infla-
zione** rate of inflation
**tasso (m) d'inter-
esse** interest rate
tasso (m) di base
prime rate

**tasso (m) di cam-
bio** exchange rate
or rate of exchange
**tasso (m) di cambio
corrente** current
rate of exchange
**tasso (m) di cam-
bio sfavorevole**
unfavourable
exchange rate
**tasso (m) di cam-
bio stabile** stable
exchange rate
**tasso (m) di
conversione**
conversion price *or*
conversion rate
**tasso (m) di pro-
duzione** rate of
production
tasso (m) di sconto
discount rate
**tasso (m) fisso di
cambio** fixed
exchange rate
**tasso (m) flut-
tuante di cambio**
floating exchange
rates
tasso (m) ridotto
reduced rate

tasso (m) su prestiti a breve call rate

tasso (m) ufficiale di sconto bank base rate

tastiera (f) keyboard (n)

tastierino (m) numerico numeric keypad

tasto (m) key *[on keyboard]*

tasto (m) delle maiuscole shift key

tasto (m) di comando control key

tavole (fpl) attuariali actuarial tables

tecnica (f) di vendita selling technique

tecniche (fpl) di marketing marketing techniques

tecniche (fpl) di propaganda canvassing techniques

tecniche (fpl) gestionali management techniques

telecomando (m) remote control

telefonare phone (v) *or* telephone (v)

telefonata (f) a carico del ricevente reverse charge call *or* collect call *[US]*

telefonata (f) d'affari business call

telefonata (f) di routine routine call

telefonata (f) in arrivo incoming call

telefonata (f) internazionale international call

telefonata (f) urbana local call

telefonista (mf) telephonist

telefono (m) phone (n) *or* telephone (n)

telefono (m) a gettoni pay phone

telefono (m) a schede card phone

telefono (m) cellulare cellular phone

telefono (m) interno internal telephone

telefono (m) per conferenze confer- ence phone

telescrivente (f) [telex] telex (n)

teleselezione (f) dial direct

teleselezione (f) internazionale international direct dialling

telex (m) telex (n)

tempo (m) di elaborazione computer time

tempo (m) impro- duttivo down time

tempo (m) libero spare time

tendenza (f) al rialzo upward trend

tendenza (f) di mer- cato market trends

tenere hold (v) *or* keep; stock *[goods]*

tenere in affitto [affittare] lease (v) *[of tenant]*

tenere in efficienza maintain *or* keep going

tenere su keep up

tenere una seduta hold a meeting *or* a discussion

terminal (m) airport terminal

terminal (m) della compagnia aerea air terminal

terminal (m) per container container terminal

terminale terminal (adj) *[at the end]*

terminale (m) di computer computer terminal

terminare [scadere] terminate; expire

termine (m) termi- nation; expiration

termine (m) [chiusura] closure

termine (m) [fine] end (n)

termine (m) ultimo [data di chiusura] closing date *or* time limit

termine (m) ultimo [data di scadenza] deadline

termini (mpl) stabiliti terms of reference
terra (f) *o* **terreno (m)** land (n)
territorio (m) territory *[of salesman]*
terza persona (f) third party
terzo trimestre (m) third quarter
tesoreria (f) treasury
tessera (f) card
tessera (f) *[di abbonamento ferroviario]* season ticket
tessera (f) prelievo contanti cash card
testa: che è in testa alle vendite top-selling
testimone (m) witness (n)
tetto (m) dei prezzi price ceiling
tetto (m) salariale credit ceiling
timbrare stamp (v) *[mark]*
timbro (m) stamp (n) *[device]*

tipografia (f) printer *or* printing company
tirare sul prezzo *[contrattare]* bargain (v)
tiratura (f) circulation *[of newspaper]*
tirocinante (m) trainee
titolare (m) holder *[person]*
titoli (mpl) securities
titoli (mpl) di prim'ordine gilt-edged securities *or* gilts
titoli (mpl) di stato government stock *or* government bonds
titolo (m) di prim'ordine blue chip
togliere lift (v) *or* remove
togliere l'embargo lift an embargo
togliere la seduta close a meeting
tonnellaggio (m) tonnage
tonnellaggio (m) lordo gross tonnage
tonnellata (f) ton *or* tonne

totale total (adj) *or* overall
totale (m) total (n) *or* sum
totale (m) corrente running total
totale (m) delle attività total assets
totale (m) generale grand total
totale (m) parziale subtotal
totale [globale] total (adj) *or* all-in
tradurre translate
traduttore (m), traduttrice (f) translator
traduzione (f) translation
traente (m) drawer
trafficare [commerciare] trade (v)
trafficare in [commerciare in] trade in [buy and sell]
traghetto (m) ferry
traghetto (m) per automezzi car ferry *or* roll on/roll off ferry
tramite (via) via

tranne (eccetto) except
transazione (f) transaction
transazione (f) a pronti spot purchase
transazione (f) commerciale business transaction
transazione (f) sul disponibile cash transaction *or* cash deal
transazioni (fpl) [operazioni] stock exchange dealing
transito (m) transit
trarre vantaggio da benefit from (v) *or* capitalize on
trascurabile negligible
trascurare [omettere] omit
trasferibile transferable
trasferimento (m) transfer (n) *or* assignment *or* cession
trasferimento (m) di capitali transfer of funds

trasferire transfer (v)

traslocare move *[house, office]*

trasloco (m) move *[to new house]*

trasmissione (f) conveyance; drive (n) *[part of machine]*

trasportare transport (v) *or* ship (v)

trasportare *[portare]* carry

trasportare a mezzo di palette palletize

trasportare merci via aerea airfreight (v)

trasportatore (m) haulage contractor

trasportatore (m) su strada road haulier

trasporti (mpl) pubblici public transport

trasporto (m) transport (n); carriage *or* freight

trasporto (m) di merci freightage

trasporto (m) di ritorno homeward freight

trasporto (m) ferroviario rail transport

trasporto (m) in container containerization *or* shipping in containers

trasporto (m) in superficie surface transport

trasporto (m) marittimo shipment

trasporto (m) mediante autocarro trucking

trasporto (m) merci via aerea air freight

trasporto (m) su strada road transport *or* road haulage

Trasporto Internazionale su Strada Transports Internationaux Routiers (TIR)

tratta (f) (bank) draft (n)

tratta (f) a vista sight draft

trattabile [controllabile] manageable

trattabile [negoziabile] negotiable

trattamento (m) equo fair dealing

trattare process (v) or deal with or negotiate

trattare [lavorare] process (v) [raw materials]

trattare con qualcuno deal with someone

trattario (m) drawee

trattativa (f) negotiation

trattative (fpl) difficile hard bargaining

trattato (m) commerciale trade agreement

trattenere hold up (v) or delay or keep back

tredicesima (f) [gratifica natalizia] Christmas bonus

treno (m) train (n)

treno (m) merci goods train or freight train

tribunale (m) law courts

tribunale (m) arbitrale arbitration board or arbitration tribunal

tribunale (m) del lavoro industrial tribunal

tribunale (m) di arbitrato adjudication tribunal

tribunale (m) di arbitrato industriale industrial arbitration tribunal

trimestrale quarterly (adj)

trimestralmente quarterly (adv)

trimestre quarter [three months]

triplicare triple (v)

triplice: in triplice copia in triplicate

triplo triple (adj)

truffa (f) [imbroglio] fiddle (n)

turno (m) [di lavoro] shift (n) [team of workers]
turno (m) di giorno day shift
turno (m) di notte night shift
tutte le spese pagate all expenses paid

Uu

UE (Unione Europea) EU (European Union)
ufficiale official (adj)
ufficiale: non ufficiale unofficial
ufficiale (m) di dogana customs official
ufficiale (m) di stato civile registrar
ufficio (m) office

ufficio: d'ufficio clerical
ufficio (m) a pianta aperta open-plan office
ufficio (m) acquisti buying department orpurchasing department
ufficio (m) addetto alla fatturazione invoicing department
ufficio (m) assistenza service department
ufficio (m) assistenza ai clienti customer service department
ufficio (m) cambio bureau de change
ufficio (m) computer computer department
Ufficio (m) Dazio e Dogana Customs and Excise Department
ufficio (m) del personale personnel department

ufficio (m) della pubblicità publicity department

ufficio (m) delle pubbliche relazioni public relations department

ufficio (m) deposito bagagli left luggage office

ufficio (m) design design department

ufficio (m) di rappresentanza representative company

ufficio (m) indennità claims department

ufficio (m) informazioni information bureau

ufficio (m) legale legal department

ufficio (m) prenotazioni booking office

ufficio (m) produzioni production department

ufficio (m) pubblico general office

ufficio (m) reclami complaints department

ufficio (m) traduzioni translation bureau

ufficio (m) vendite sales department

ufficiosamente off the record

ufficioso *[non ufficiale]* unofficial

uguagliare equal (v)

uguale equal (adj)

ultima offerta (f) *[di licitazione]* closing bid

ultimo a entrare, primo a uscire last in first out (LIFO)

ultimo trimestre (m) last quarter

unico one-off *or* unique

unico proprietario (m) sole owner

uniforme *[indiscriminato]* general *or* across-the-board

unilaterale unilateral

**unione (f) doga-
nale** customs union
**Unione (f) Europea
(UE)** European
Union (EU)
unire join
unire [attaccare]
attach *or* join
unità (f) unit *or* item
**unità (f) a dischi
magnetici** disk
drive
unità (f) monetaria
monetary unit
unito [congiunto]
joint; united
uomo (m) man (n)
uomo (m) d'affari
businessman
**uomo (m) delle con-
segne** deliveryman
**uomo (m) di fidu-
cia** right-hand man
urgente urgent
usare use (v)
**usato [di seconda
mano]** secondhand
uscente retiring
uscita (f) exit
uscita: in uscita
outgoing

uso (m) use (n)
usuale [comune]
common *or* frequent
usuale [standard]
stock (adj) *or* normal
**usufrutto (m) [ren-
dita vitalizia]** life
interest
**usurpare un breve-
tto** infringe a patent
**usurpazione (f) di
brevetto** infringe-
ment of patent
utente (m) user
utente (m) finale
end user
utile useful
utile (m) [profitto]
profit
**utile (m) al lordo
delle imposte**
pretax profit *or*
profit before tax
**utile (m) al netto
delle imposte**
profit after tax
utile (m) d'esercizio
operating profit *or*
trading profit
utile (m) in aumento
increasing profits

utile (m) lordo
gross profit
utile (m) netto net
profit
utile (m) per
azione earnings per
share or earnings
yield
utili (mpl) dis-
tribuibili distrib-
utable profit
utili (mpl) ipotetici
paper profit
utili (mpl) netti
net earnings or net
income
utili (mpl) record
record profits
utili (mpl) societari
corporate profits
utilità (f) [benefi-
cio] usefulness or
benefit (n)
utilizzazione (f)
utilization
utilizzo (m) della
capacità produttiva
capacity utilization

Vv

vacante vacant
vaglia (m)
[mandato di paga-
mento] money order
vaglia (m) postale
postal order
valere be worth
validità (f) validity
valido valid
valido: essere
valido be valid or
be in force
valigia (f) case or
suitcase
valore (m) value
(n) or worth
valore: in base al
valore di ad valorem
valore (m) attuale
present value
valore (m) con-
tabile book value
valore (m) di mer-
cato market value
valore (m) di
riscatto surrender
value

valore (m) di sostituzione replacement value

valore (m) dichiarato declared value

valore (m) massimo peak (n)

valore (m) mediano median

valore (m) nominale nominal value *or* face value *or* par value

valore (m) patrimoniale asset value

valore (m) patrimoniale netto net assets *or* net worth

valore (m) totale della fattura total invoice value

valorem: ad valorem ad valorem

valuta (f) currency

valuta (f) bloccata blocked currency

valuta (f) convertibile convertible currency

valuta (f) debole soft currency

valuta (f) di riserva reserve currency

valuta (f) estera foreign exchange *[currency]*

valuta (f) solida hard currency

valutare value (v) *or* evaluate

valutare *[stimare]* estimate (v)

valutare i costi evaluate costs

valutato estimated

valutazione (f) valuation; evaluation; estimate

valutazione (f) approssimativa rough estimate

valutazione (f) dei costi costing

valutazione (f) del mercato azionario stock market valuation

valutazione (f) della prestazione performance rating

valutazione (f) delle scorte stock valuation

vantaggioso economic *or* profitable
variare *[estendersi]* vary; range (v)
variazione (f) variation; variance
variazioni (fpl) *[scala]* range (n) *or* variation
variazioni (fpl) stagionali seasonal variations
vario *[miscellaneo]* various *or* miscellaneous
vecchio old
vecchio: di vecchia data long-standing
vecchio: di vecchia istituzione old-established
vecchio: più vecchio senior
veicolo (m) vehicle
veicolo (m) per merci pesanti heavy goods vehicle (HGV)
veicolo (m) articolato articulated vehicle
veloce fast (adj)

velocemente *[rapidamente]* fast (adv) *or* rapidly
vendere sell
vendere *[commercializzare]* market (v) *or* put on the market
vendere a minor prezzo di un concorrente undercut a rival
vendere a termine sell forward
vendere al dettaglio retail (v) *[goods]*
vendere all'asta auction (v)
vendere sotto costo discount (v); undersell
vendere tutto *[esaurire]* sell out *[all stock]*
vendersi be sold; move
vendersi a retail for (v) *or* sell for a price
vendibile saleable
vendibilità (f) saleability

vendita (f) sale (n) *or* selling

vendita: in vendita for sale

vendita (f) a domicilio house-to-house selling

vendita (f) al dettaglio retailing

vendita (f) all'asta sale by auction

vendita (f) coatta forced sale

vendita (f) con carta di credito credit card sale

vendita (f) con possibilità di resa see-safe

vendita (f) di merce sotto costo distress sale

vendita (f) di realizzo bargain made (n) *[on stock exchange]*

vendita (f) diretta direct selling

vendita (f) diretta tramite corrispondenza direct mail

vendita (f) per contanti cash sale

vendita (f) porta a porta door-to-door selling

vendite (fpl) *[fatturato]* sales

vendite (fpl) a termine forward sales

vendite (fpl) basse low sales

vendite (fpl) interne domestic sales

vendite (fpl) nazionali ovendite sul mercato interno home sales

vendite (fpl) per telefono telesales

vendite (fpl) presunte estimated sales

vendite (fpl) previste projected sales

vendite (fpl) record record sales

vendite (fpl) registrate book sales

venditore (m) salesman; seller *or* vendor

venditore (m) a domicilio door-to-door salesman

venditore (m) di assicurazioni insurance salesman

venditori (mpl) sales people

venduto: essere venduto be sold *or* change hands

venduto con possibilità di resa sale *or* return

venire a un compromesso compromise (v)

ventiquattrore (f) personalizzata personalized briefcase

verbale verbal

verbale (m) *[di assemblea]* minutes (n) *[of meeting]*

verbalizzare *[mettere a verbale]* minute (v)

verde: al verde broke (informal)

verdetto (m) *[decisione]* judgement *or* judgment; verdict

verifica (f) *[controllo]* verification; control (n) *or* check

verificare verify; audit (v)

verificare i conti audit the accounts

verificato: non verificato unaudited

vero *[autentico]* genuine *or* true

versamento (m) d'acconto down payment

versare denaro deposit (v)

vertenza (f) di lavoro labour disputes

vertenza (f) operaia industrial disputes

veto (m) veto (n)

veto: porre il veto a una decisione veto (v) a decision

vetrina (f) shop window

vetrinetta (f) display case

vetta (f) (cima) top (n) *or* highest point

vettore (m)
common carrier
via (tramite) via
viaggio (m) d'affari
business trip
**viaggio (m) di
ritorno** homeward
journey
**vice amministra-
tore (m) delegato**
deputy managing
director
vice direttore (m)
assistant manager
or deputy manager
vicino a close to
videoscrittura (f)
word-processing
video-unità (f) dis-
play unit
vie (fpl) legali
legal proceedings
vietare [interdire]
ban (v)
**vigilanza (f)
[supervisione]**
supervision
**vigore: essere in
vigore** rule (v) *or*
be in force

**vincere un con-
tratto** win a con-
tract
vincolante binding
violare la legge
break the law
**violazione (f) dei
regolamenti
doganali** infringe-
ment of customs
regulations
**violazione (f) di
garanzia** breach of
warranty
**virgola (f) deci-
male** decimal point
visita (f) visit *or*
call (n)
visita (f) a freddo
cold call
vista (f) sight
vista: tratta a vista
sight draft
visto (m) consolare
visa
**visto (m) consolare
di transito** transit visa
**visto (m) consolare
multiplo** multiple
entry visa

visto (m) d'in-gresso entry visa
vita (f) ciclica di un prodotto product cycle
viziare *[rovinare]* spoil
viziato *[privo di validità]* defective or not valid
voce (f) item *[of information]*
voci (fpl) straordi-narie extraordinary items or exceptional items
volantino (m) leaflet
volere *[richiedere]* take (v) or need
volo (m) flight *[of plane]*
volo (m) a lunga percorrenza long-distance flight
volo (m) a lungo raggio long-haul flight
volo (m) charter charter flight

volo (m) di coinci-denza connecting flight
volo (m) di linea scheduled flight
volume (m) volume
volume (m) *[grande quantità]* bulk or mass
volume (m) d'af-fari sales figures or turnover
volume (m) degli scambi commerciali volume of trade or volume of business
volume (m) delle vendite sales volume or volume of sales
voluminoso bulky
voto (m) decisivo casting vote
voto (m) per del-ega proxy vote
vuotare empty (v)
vuoti (mpl) a ren-dere returned empties
vuoto empty (adj)

vuoto (m) *[spazio]*
blank (n)
vuoto *[in bianco]*
blank (adj)

Zz

zero (m) *[nulla]*
zero *or* nil
zona (f) *[quartiere]*
zone; area *or* district
[of town]

**zona (f) commer-
ciale** shopping
precinct
**zona (f) di
libero scambio** free
trade area
**zona (f) di
libero scambio** free
trade zone
zona (f) franca
free zone
zona (f) industriale
industrial estate

Business correspondence

La corrispondenza commerciale

Sample Curriculum Vitae

CURRICULUM VITAE
Giuseppina Cataldo
Via Colfosco 15
00151 Roma
Tel: 00 44 20 8868 9854 Cellulare: 00 44 7914 248553
E-mail: giusecaldo@scalinet.it

<u>**Interessi**</u>
Assunzione con ruolo direttivo e di capo
squadra di un ufficio personale, all'interno di
una affermata società di informatica

<u>**Esperienza lavorativa**</u>
1999 ad oggi
Costello Commerci Marittimi srl |Genova
Consulente per le Risorse Umane
Ha lavorato come consulente in questioni di politica del personale. I suoi compiti comprendevano
l'amministrazione della politica delle relazioni e
del tirocinio del personale. Ha collaborato
all'ideazione e l'implemento di nuove strategie
all'interno della compagnia, su territorio italiano.

1996 - 1998
Costello Commerci Marittimi srl |Genova
Consulente per le Risorse Umane nel campo
marittimo, navale e d'aviazione
Ha lavorato come consulente per tre reparti della
compagnia a livello globale: prodotti marittimi,
spedizioni marittime e spedizioni aeree. Ha coor-
dinato diversi processi d'assunzione, dalla fase di

---

richiesta di personale al momento delle selezioni dei candidati.

1993 - 1995
Costello Scavi Petrolifici srl |Genova
Consulente per le Risorse Umane nel campo dell'ingegneria petrolifica
Fra le altre cose, ha offerto consulenza in un importante processo di trasferimento della compagnia.

Studi

1999 — 2001 Diploma di specializzazione in Relazioni Umane Università della Sapienza - Roma

1996 — 1998 Diploma di specializzazione in Risorse Umane e Sviluppo Istituto di Ricerca delle Risorse Umane e

Sviluppo
1990 — 1993 Diploma di Laurea in Psicologia Sperimentale Università di Bologna

1982 — 1990 Conseguimento di diploma di maturità scientifica Liceo Scientifico Statale G.B. Morgagni -

Prototipo di Curriculum Vitae

CURRICULUM VITAE for Ms. Josephine Catterall
5A, Hanton Street, London, SE13 1DF
Tel: (020) 8868 9854 Mobile: (07914) 248553
E-mail: jfcatterall@hotmail.com

Objective:

To become a professional HR manager with a team-leader role within a blue-chip company. Future positions to involve managing employee relations on a UK or global basis.

Work History:

Dec 1999 — present   GP International Trading and Shipping Company Ltd., London

Human Resources Policy Adviser
Provided professional advice on all HR policy matters including employee relations and training. Developed UK policy and implemented policy changes within the business.

May 1996 — Nov 1999   GP International Trading and Shipping Company Ltd., London

Human Resources Adviser: Marine, Shipping, and Aviation
Provided recruitment advice to 3 departments of the Global Businesses group: Marine Products,

Shipping, and Aviation. Coordinated several internal and external recruitment processes through all stages from advertising to candidate selection.

Sept 1993 — April 1996 GP UK Exploration and Production, Southampton

Human Resources Consultant: Oil-well Engineering
Provided advice on a range of issues, including helping to manage a large-scale company relocation.

Education/Qualifications:

1999 — 2001	MSc in Employee Relations, *University of Westminster, London*
1996 — 1998	Graduate of the Chartered Institute of Personnel and Development
1990 — 1993	BA (Hons) Experimental Psychology (Class Iii), *University of Bristol*
1982 — 1990	'A' Levels: Biology (A), French (A), German (B), *St Stephen's School, Ely, Cambs*

Sample covering letter for job application

Antonella Grimaldi
Vicolo Marino
00 160 Ostia   25 marzo 2003

Gentile sig.ra Gianna Stefanelli
      Ufficio Assunzioni
      Infodati spa
      Via Merlo 1
      20 122 Milano

      Gentile signora Stefanelli

Riscontro all'inserzione da voi pubblicata su Repubblica del 20 marzo con l'offerta di un posto di Capo Area Vendite presso la Infodati spa.

In merito, essendone interessata, mi preme segnalare che, in qualità di Vice Direttore Vendite presso la Promedia spa, ho personalmente prodotto un incremento pari al 15% sul valore delle azioni del passato anno.
Dal vostro resoconto annuale, secondo i dati della vostra web-site, risulta che anche le azioni della Infodati spa hanno goduto di un incremento per cui si è decisa una programmazione di rialzo delle azioni per il nuovo anno finanziario. Sono certa che, con la mia esperinza e le mie qualifiche, potrei collaborare alla realizzazione di quanto da voi programmato.

Come da vostra richiesta, allego copia di mio
curriculum completo e aggiornato.

Sperando di essere presa in considerazione per
l'incarico offerto, in attesa di gentile riscontro
invio distinti saluti

Antonella Grimaldi

Prototipo di lettera per domanda di assunzione

Adrienne Griffiths
20 Shakespeare Road
London
SE18 2PB

Jane Stevenson
Senior Personnel Officer
DataTech Ltd
Botley Road
Oxford
OX2 1ZZ

25 March 2003

Dear Ms Stevenson

I am very interested in the position of sales manager at DataTech Ltd as described in your advertisement of 20 March in the Guardian newspaper.

In my current position of deputy sales manager for Parker Smith Plc I have helped to increase our market share by 15% in the past year. I see from your website and annual report that DataTech have also increased their market share this year and are aiming to do the same in the next financial year, and I feel my track record and qualifications would fit in well with these plans for growth.

As requested in the advertisement, I enclose a copy of my CV which gives full details of my qualifications and work history. I would be very pleased to be considered for this position and I look forward to hearing from you.

Yours sincerely

Adrianne GrEiffiths

Encl.

Sample letter making a job offer

Infodati spa
Via Merlo 1
20 122 Milano   10 aprile 2003

Gentile sig.ra Antonella Grimaldi
Vicolo Marino
00 160 Ostia

**Oggetto: conferma assunzione a
        Capo Area Vendite**

Gentile signora Grimaldi

Facendo seguito al nostro ultimo colloquio, sono lieto di comunicarle la sua assunzione presso la nostra società, con l'incarico di Capo Area Vendite.

Il signor Davide Merlo, nostro Direttore Vendite, sara il suo interlocutore diretto.

Per l'incarico da lei svolto, le sue spettanze ammonteranno € 18.000 annuali, che saranno revisionate in occasione del primo rinnovo contrattuale.

I termini di assunzione le verranno puntualizzati in sede.

Auspicando una proficua collaborazione, le invio distinti saluti

Gianna Stefanelli
Direttore del Personale
Infodati spa

Prototipo di lettera d'offerta di lavoro

DataTech Ltd
Botley Road
Oxford
OX2 1ZZ

Ms Adrianne Griffiths
20 Shakespeare Road
London SE18 2PB

10 April 2003

Dear Ms Griffiths

Re: Post of Sales Manager

Further to your interview last week I am pleased to be able to offer you the post of Sales Manager, reporting directly to David Wardlock, our Company Sales Director.

Your starting salary will be £29,635, with an annual salary review on the date of your joining the company. Other terms and conditions will be as outlined in the interview.

If this offer is acceptable to you I would be grateful if you could send me confirmation in writing. We can then finalize details of your contract and starting date and discuss any relocation expenses you may have to claim.

Best wishes

Yours sincerely

Jane Stevenson
Senior Personnel Officer
DataTech Ltd

Sample reply to request for information

Emilia Del Fosco
Direttore Vendite
Infocarta spa
Via di Donna Olimpia 8
00 151 Roma   10 aprile 2003

Egregio signor Luigi Volpe
Via Albaro 18
16 124 Genova

Egregio signor Volpe

Facendo seguito alla nostra conversazione telefonica odierna, ho il piacere di inviarle il nostro catalogo con tutte le informazioni da lei gentilmente richieste, dove troverà una lista dei nostri prodotti disponibili e relativi costi.

Per ulteriori informazioni, non esiti a contattarmi al seguente indirizzo e-mail: info@scalaro.it.

Nel ringraziarla sentitamente per essersi rivolto a noi, le invio i piu distinti saluti

Emilia Del Fosco
Direttore Vendite

Prototipo di lettera di richiesta informazioni

12 Smith Street
Manchester
M90 1AA

Customer Sales
New DIY Ideas Ltd
Butler Industrial Estate
Manor Park
Manchester SE12 8NU

24 June 2003

Dear Sir or Madam

I recently saw an advert for your new range of DIY products in my local paper and would be very interested to have more information on prices.

Could you send a copy of your catalogue to my home address above?

Thanking you in advance.

Yours faithfully

James Fox

Sample letter of complaint

Eleonora Giordano
Via del Tuorlo 22
00 153 Roma   20 marzo 2003

Gentile sig.ra Silvia Rossi
Computer & Accessorii
P.le Aurelio 15
00198 Roma

**Oggetto: Malfunzionamento della stampante
a getto (modello A1234)**

Gentile signora Rossi

Giovedì 13 marzo, presso il suo negozio, ho
acquistato una stampante a getto modello
A1234 (allego fotocopia della ricevuta).

Purtroppo la stampante risulta difettosa, e i
vostri due tecnici non sembrano essere in grado
di individuare il problema.

Chiedo pertanto il rimborso immediato della spesa da
me sostenuta nell'acquisto della suddetta stampante.

La prego di contattarmi all'indirizzo sopraindi-
cato così da potere fissare un appuntamento a
perché lei venga a riprendere la stampante.

Nell'attesa le invio distinti saluti

Eleonora Giordano

Prototipo di lettera di reclamo

47 Highfield Road
York
YO2 3BP

Ms H Naughton
The Computer Shop Ltd
123 High Street
York
YO1 7HL

20 March 2003

Dear Ms Naughton

Faulty inkjet printer (model number A1234)

I purchased an inkjet printer (model number A1234) from your shop on Thursday 13 March (copy of receipt enclosed). Unfortunately, the printer appears to be faulty, and two engineers from your shop have not been able to isolate the cause of the problem. I would, therefore, appreciate a full refund on the faulty printer at your earliest convenience.

Please contact me at the above address so that we may arrange a time when the printer can be picked up and returned.

I look forward to hearing from you.

Yours sincerely

Elizabeth Kendall